Education,
Literacy, and
Humanization

Critical Studies in Education and Culture Series

Wittgenstein: Philosophy, Postmodernism, Pedagogy
Michael Peters and James Marshall

Policy, Pedagogy, and Social Inequality: Community College
Student Realities in Post-Industrial America
Penelope E. Herideen

Psychoanalysis and Pedagogy
Stephen Appel, editor

The Rhetoric of Diversity and the Traditions of American Literary Study:
Critical Multiculturalism in English
Lesliee Antonette

Becoming and Unbecoming White: Owning and Disowning a Racial Identity
Christine Clark and James O'Donnell

Critical Pedagogy: An Introduction, 2nd Edition
Barry Kanpol

Michel Foucault: Materialism and Education
Mark Olssen

Revolutionary Social Transformation: Democratic Hopes, Political Possibilities,
and Critical Education
Paula Allman

Critical Reflection and the Foreign Language Classroom
Terry A. Osborn

Community in Motion: Theatre for Development in Africa
L. Dale Byam

Nietzsche's Legacy for Education: Past and Present Values
Michael Peters, James Marshall, and Paul Smeyers, editors

Rituals, Ceremonies, and Cultural Meaning in Higher Education
Kathleen Manning

Education, Literacy, and Humanization

Exploring the Work of Paulo Freire

PETER ROBERTS

Critical Studies in Education and Culture Series
Edited by Henry A. Giroux

BERGIN & GARVEY
Westport, Connecticut • London

Library of Congress Cataloging-in-Publication Data

Roberts, Peter, 1963–
    Education, literacy, and humanization : exploring the work of Paulo Freire /
Peter Roberts.
      p. cm.—(Critical studies in education and culture series, ISSN 1064–8615)
    Includes bibliographical references (p.) and index.
    ISBN 0–89789–571–1 (alk. paper)
    1. Freire, Paulo, 1921– 2. Education—Philosophy. 3. Popular education.
    4. Critical pedagogy. I. Title. II. Series.
    LB880.F732R62 2000
    370'.1—dc21   99–055889

British Library Cataloguing in Publication Data is available.

Library of Congress Catalog Card Number: 99–055889
ISBN: 0–89789–571–1
ISSN: 1064–8615

First published in 2000

Bergin & Garvey, 88 Post Road West, Westport, CT 06881
An imprint of Greenwood Publishing Group, Inc.
www.greenwood.com

Printed in the United States of America

∞™

The paper used in this book complies with the
Permanent Paper Standard issued by the National
Information Standards Organization (Z39.48–1984).

10 9 8 7 6 5 4 3 2

OCLC 42717608
Aug. 2001

Copyright Acknowledgments

Contents

Series Foreword *by Henry A. Giroux*   ix

Acknowledgments   xiii

Introduction   1

1. Reading Freire   23

2. Knowledge, Dialogue, and Humanization:
   Exploring Freire's Philosophy   35

3. Ethics, Politics, and Pedagogy: Freire on Liberating
   Education   53

4. Freirean Adult Literacy Education   75

5. Extending Literate Horizons: Freire and the
   Multidimensional Word   87

6. Critiques of Freire's Modernism   97

7. Defending Freirean Intervention   119

8. Rethinking Conscientization   137

Bibliography   157

Index   169

Series Foreword

Educational reform has fallen upon hard times. The traditional assumption that schooling is fundamentally tied to the imperatives of citizenship designed to educate students to exercise civic leadership and public service has been eroded. The schools are now the key institution for producing professional, technically trained, credentialized workers for whom the demands of citizenship are subordinated to the vicissitudes of the marketplace and the commercial public sphere. Given the current corporate and right-wing assault on public and higher education, coupled with the emergence of a moral and political climate that has shifted to a new Social Darwinism, the issues which framed the democratic meaning, purpose, and use to which education might aspire have been displaced by more vocational and narrowly ideological considerations.

The war waged against the possibilities of an education wedded to the precepts of a real democracy is not merely ideological. Against the backdrop of reduced funding for public schooling, the call for privatization, vouchers, cultural uniformity, and choice, there are the often ignored larger social realities of material power and oppression. On the national level, there has been a vast resurgence of racism. This is evident in the passing of anti-immigration laws such as Proposition 187 in California, the dismantling of the welfare state, the demonization of black youth that is taking place in the popular media, and the remarkable attention provided by the media to forms of race talk that argue for the intellectual inferiority of blacks or dismiss calls for racial justice as simply a holdover from the "morally bankrupt" legacy of the 1960s.

Poverty is on the rise among children in the United States, with 20 percent of all children under the age of eighteen living below the poverty line. Unemployment is growing at an alarming rate for poor youth of color, especially in the urban centers. While black youth are policed and disciplined in and out of the nation's schools, conservative and liberal educators define education through the ethically limp discourses of privatization, national standards, and global competitiveness.

Many writers in the critical education tradition have attempted to challenge the right-wing fundamentalism behind educational and social reform in both the United States and abroad while simultaneously providing ethical signposts for a public discourse about education and democracy that is both prophetic and transformative. Eschewing traditional categories, a diverse number of critical theorists and educators have successfully exposed the political and ethical implications of the cynicism and despair that has become endemic to the discourse of schooling and civic life. In its place, such educators strive to provide a language of hope that inextricably links the struggle over schooling to understanding and transforming our present social and cultural dangers.

At the risk of overgeneralizing, both cultural studies theorists and critical educators have emphasized the importance of understanding theory as the grounded basis for "intervening into contexts and power . . . in order to enable people to act more strategically in ways that may change their context for the better."[1] Moreover, theorists in both fields have argued for the primacy of the political by calling for and struggling to produce critical public spaces, regardless of how fleeting they may be, in which "popular cultural resistance is explored as a form of political resistance."[2] Such writers have analyzed the challenges that teachers will have to face in redefining a new mission for education, one that is linked to honoring the experiences, concerns, and diverse histories and languages that give expression to the multiple narratives that engage and challenge the legacy of democracy.

Equally significant is the insight of recent critical educational work that connects the politics of difference with concrete strategies for addressing the crucial relationships between schooling and the economy, and citizenship and the politics of meaning in communities of multicultural, multiracial, and multilingual schools.

Critical Studies in Education and Culture attempts to address and demonstrate how scholars working in the fields of cultural studies and the critical pedagogy might join together in a radical project and practice informed by theoretically rigorous discourses that affirm the critical but refuse the cynical, and establish hope as central to a critical pedagogical and political practice but eschew a romantic utopianism. Central to such a project is the issue of how pedagogy might provide cultural studies theorists and educators with an opportunity to engage pedagogical practices that are not only transdisciplinary, transgressive, and oppositional, but also connected to a wider project designed to further racial, economic, and political democracy.[3] By taking seriously the relations between culture and power, we further the possibilities of resistance, struggle, and change.

Critical Studies in Education and Culture is committed to publishing work that opens a narrative space that affirms the contextual and the specific while simultaneously recognizing the ways in which such spaces are shot through with issues of power. The series attempts to continue an important legacy of theoretical work in cultural studies in which related debates on pedagogy are understood and addressed within the larger context of social responsibility, civic courage, and the reconstruction of democratic public life. We must keep in mind Raymond Williams's insight that the "deepest impulse (informing cultural politics) is the desire to make learning part of the process of social change itself."[4] Education as a cultural pedagogical practice takes place across multiple sites, which include not only schools and universities but also the mass media, popular culture, and other public spheres, and signals how within diverse contexts, education makes us both subjects of and subject to relations of power.

This series challenges the current return to the primacy of market values and simultaneous retreat from politics so evident in the recent work of educational theorists, legislators, and policy analysts. Professional relegitimation in a troubled time seems to be the order of the day as an increasing number of academics both refuse to recognize public and higher education as critical public spheres and offer little or no resistance to the ongoing vocationalization of schooling, the continuing evisceration of the intellectual labor force, and the current assaults on the working poor, the elderly, and women and children.[5]

Emphasizing the centrality of politics, culture, and power. *Critical Studies in Education and Culture* will deal with pedagogical issues that contribute in imaginative and transformative ways to our understanding of how critical knowledge, democratic values, and social practices can provide a basis for teachers, students, and other cultural workers to redefine their role as engaged and public intellectuals. Each volume will attempt to rethink the relationship between language and experience, pedagogy and human agency, and ethics and social responsibility as part of a larger project for engaging and deepening the prospects of democratic schooling in a multiracial and multicultural society. *Critical Studies in Education and Culture* takes on the responsibility of witnessing and addressing the most pressing problems of public schooling and civic life, and engages culture as a crucial site and strategic force for productive social change.

Henry A. Giroux

NOTES

1. Lawrence Grossberg, "Toward a Genealogy of the State of Cultural Studies," in Cary Nelson and Dilip Parameshwar Gaonkar, eds., *Disciplinarity and Dissent in Cultural Studies* (New York: Routledge, 1996), 143.

2. David Bailey and Stuart Hall, "The Vertigo of Displacement," *Ten 8* 2:3 (1992), 19.

3. My notion of transdisciplinary comes from Mas'ud Zavarzadeh and Donald Morton, "Theory, Pedagogy, Politics: The Crisis of the "Subject" in the Humanities," in *Theory Pedagogy Politics: Texts for Change*, Mas'ud Zavarzadeh and Donald Morton, eds. (Urbana: University of Illinois Press, 1992), 10. At issue here is neither ignoring the boundaries of discipline-based knowledge nor simply fusing different disciplines, but creating theoretical paradigms, questions, and knowledge that cannot be taken up within the policed boundaries of the existing disciplines.

4. Raymond Williams, "Adult Education and Social Change," in *What I Came to Say* (London: Hutchinson-Radus, 1989), 158.

5. The term "professional legitimation" comes from a personal correspondence with Professor Jeff Williams of East Carolina University.

Acknowledgments

This book is intended to serve as an introduction to the philosophy and pedagogy of the prominent Brazilian educationist, Paulo Freire. I first encountered Freire's work in the early 1980s, and have continued to reflect on his writings for almost two decades. Although Freire has sometimes been regarded as an educational guru with disciples, or as a cultural and political hero with followers, I prefer to see him as a teacher, writer, and activist who opened avenues for others to explore. When viewed in this light, Freire becomes a thinker with whom one might travel—respectfully but not always agreeably—on one's own intellectual journey. Such journeys, as Freire would have reminded us, are often demanding and can never be completed alone.

I wish to acknowledge the special assistance provided by the following people, while also recognizing that I am indebted to many others not named here. I am grateful to Paulo Freire for encouraging others to address his work critically and for creating, through his actions and words, a legacy *worthy* of ongoing discussion and debate. Colin Lankshear prompted my initial exploration of Freirean ideas and has consistently demonstrated, better than anyone else I know, the importance of combining political commitment with scholarly rigor and philosophical clarity. Working with Michael Peters, my endlessly energetic colleague, has been an educative and valuable experience. Martin Sullivan has been a close friend and constant source of support since 1985. I would like to thank students who have participated in my classes on Freire at the University of Waikato and the University of Auckland for many stimulating and rewarding dialogues over the years. Jane Garry, Lynn Zelem, and Diane Burke have provided very prompt, professional, and helpful service in seeing this book through to publication with the Greenwood Publishing Group. Henry Giroux's immediate interest in the project, as editor of the *Critical Studies in Education and Culture* series, was a welcome boost. Thanks also to Ira Shor, Pamela Gay, Trevor Gale, Harvey Graff, Bill Pinar, Peter Mayo, Nicole Bishop, Megan Boler, Nicholas Burbules, Peter McLaren, Carlos Alberto Torres, Donaldo Macedo, James Paul Gee, and Michael Apple for helpful discussions and/or words of encouragement over the past few years. Finally, this book is dedicated to my wife, Linda, and our children, Ben and Emma, in heartfelt appreciation.

Introduction

Few educational thinkers have been more widely influential than Paulo Freire.[1] Freire's classic text, *Pedagogy of the Oppressed* (1972a), has been studied by numerous political activists, Left intellectuals, liberation theologians, and radical educationists over the last three decades. His ideas have been applied by school teachers, academics, adult literacy coordinators, development theorists, church leaders, counselors, psychologists, social workers, health professionals, prison rehabilitation workers, and language learning specialists, among others. Thousands of books, articles, theses, videos, interviews, and even theater productions have been directly or indirectly inspired by Freire. When Freire died on May 2, 1997 he left an extensive body of written work, much of it produced in the latter part of his life, and a legacy of memorable educational and political achievements.[2]

Drawing on his experiences with rural peasant communities and the urban poor in Brazil and Chile, Freire theorized an intimate connection between education and the process of becoming more fully human. For Freire, education is humanizing when it is critical, dialogical, and praxical. Repudiating the notion that education can be neutral, Freire calls on teachers to *disclose*, but *not impose*, their political views in seeking, with students, to more deeply understand a given object of study. To educate, in the Freirean sense, is to foster reflection and action on both "word" and "world." This entails the rigorous interrogation of texts and contexts, through structured, purposeful dialogue, coupled with practical involvement in the struggles of everyday life. Freire rejects a "banking" model of the teaching process in favor of a problem-posing approach, and encourages students to adopt a curious, questioning, probing stance in exploring educational issues. Freirean education demands a deep commitment to the goal of building a better social world, and necessitates active resistance against oppressive structures, ideas, and practices.

Part of the explanation for Freire's (ongoing) popularity, I believe, lies in the profoundly *hopeful* nature of his work. The title of one of Freire's later works, *Pedagogy of Hope* (1994), attests to the importance of this theme in his theory and practice. It is possible to read Freire's entire pedagogical history, from his initial adult literacy programs to his stint as Secretary of Education in São Paulo during the late 1980s and early 1990s, as a narrative of hope. Hope, for Freire, is "not just a question of grit or courage. It's an ontological dimension of our human condition" (Freire, 1998c, p. 47). Even in the most oppressive social circumstances, and perhaps *particularly* in such situations, Freire never resigned himself to a position of despair (cf. Freire, 1997a, p. 106). In *Pedagogy of the City*, he draws attention to the enormous obstacles facing democratic educators in contemporary Brazil. Other difficulties of a similar magnitude have been to the fore in Chile, Guinea-Bissau, Nicaragua, and Grenada: all countries to which Freire contributed as an adult educator or consultant. Yet, Freire always retained what he unashamedly refers to as a "utopian dream": a hope that through myriad forms of struggle, a society that is "less unjust, less cruel, more democratic, less discriminatory, less racist, [and] less sexist" might emerge (Freire, 1993a, p. 115).

Freire's work has attracted various criticisms over the years. Those who regard education as a neutral or technical process have complained that Freirean approaches "politicize" teaching and learning. Freire's refusal to provide "packages" has irritated those who seek clear-cut methodological solutions to educational problems. The use of the male pronoun in *Pedagogy of the Oppressed* and other early writings has been attacked. The notion of promoting a critical mode of consciousness has been questioned. Freire's focus on social class (at the expense of gender and ethnicity) in his early analyses of oppression has been rendered problematic by a number of contemporary educational theorists. Others suggest that Freire should have devoted more space in his books to class theory. Some critics have argued that Freirean pedagogy, contrary to its professed aims, constitutes a form of cultural invasion. Finally, as postmodern ideas have gained increasing currency in recent times, universalist assumptions in Freire's ethic, epistemology, and pedagogy have come under fire.

Some of these criticisms were addressed directly by Freire in his later books; others remain the subject of continuing debate. Freire commented on occasion that when confronted with criticisms of his work, he would try to avoid the temptation to assume the posture of a person who had been "wounded." His attempt to deal with criticism openly and honestly applied, by his own account, to all his dealings with others—even if he was not always as successful as he would like to have been in this. In *Pedagogy of Freedom*, he says:

> I have never been afraid of being criticized by my wife, by my children, or by the students with whom I have worked down the years because of my profound conviction of the value of freedom, hope, the word of another, and the desire of someone to try and try again as a result of having been more ingenuous than critical. (Freire, 1998c, p. 98)

Constructive criticism, for Freire, represented a positive invitation to examine hitherto accepted ideas afresh and to engage in dialogue—written or verbal—with others holding contrary positions (compare, Freire, 1985, pp. 151–152).

This book aims to make a modest contribution to this tradition of critical scholarship while also providing an introduction to some of Freire's major ideas. It does not claim to cover all dimensions of Freire's thought, nor does it deal comprehensively with a number of ongoing theoretical difficulties and important new lines of critique. Although Freire would have insisted that some readings of his work might be better than others, there can be no complete or final account of his theory and practice. The themes, events, and issues highlighted in these pages seem to me to be of enduring importance in attempting to understand Freire's philosophy and pedagogy. It is recognized, however, that many other interpretations of Freirean ideas are possible, and that a great deal of further work remains to be done.[3]

After brief biographical comments, this introduction discusses the question of how Freire's work might be approached by educationists from the First World. I argue that if we are to avoid the danger of domestication, both Freire's writings and his pedagogical practice must be properly contextualized. There are good reasons, I maintain, for studying Freire's ideas in a holistic and critical manner. In applying Freirean pedagogical principles, an antitechnocratic stance toward educational questions, issues, and problems is necessary. The introduction concludes with a summary of the structure and content of the book.

FREIRE: A BRIEF BIOGRAPHY

Paulo Reglus Neves Freire was born in Recife, Brazil, in 1921. He came from a middle-class family of four children. He retained fond memories of his childhood despite experiencing a number of significant hardships. As Freire notes in *Letters to Cristina* (1996, p. 21), he was connected to two groups during his childhood: the world of those who ate well (to whom his family was linked by their class position) and the poorer children from the outskirts of town (to whom he and his siblings were linked by hunger). The Freire family moved to Jaboatão when Freire was ten. Freire's father had spent some time in the army and later joined the Pernambuco Military Police. Arterial sclerosis forced him into retirement and eventually led to his death in 1934. As his mother battled, on only an "insignificant" widow's pension (p. 75), to support herself and her children, Freire experienced genuine hunger. He remembers falling asleep at the table, as if he had been drugged, while trying to complete his homework under the cloud of hunger (p. 15). He made dramatic improvements at school as more food returned to the family table (Freire and Shor, 1987, p. 29). Eventually, Freire was able to give supplementary lessons in Portuguese to other young people to enable him to complete his secondary education. After leaving school, he attended the University of Recife, where he enrolled in the secular School of Law.

Freire married Elza Oliveira—whose influence and encouragement Freire has frequently acknowledged[4]—while in his early twenties, and after completing his degree attempted only one case before abandoning his career as a lawyer (A.M.A. Freire and Macedo, 1998, p. 14). He had developed a strong interest in education, sparked initially by his study of linguistics and Portuguese grammar (Freire, 1996, p. 79). He and Elza became involved with the Catholic Action Movement, but quickly rejected the social conservatism characteristic of the established church at the time. Freire became closely associated with the Basic Church Communities, a movement that had "grown to accept the need for a clearer identification with the poor, and for a theology of liberation relevant to ordinary people" (Taylor, 1993, p. 22). In 1947, Freire started work with the Social Service of Industry (SESI) at the Regional Department of Pernambuco, where he was to stay for ten years. During his time with SESI, he coordinated a popular education program for working class adults. In later reflections, Freire was critical of the domesticating, paternalistic, and bureaucratic nature of SESI, but he also recognized that the organization's leader, Cid Sampaio, was more progressive than many of his industrial colleagues at the time (Freire, 1996, pp. 81–82). More than once he has noted that his contact with laborers, peasants, and fisherman at this time was seminal in the development of his ideas (see, for example, Freire, 1985, pp. 175–176; Freire and Shor, 1987, pp. 29–30). It was with SESI that Freire started to learn about the contradictions between different social classes (Freire, 1996, p. 83). Freire's emerging ideas on education and adult literacy were presented in his doctoral thesis in 1959, and, shortly after this, he accepted a chair in the history and philosophy of education at the University of Recife.

Following the success of a pilot adult literacy project in Recife in 1961,

Freire was appointed director of the Cultural Extension Service at the University of Recife. In this capacity, he developed the "culture circles" which were later to become famous. The prominence of his work with illiterate adults in the northeast was such that in 1963 Freire became director of Brazil's National Literacy Program. His goal from the start was that literacy should enable adults to learn how to read and write while simultaneously promoting a (more) critical understanding of oppressive social conditions. The program was highly effective in enabling adults to attain a basic competence with print in a very short period of time (see Brown, 1974; Sanders, 1972), but with the overthrow of the Goulart government by the military in 1964, the campaign was brought to an abrupt halt. Freire's approach to adult literacy education was seen as subversive, and he was twice placed under arrest (Mackie, 1980a, p. 5; Freire, 1985, p. 180). He was forced to travel to Rio de Janeiro to testify in a military-police inquiry (A.M.A. Freire and Macedo, 1998, p. 20).

After a short stay in Bolivia, Freire sought exile in Chile, where he was to remain for five years. He secured a post at the University of Santiago, and became involved in educating extension workers for the Chilean Agrarian Reform Corporation. During his time in Chile, he completed *Education: The Practice of Freedom* (Freire, 1976), incorporating parts of his doctoral thesis (see Freire, 1996, p. 87). In 1969, after receiving invitations from both Harvard University in the United States and the World Council of Churches in Switzerland, Freire decided to take up residence at the former for some months before moving to Geneva in February of the following year (Freire and Faundez, 1989, pp. 11–12). While at Harvard, he worked on the two essays that later became *Cultural Action for Freedom*,[5] and in 1970 the first English language version of *Pedagogy of the Oppressed* was released.[6] In his decade with the World Council of Churches, Freire was able to travel widely, visiting Africa, Asia, Latin America, the Caribbean, North America, Europe, and Australasia (p. 13). Throughout the 1970s, he continued to contribute to adult education programs in a number of Third World countries. His extensive involvement in adult literacy work in Guinea-Bissau in the mid-1970s provided the basis for *Pedagogy in Process: The Letters to Guinea-Bissau*, published in 1978. Freire also played a substantial role in literacy activities in São Tomé and Príncipe. Additionally, he served as a consultant for the Nicaraguan literacy crusade of 1980 and for adult education initiatives in Grenada.

During the 1980s, Freire was once again based in Brazil, and resumed university teaching duties in São Paulo. He made periodic visits to the United States following his return to Brazil, conducting seminars, lectures, and interviews. After a long period with no new publications of note,[7] Freire became more productive in his writing than ever before, collaborating in a series of coauthored, "talking" books with Ira Shor,

Donaldo Macedo, Antonio Faundez, Myles Horton, and others.[8] In the middle of this decade, Elza passed away, and in 1988, Freire married Ana Maria Araujo, a friend he had known since childhood. The late 1980s witnessed the emergence of a new phase in Freire's contribution to Brazilian politics with his appointment as Secretary of Education for the municipality of São Paulo in January 1989. A foundation member of the Brazilian Workers' Party, Freire supported Luis Inacio Lula da Silva, who narrowly lost the national presidential elections to Collor de Melo in 1989 (Torres, 1994a, p. 184). Freire resigned from his position in the Municipal Bureau of Education in 1991, convinced "his real skills and ambitions . . . [lay] in being a political educator rather than an educated politician" (Taylor, 1993, p. 33), and returned to his writing. He died of a heart attack on May 2, 1997.

From any account of Freire's life, it is clear that his prime commitment in education and politics was always to the Third World. The roots of Freire's pedagogy—his theory of what it means to be human, his ethical position, and his views on oppression—are deeply embedded in his experiences in Brazil, Chile, and other Third World countries. Since 1970, his ideas have been enthusiastically embraced by an increasing number of theorists and activists in the First World. Care needs to be taken, however, in interpreting and applying Freirean ideas in Western settings. The next section highlights some of the risks associated with this enterprise, and argues against the domestication of Freire's work.

APPROACHING FREIRE FROM THE FIRST WORLD

Western scholars have always enjoyed an ambivalent relationship with their Third World colleagues. On the one hand, the work of activists and intellectuals from Latin America and Africa (among other parts of the world) has been a source of fascination and inspiration for First World academics of a radical persuasion. Revolutionary leaders have been, if not revered, at least cautiously admired by many Left intellectuals struggling against dominant ideas (and social structures). There appears to be much that can be learned from Third World writers in seeking avenues for resistance in the First World. On the other hand, the problems that beset Third World countries are significantly different—sometimes if only in degree but often in kind—to those which confront the United States, Canada, Britain, Australia, and New Zealand. In applying the insights of Third World thinkers to First World settings, special care must be taken not to domesticate their ideas.

Certainly it can be claimed that within most First World countries there is—in effect—a Third World: the existence of genuine poverty in ostensibly "civilized" societies has become (even more) readily apparent in recent years as an increasing number of people turn to food banks and other emergency sources to satisfy basic human needs. Unemployment and underemployment are now seemingly permanent features of most industrialized societies. While at one end of the social scale a growing underclass emerges, at the other multinational corporations seek to gain a stranglehold over the production and circulation of essential goods and services. Legislative moves to lower wages and crush the power of unions—the Employment Contracts Act in New Zealand, for instance—have exacerbated existing disparities between the rich and the poor.

Paulo Freire speaks of both a Third World within the First World and a First World within the Third World. From Freire's point of view, the notion of a Third World is ideological and political, not (merely) geographic: "The Third World is in the last analysis the world of silence, of oppression, of dependence, of exploitation, of the violence exercised by the ruling classes on the oppressed" (1985, p. 140). These conditions are clearly evident in Western countries, just as within so-called "underdeveloped" nations elite groups enjoy a life of luxury and opulence. It could be suggested, moreover, that given the continuing growth of global networks of trade and communication, and the breakdown of the Cold War, the very categories of "Third World" and "First World" are now highly problematic. There can be little doubt that the world is changing (rapidly and dramatically), yet the manifestation of gross inequities between nations is, I believe, still sufficiently self-evident to retain certain distinctions. Hunger, exploitation, and oppression are rife throughout the First World, but the difficulties endured by millions of people in the Third World (widespread malnutrition, diseases almost out of control, alarming rates of infant mortality, appalling housing conditions, staggeringly low or nonexistent wages, etc.) are, in both scale and severity, of a magnitude few in Western societies could imagine. Freire changed his terminology in some of his later works, adopting the "North/South" nomenclature in discussing relations between groups of countries (see Freire, 1996, pp. 179–180), but remained opposed to narratives claiming the disappearance of structural inequalities between nations. The Third World, despite all the recent talk of globalization, is still a *different* world, and any attempt to apply theoretical frameworks, methodological principles, or innovations in practice from that world to the First World must proceed cautiously.

Education is one area of human endeavor where the hazards of domestication have particular significance, and Freire's pedagogy seems to have been especially prone to this problem. As word of Freire's success in adult literacy work spread and his reputation as an educationist grew, the risk of distortion in conveying his ideas also increased. Among other problematic tendencies, failing to consider Freire's work in its social context, fragmentation in reading his texts, and reductionism in appropriating Freirean concepts, principles, and practices are especially common. To counter these possibilities, I want to suggest that Freire should be read contextually, holistically, and critically.

Considering Freire's Work in Its Social Context

Any comprehensive assessment of Freire's pedagogy must take into account the historical, cultural, and political contexts in which he worked. During the 1950s and early 1960s, Brazil was characterized by immense inequalities in the distribution of resources, with a high concentration of wealth in the hands of a few elite landowners and grinding poverty among rural peasant communities and the urban poor. Inequities between different groups in housing, food and water supplies, and provisions for health care and education were glaringly apparent. Then, as now, Brazil was a deeply divided society. Writing about the situation Freire faced as Secretary of Education, Torres talks of São Paulo's

> seemingly insurmountable problems of abandoned children living in the streets, growing poverty and urban violence, fiscal constraints, particularly due to Brazil's growing external debt, and the peculiarities of post-dictatorship Brazilian politics and electoral struggle. (Torres and Freire, 1994, p. 105)

In later texts, Freire speaks of corruption and violence at the highest levels of the Brazilian political system. Referring in 1996 to the "Collored or de-Collored PC's" in the 1990s, he says: "they steal, they kill, they violate, they kidnap, and nothing or almost nothing happens" (Freire, 1996, p. 46).

Although Freire was careful from the beginning not to see literacy as a cure-all for Brazil's social ills, he believed widespread illiteracy was a symptom of deep structural injustices. For Freire, illiteracy did not "cause" poor health or nutrition; nor did it "explain" the sharp divisions between classes in Brazil. Rather, the high rates of illiteracy among the poor reflected and reinforced wider imbalances in power and control. Patterned illiteracy, from Freire's point of view, was a direct consequence of political policies and an oppressive social order. Under these circumstances, becoming literate was always going to be about much *more* than "simply" learning how to read and write. For Freire, literacy was inextricably linked with the broader process of social transformation. The very character of the literacy learning promoted by Freire was shaped by a particular conception of Brazilian reality and a distinct vision of life under more liberating social conditions.

As chapter 4 demonstrates, in content and style the literacy campaign was profoundly Brazilian. The words and themes which formed the core of the program were derived in large measure from the people with whom the literacy facilitators were working. The discussion of nature, culture, work, and human relationships, which preceded what is sometimes (erroneously) called "the actual literacy training," was, according to one commentator at least, well suited to the willingness among Brazilians—when appropriately prompted—to talk about their world (Sanders, 1972, p. 593). Although many of the issues problematized in Freire's culture circles were, it might be claimed, of universal human significance, the aims of the program were quite specific: it was liberation from the particular forms of hardship and exploitation endured by the oppressed in Brazil during a given historical period with which Freire was concerned in the first instance.

The risks associated with decontextualized analyses of Freirean concepts have been vividly displayed in certain interpretations of "conscientization." (This issue is addressed at length in chapter 8.) Freire's depiction of three levels of consciousness (magical, naive, and critical) in his early works is certainly ripe for philosophical interrogation. When this framework is divorced from the social situation in which it was initially grounded, however, new difficulties arise. The translation of "conscientization" into "consciousness raising" is especially problematic, as is the systematization of Freire's three levels into distinct, sequential stages of predefined personality and behavioral characteristics. Freire used the terms "magical" and "naive" to try and capture the essence of modes of thinking and acting among specific groups within Brazilian society during given historical periods. His theory of conscientization, as it was originally developed, was intended to explain (in the case of magical and naive levels of consciousness) that which already existed in a particular society; it was *not* meant to serve as a blueprint for categorizing individuals in *all* societies.

Although Freire welcomed critical engagement with all aspects of his work (a point I discuss further below), he positively urged readers to consider the context within which his ideas emerged when examining his texts. In one interview, he expressed dismay at the form of anger generated by his use of the male referent in *Pedagogy of the Oppressed*:

> I received not long ago a letter from a young woman who recently came across *Pedagogy of the Oppressed* for the first time, criticizing my *machista* language. This letter was very insulting and somewhat vulgar but I was not upset by it. I was not upset by her letter because, most certainly, she has only read *Pedagogy of the Oppressed* and evaluated my language as if this book were written last year. (Freire and Macedo, 1993, p. 171)

Freire is quick to point out that he is *not* making excuses for the sexist language in the book but simply stressing that his work must be viewed in the light of his social and cultural background.[9] During his formative years, he "did not escape the enveloping powers of a highly sexist culture"; in later publications, Freire insisted that those translating his books into English use nonsexist language (p. 171). He acknowledges his debt to North American feminists in developing a greater awareness of issues of gender oppression. Both theoretical and social/cultural influences on an author's ideas (and the author's communication of them) need to be taken into account. Freire admits that his major focus when writing *Pedagogy of the Oppressed* was social class. This not only reflected the visibility of "incredibly cruel" class oppression in Brazil, but also the towering influence of Marx over Freire's intellectual development (p. 172). If Freire neglected questions of gender in his early writings, this can be explained (he claims), at least in part, by the lack of feminist works available to him at the time. Were he to write *Pedagogy of the Oppressed* today, Freire notes, "and ignore the immense world of information regarding sex discrimination and the level of awareness concerning sexism that both men and women have today, some of the criticism leveled against . . . [the book] would not only be valid but would be most necessary" (p. 173).[10]

Reading Freire Holistically

Freire first gained widespread international recognition in the early 1970s. With the publication of *Pedagogy of the Oppressed* in English, his ideas became the subject of much discussion among educationists, political activists, and social theorists in the West. Riding a wave of discontent with conventional teaching methods and state-funded systems of education,[11] Freire enjoyed a popularity uncommon among radical thinkers. *Pedagogy of the Oppressed* appeared at "an intensely troubled moment in history" (Freire, 1994, p. 120). Social movements—against sexism, racism, nuclear arms, and the destruction of the natural environment—were already well underway. The deschooling movement had taken off, and Freire was frequently seen as an ally to two of its most prominent spokespersons, Ivan Illich and Everett Reimer. Although a retrospective assessment suggests Freire's theoretical and political kinship with the deschoolers was rather more tenuous than formerly believed,[12] he shared with Illich and Reimer grave concerns about the formal educational institutions of the time, a commitment to improving the living conditions of people in Latin America, and a desire to enhance worthwhile modes of learning and being. Along with many other radical educationists— particularly, though not exclusively, marxists—Freire saw existing schools as (primarily) sites for reproducing rather than resisting existing social inequities. Freire believed the alternative approach to education articulated in his books and embodied in his practice was based on a deeper understanding of human beings and the learning process than traditional systems of instruction in schools and other formal educational settings.

Pedagogy of the Oppressed became a bible for those dissatisfied with prevailing forms of pedagogy: "Banking education" emerged as an academic buzzword, and "problem-posing education" quickly joined conscientization and dialogue as one of the least understood constructs in Freire's work. At seminar after seminar and in paper after paper, Freire was compelled to explain what these terms meant in his philosophy, yet confusion persisted. The frustrations he experienced in trying to clarify complex concepts may have contributed to the dramatic decline in Freire's use of the most controversial of these terms, conscientization, in his writings from the mid-1970s to the mid-1980s.

Freire refined and reworked other key notions in his many publications following the release of *Pedagogy of the Oppressed* in English. Yet many educationists and activists continued to base their understanding of his ideas on a reading of only very limited segments of his work. *Pedagogy of the Oppressed* is without doubt Freire's most famous book; it also provides perhaps the best concise presentation of key dimensions of his philosophy—particularly his ontological distinction between humanization and dehumanization. In any major study of Freire, this book is bound (and ought) to feature prominently in discussion. Yet, in the years after the publication of this classic text, there were significant changes both in Freire's own thinking and wider theoretical developments in education and other fields. By the early 1990s, Freire could call on the experience of extensive work in Guinea-Bissau, he had returned to Brazil and again become active in national politics, and he had continued—particularly via his coauthored "talking" books—to reflect critically on his earlier ideas. Whether agreeing or disagreeing with Freire, it is vital that readers address his work holistically. Freire's influence has extended to a wide range of educational, political, and theological groups. From one point of view, this diversity is positive testament to Freire's eclecticism and the broad appeal of his ideas. There is, however, also a danger that Freirean theory may be spread too thinly. Freire cannot be all things to all people. More importantly, still, his work should not be turned into something it is not. Distortions of the Freirean educational ideal have resulted not infrequently from superficial and selective readings of mere fragments of Freire's work or, worse, from the passing of purportedly Freirean ideas from person to person in increasingly "watered-down" form. In some cases, those who declare themselves Freireans possess, at best, a "secondhand" knowledge of Freire's texts. Any reasonably attentive reading of *Pedagogy of the Oppressed* negates, for example, the hypothesis that Freire supported a laissez-faire style of pedagogy; for an elaboration of the *reasons* behind Freire's rejection of such an approach, though, one must turn to later books.

Of course, a fragmented reading or secondhand knowledge of Freire does not always result in the gross misrepresentation of his ideas. Nevertheless, to judge by Freire's own comments, serious distortions were not uncommon (see, for example, Freire, 1985, pp. 123–125, 152; 1994, pp. 73–77; Fonseca, 1973, p. 94). Freire often championed the value of a well-rounded, global approach to texts. He acknowledged the importance of not sacrificing depth in favor of breadth in reading, but also suggested that any serious, comprehensive effort to understand a given theorist's thought demands careful, critical scrutiny of as many dimensions of that thinker's work as time and resources allow. Educators who attempt to get to grips with Freire's ideas through finding out about them secondhand, or by giving his publications only a very partial reading, not only run the risk of doing a disservice to Freire but also to the students with whom they work.

A holistic approach to studying Freire is necessary if inconsistencies and shifts in his theory are to be identified and analyzed. By way of illustration, reference might be made to Freire's delineation of three "moments" in his understanding of the relationship between education and politics. The first shift in his political position is highlighted by the contrast between the liberalism of *Education: The Practice of Freedom* and the revolutionary ethics of *Pedagogy of the Oppressed*. Where in the former Freire "did not speak about politics and education," in the latter he addressed the "political aspects" of education. By 1987, Freire was able to talk of a third moment, noting that he then believed "education *is* politics" (Freire and Shor, 1987, p. 61).

Freire always saw himself as a reflexive thinker (even if some of his critics may have disagreed with this assessment), constantly restless in his search for a deeper understanding of social reality, and ever-prepared to reexamine and repudiate earlier assumptions where necessary (compare, Freire, 1976, p. 195; 1985, p. 180). It is to be expected of any theorist that some of his or her ideas might change over the course of a long career. Paradoxically, it is entirely consistent with Freirean principles that inconsistencies of a kind occur from time to time. The critical reflection Freire advocates applies as much to his own work as it does to any other sphere of activity. In many cases, the impetus for this interrogation has been provided by others who have read and responded critically to his texts. Feminists provided the impulse for a change in Freire's written expression (and his perception of oppression); marxist critics enabled him to deepen his understanding of class; and, although Freire remained essentially a modernist thinker, he did acknowledge and incorporate a number of postmodern insights in his later works (see, for example, Freire, 1993b, 1994, 1998b).

Avoiding Reductionism in Applying Freire's Ideas

Freire always maintained that his pedagogy could not be reduced to a set of techniques, skills, or methods. In his literacy work in Brazil, for instance, the "mechanical" aspects of reading and writing (learning how to form and decode letters, words, and sentences) were but one part of the program, inseparable from the wider discussions of nature, culture, work, and human relationships, and intimately connected with the enhancement of political consciousness among participants. Yet, as Aronowitz (1993, p. 8) notes, "Freire's ideas have been assimilated to the prevailing obsession of North American education, following a tendency in all the human and social sciences, with *methods*—of verifying knowledge and, in schools, of teaching, that is, transmitting knowledge to otherwise unprepared students." This propensity is one aspect of the wider tendency—not only in the United States but in Canada, Britain, Australia, and New Zealand as well—to translate Freirean theory and practice into technocratic terms. The term "pedagogy"—employed by Freire to denote a complex philosophy, politics, and practice of education—has been narrowly conceived by some as merely "teaching methods." This had led to a proliferation of supposedly Freirean courses and programs, where teachers, often with the best of intentions, have assumed that modifications in teacher-student roles and changes in subject matter suffice as examples of liberating education.

Incomplete readings of Freirean texts serve to compound this problem. A misappropriation of Freire's list of characteristics of "banking education" in *Pedagogy of the Oppressed* (1972a, pp. 46–47), for example, might lead to the mistaken belief that the Freirean critique of dehumanizing pedagogical approaches can be *completely* summarized and explained in a list of ten methods and attitudes. Neither banking education nor problem-posing education can be encapsulated in a set of prescriptive rules (cf. Brady, 1994, p. 144). Of course, there *are* certain attitudes, methodological principles, and techniques (e.g., for teaching reading and writing) that contribute to the distinctive character of Freirean education; the point is, however, that Freire's philosophy and practice imply *more* than this. In particular, Freire built his pedagogy on a deep understanding of social theory (especially those strands derived from Marx), and demanded of educators a clear ethical and political commitment to transforming oppressive social conditions. The risks of such a stance were lucidly highlighted by Freire's own experiences: he was arrested, exiled from his homeland, and savagely criticized. Others have been killed in their efforts to assist in the liberation of marginalized and exploited groups. Methods and techniques flow from revolutionary commitment, but they do not define it.

A second (closely related) problem is that Freire has been used to justify or legitimate classroom practices which have, at best, only a limited or spurious connection with his pedagogy. In some cases, the use of Freire's name as a banner for support is mischievous or positively misleading. For example, teachers who describe themselves as "Freireans" simply because they encourage students to discuss ideas among themselves or allow the political issues of the day to become a subject for student projects unwittingly make a mockery of the depth of Freire's theory and practice. Frequently, avowedly Freirean educators ask students to share their own experiences with others, working earnestly to set up a caring, supportive environment for this purpose. Yet many eschew the clear Freirean imperative to examine personal experiences *critically*; this demands reflection on, rather than mere affirmation of, existing views and assumptions. Freire was not against educators adapting his ideas to suit their own circumstances; indeed, he spoke of some efforts in this direction as "exceedingly productive work" (Freire, 1993b, p. ix). But he did object to his name being falsely invoked, and sometimes expressed surprise at the number of programs, courses, practices, and attitudes which were *purportedly*, but not demonstrably, Freirean in orientation.

There is a flip-side to this problem. Classroom processes have changed dramatically over the past three decades in many Western countries. Many of these changes bear a certain similarity to transformations suggested by Freire in his discussion (and implementation) of problem-posing education. Far from being excessively eager to call upon Freire's name, politicians, policy makers, and those responsible for training teachers have sometimes not even heard of Freire, let alone read his work. Just as Illich (1971) has long been forgotten in many references to the "hidden curriculum," so too is Freire often invisible in criticisms of "banking" education. This problem reflects a wider ignorance of the history of educational thought. It is a matter for amusement as well as mild annoyance that students graduating from colleges of education frequently make reference to the *new* interactive, experience-based approaches to teaching currently being promoted in schools, as if Steiner, Dewey, Freire, and a host of other educationists had never existed. Of course, there are important differences between these theorists, and between their ideas and those being promulgated in new curriculum developments. But credit should be given where credit is due. Thus, it is crucial that practices which only vaguely or partially resemble Freirean pedagogy be identified as such and described as, at most, "reworkings" or "revisions" or "modifications" of Freirean ideas. On the other hand, it is equally important that past contributions to educational theory and practice be accorded the recognition they deserve, and that ideas which masquerade as original or groundbreaking developments in pedagogical theory be placed in their proper historical context.

At a different level, reductionist tendencies in the application of Freirean theory are signified by the "watering down" of complex concepts to a point where they lose their original force. This phenomenon is not confined to adaptations of Freirean ideas. Dale has noted that

> "the state" may be in danger of becoming an example of a vital concept drained of its original value through promiscuous use in exercises of theoretical painting by numbers, and consequently at risk of joining "resistance" and "critical" ... on the shelves of theoretical banality. The danger is that, like them, "the state" has come to be used to *name* the space where theoretical work is needed rather than to fill that space, and worse, by such naming, to apparently preclude the need for more theoretical work. (cited in Lankshear and McLaren, 1993, pp. xvi–xvii)

The theoretical impoverishment of many contemporary discussions of "empowerment"—an ideal often associated with Freire's work—has also been the subject of some attention. Lankshear (1994a, p. 59) argues that the notion of empowerment is "in danger of being trivialized through unreflective over-use and, consequently, of losing its semantic viability and persuasive force." Freirean concepts seem to be particularly susceptible to the problems identified by Dale and Lankshear.[13] The fate of conscientization has already been noted. "Dialogue," too, has frequently been reduced to a shadow of its former self in (mis)appropriations of Freirean ideas in First World settings. Almost any form of discourse between two or more people now appears to count in some educational arenas as an example of Freirean dialogue in action. Yet, as I argue in later chapters, Freire is adamant that educational dialogue should have a clear purpose, a sense of structure, and a definite direction (see Freire, 1972a, pp. 61, 65; Freire and Shor, 1987, pp. 102, 109, 171–172). Freirean dialogue is *not* an "anything goes" affair; that is, it cannot be equated with (and indeed must be opposed to) mere "idle conversation."

Finally, if Aronowitz's (1993) appraisal of the U.S. education scene is accurate (and indicative of trends elsewhere in the Western world), Freire appears to have often been viewed through distinctly atheoretical lenses. By this I do not mean that the self-proclaimed Freireans to whom Aronowitz refers bring no theoretical assumptions to bear on their interpretation or adaptation of Freire's work; this, Freire himself would have reminded us, is an impossibility. Rather, it is a case of forgetting "where Freire comes from" in not only the physical, social, and cultural

senses but the intellectual as well. Freire draws on a wide range of intellectual traditions (Mackie, 1980b), and regularly refers to other theorists' ideas. His pedagogy is a *synthesis* of theory and practice:
attempting to practice supposedly Freirean "methods" in schools and
other settings without examining Freirean theory denies this dialectical
relationship.

Reading Freire's Work Critically

People who met Freire or heard him speak often identified the quality
of humility as one of his distinguishing character traits. Despite the numerous official honors and collegial tributes bestowed on him,[14] he never
claimed to have anything especially original or insightful to offer; instead, he preferred to think of himself as a "vagabond of the obvious"
(Shallcrass, 1974, p. 24). When asked in 1974 why his books had become
so popular and widely read, Freire replied, "Mainly because they are
saying obvious things, which a lot of people have inside them, but which
they have not been able to express. They discover themselves when they
read the books and think—'that is precisely what I thought'" (*New Citizen*, 1974).

Freire frequently acknowledged his indebtedness to numerous people,
including not only his intellectual forbears, but also those with whom he
has worked (as both a teacher and colleague) over the years. The success
of his literacy efforts in Brazil and Chile, together with the enormous
impact of *Pedagogy of the Oppressed*, brought Freire international recognition and widespread acclaim. Freire provided the inspiration for a
fresh examination of pedagogy and literacy, and gave many educationists a model of how theory and practice might be dynamically intertwined. However, this sudden attention also had the effect of
mythicizing Freire and his approach to education.[15] Conscientization
quickly came to be perceived by some as some kind of magic bullet,
capable of miraculously curing social ills overnight (see Freire's comments in *LP News Service*, 1971). Freire was elevated to gurulike status
and spoken of in reverential tones in some quarters. In the field of adult
education, especially, Freire became almost an academic god. His work
injected a scholarly rigor—supported by practical experience—into adult
learning discourses, strengthening the legitimacy of the field as a serious
area for inquiry within universities and other institutions (Findsen, 1999).
Such adoration has always made Freire nervous (compare, Hill, 1974;
Rowe, 1974, p. 7). It is undeniable that Freire has been regarded as a
"radical hero" by some (see Coben, 1998), but such heroization is highly
problematic (Boler, 1999). Freire resisted—perhaps not altogether successfully—attempts by others to turn him into a myth during the 1970s,

seeking instead to let his actions speak for themselves via his commitment to a range of educational and political initiatives.

The uncritical acceptance of Freirean principles contradicts Freire's insistence that readers actively engage and debate his work. At the end of
The Politics of Education, for example, he advises readers to reread his
book, with the second reading being far more critical than the first (Freire, 1985, p. 198). The caveats noted earlier in this introduction confirm
rather than contradict this objective, for, among other features, a critical
approach to texts implies reading them globally and in context. Freire
wanted readers to neither reject nor accept anything he says at face value:
in reading his books, as with all other texts, he believed an effort should
be made to get beneath the surface, searching, as he would put it, for
the raison d'être or essence which explains the object of study. He was
fundamentally opposed to mythicizing activity, whether it involved himself or anyone else. Freire spoke disparagingly of the ideological misrepresentation of reality by dominant groups and urged educators and
others to break myths down. His pedagogy does not provide a panacea
for oppression: Freire was always careful not to overestimate the potential of education for bringing about structural change (see Freire, 1975,
p. 16; 1998c, p. 110; Freire and Shor, 1987, pp. 31–32). The same could be
said of our expectations of Freire as social theorist. Freire's work has
much to offer in seeking to understand relationships between education,
literacy, oppression, and liberation, but of course it also has its limits.
Many of the metaphysical, ontological, epistemological, ethical, and political questions addressed by Freire have been investigated in a more
sophisticated and extended way by others (e.g., philosophers and political scientists) who have been less concerned with pedagogical issues.
Freire was aware of some of his own weaknesses and welcomed opportunities to read the work of peers who had engaged and extended his
ideas.

EDUCATION, LITERACY, AND HUMANIZATION

Freire's work, flawed though it may be, has much to offer First World
theorists and practitioners in education and a diverse range of other
fields. Freire encourages Western educators to "reinvent" his ideas in
addressing the themes and tasks that characterize their own struggles.
He also stresses, however, that this process of reinvention should be
based on a *thorough* reading of his books and an acknowledgment of the
particular social circumstances under which his pedagogy was forged.
In adapting Freirean theory to suit specific First World educative situations the risk of domesticating his ideas is ever-present. There *are* certain
key ideas in Freire's theory which (he would argue) transcend national

and cultural boundaries, but to comprehend the full significance of these principles *for* Freire, his work must be studied holistically, contextually, and critically.

With these comments in mind, chapter 1 provides a broad overview of Freire's major writings, concentrating in particular on the relationship between *Pedagogy of the Oppressed* (1972a) and later books in the Freirean corpus. While the importance of *Pedagogy of the Oppressed* is noted, the chapter also points to some of the potential dangers in placing excessive emphasis on this book over others. Three periods in Freire's publishing career are identified: an early phase (from the mid-1960s to the mid-1970s) dominated by the release of *Pedagogy of the Oppressed* in the English-speaking world; a quieter period (the decade between 1976 and 1986) where *Pedagogy in Process: The Letters to Guinea-Bissau* (1978) was the only publication of note; and an extraordinarily productive final phase beginning with Freire and Shor's *A Pedagogy for Liberation* in 1987. The chapter stresses the significance of these often-neglected later works for understanding Freire's views on the nature of critical reading, Left and Right politics, the relationship between teachers and students, questions of unity and diversity, and a host of other issues.

Chapter 2 addresses the metaphysical, ontological, epistemological, and ethical dimensions to Freire's thought. Comparisons with Plato, Aristotle, and others are drawn to elucidate distinctive elements of Freire's theory of knowledge and his ideal of humanization. A number of key moral principles in Freire's work are identified. The analysis in this chapter suggests that Freire's philosophy is built on a dialectical approach toward the world and a deep commitment to the liberation of the oppressed. Freire speaks of a dynamic process of interaction and constant change between the objective (material) and subjective (conscious) spheres of reality. Humans, for Freire, are necessarily incomplete, imperfect beings. The quest to "know," similarly, is an unending process, and "absolute knowledge" is unattainable. The essence of humanization, from a Freirean point of view, lies in the concept of praxis: critical, dialogical reflection and action on the world to transform it.

In chapter 3, the arguments advanced in this introduction and the first chapter find further elaboration in relation to Freire's educational theory. Freire's discussion of banking education and problem-posing education in *Pedagogy of the Oppressed* has exerted considerable influence among educators in both the Third World and the First World over the past three decades. This classic account needs, however, to be read alongside subsequent publications which, collectively, provide a richer and more complex set of ideas on teaching and learning. Freire's emphasis, especially in later books, on the need for structure, direction, and rigor in liberating education is discussed. I argue that Freire's pedagogy can best be understood not as a "method" but as a distinctive approach to human beings and the world. It is possible to generate a set of broad pedagogical principles from a reading of Freire's work, but the development of appropriate methods for teaching and learning will vary from one context to another.

Chapters 4 and 5 address different dimensions of Freire's literacy work. Freire's experiences with Brazilian and Chilean adults in the 1960s are succinctly described in two of his early books, *Education: The Practice of Freedom* (1976) and *Cultural Action for Freedom* (1972b), and have attracted extensive comment over the last thirty years. Chapter 4 furnishes a summary of Freire's initiatives in these countries and comments briefly on other literacy programs with which Freire was involved in the 1970s. Chapter 5 attempts to integrate insights from Freire's later texts and earlier practical experiences via the notion of the multidimensional "word." The word, for Freire, comprises spoken, written, and active dimensions, and provides the pivot on which programs of literacy education turn. I argue that Freire's concept of literacy is considerably broader than the conventional view. From a Freirean standpoint, literacy is a political phenomenon, intimately related to personal and collective experience. Freirean *critical* literacy implies not merely engagement with printed texts, but the development of a reflective, dialogical, praxical mode of social being, grounded in a narrative of hope, an ethic of struggle, and a pedagogy of transformation.

Chapter 6 outlines and addresses some of the major criticisms of Freire's work from the past three decades. Several thinkers have focused on questions pertaining to Freirean pedagogical intervention: Bowers concentrates on cultural and linguistic issues; Berger attacks the concept of conscientization; and Walker identifies antidialogical currents in Freire's politics. Others—Ellsworth and Weiler among them—argue that Freire relies on a universalist philosophical language and ignores the particulars of oppression and liberation. Taken together, these critiques ask searching questions about the very foundations on which Freire's pedagogy rests. I provide preliminary comments on some of these criticisms in this chapter, and develop my ideas further in chapters 7 and 8. Chapter 6 is concerned, in part, with Freire's responses to his critics. From the views he expressed on the different positions assumed by the Right and the Left in contemporary politics, the "fatalism" of neoliberal discourses, and the need for "unity in diversity," it is clear that although Freire accepted a number of postmodern insights, he remained a modernist thinker: a philosopher, educationist, and activist committed to what he called, in one of his last works (Freire, 1998c), a "universal human ethic."

Chapter 7 responds in more detail to the challenges Bowers poses for Freirean educators. Bowers sees Freire as a "carrier" of a highly problematic Western mind set: one that has a "cultural bias" toward progressive change, critical reflection, and intervention. Bowers maintains that Freirean adult literacy programs, in challenging traditional systems of authority and belief, are potentially invasive and hegemonic. The chapter critiques Bowers's analysis and defends Freire's pedagogical interventionism. I argue that Bowers homogenizes Western modes of thought and action, distorts Freirean theory, romanticizes "traditional" cultures, and ignores the concrete realities of the situations with which Freire was dealing. The chapter develops the view that programs of education are necessarily interventionist, and concludes that Freire's pedagogical approach, while not without its difficulties, can be strongly defended.

Freire's concept of conscientization has been the subject of considerable debate since the early 1970s. One way of interpreting conscientization is to see it as a process of consciousness raising, whereby individuals move through a sequence of distinct stages. The final chapter critiques the "stages" model and advances an alternative perspective on conscientization. Rejecting an individualist view of critical consciousness, I concentrate on the link between conscientization and praxis, and reassess Freire's ideal in the light of the postmodernist notion of multiple subjectivities.

NOTES

1. For an indication of how extensive Freire's influence across the globe has been, see the fall issue of *Taboo: The Journal of Culture and Education*, volume 2, published in 1997. The journal contains a wide range of tributes to Freire—varying in length from a few words to several pages—from people in Brazil, Mexico, the United States, Canada, England, Australia, Malta, and New Zealand, among other countries.

2. Events in Freire's life will be described in the past tense, but his books will be discussed in the present tense. This seems appropriate when addressing a theorist who urged readers to engage in a "live" dialogue with texts rather than treating them as "dead documents."

3. The book is part of a wider project on the theory and practice of Freirean education. This text deals, in an introductory way, with major philosophical and pedagogical principles in Freire's work. It is hoped that another book with a more applied focus—the application of Freirean ideas to debates over curriculum reform, political correctness, and higher education—will be published in the near future. The present volume draws on a range of previously published essays. Part of the introduction is based on an article published in the *International Journal of Lifelong Education* (Roberts, 1996a). Earlier versions of chapters 1 and 2 appeared in *The New Zealand Journal of Adult Learning* (Roberts, 1998a) and the *Journal of Educational Thought* (Roberts, 1998b), respectively. Chapter 3 has been adapted from a longer essay in the *Oxford Review of Education*

(Roberts, 1996b). Parts of a paper from *Educational Studies* (Roberts, 1994) have been used in chapter 4. Chapter 5 originally appeared, in substantially similar form, in *Educational Review* (Roberts, 1998c). Small sections of chapter 6 were drawn from an article in *The Review of Education/Pedagogy/Cultural Studies* (Roberts, 1995a). Chapters 7 and 8 are based on papers first published in *Educational Theory* (Roberts, 1996d) and the *Journal of Philosophy of Education* (Roberts, 1996e).

4. See, for example, Freire (1985, p. 175).

5. One of the most widely circulated versions is the 1972 edition released by Penguin (Freire, 1972b). *Cultural Action for Freedom* comprises essays initially published in *Harvard Educational Review* in 1970.

6. The 1970 publication date refers to the Herder and Herder edition of the book. All citations in the present study are from the Penguin edition (Freire, 1972a).

7. Apart from his interview with Donaldo Macedo and the introduction by Henry Giroux, all of the material in Freire's *The Politics of Education* (1985) had been previously published.

8. Freire and Shor (1987); Freire and Macedo (1987); Horton and Freire (1990); Escobar et al. (1994).

9. Colin Lankshear recalls that his use of the female pronoun in *Freedom and Education* (1982) caused a "furore." The male referent was dominant in Anglo-American contexts until the mid-1980s. In private communication.

10. Mayo (1994) makes some helpful critical comments on Freire's analysis of gender issues in this conversation.

11. There were many different positions represented in the emerging "alternative" educational literature at the time. Some of the best known books were strongly polemical and deliberately provocative, rather than thoroughly argued academic treatises. Compare, for example, the following: Illich (1971); Reimer (1971); Goodman (1971); Postman and Weingartner (1971); Holt (1969, 1970, 1971).

12. If the major early texts by Illich and Freire are compared, it is clear that the latter's pedagogical ideas rest on a more thoroughly argued ontological, ethical and political theoretical base than the former's. Compare, for example, Illich (1971) and Freire (1972a). See also Freire's comments in Makins (1972, p. 80) and Lister (1973, p. 14).

13. Arguably, a litany of other concepts in social theory have been sapped of their original force and intent: empowerment, conscientization, and dialogue could be joined with critical thinking, liberation, collaboration, participation, and so on in a broader discussion of this issue.

14. For a list of many of these honors and awards, see A.M.A. Freire and Macedo (1998).

15. For one perspective on the myths associated with Freire, see Weiler (1996).

CHAPTER 1

Reading Freire

When Paulo Freire's name is mentioned, reference to his classic work—*Pedagogy of the Oppressed* (1972a)—almost invariably follows. People who know very little else about Freire are often at least aware that he was the author of this highly influential book. When Freire passed away on May 2, 1997, we were reminded of just how significant this text has been in the international scholarly community. Tributes to Freire poured in from around the globe. Many made some mention of *Pedagogy of the Oppressed*. Over the years, *Pedagogy of the Oppressed* not only has been read or cited by educationists but also activists and scholars in numerous other fields.[1] The book has been translated into a number of different languages, and in some—English, Spanish, and Portuguese—it has been reprinted numerous times since its initial publication three decades ago. *Pedagogy of the Oppressed* is, in short, one of the most widely read books by an educationist this century, and deserves to occupy a special place in the history of pedagogical thought.

This chapter acknowledges the importance of *Pedagogy of the Oppressed*, both for Freire and for others who have responded (sometimes critically) to the book, while at the same time drawing attention to some dangers associated with concentrating on this book at the expense of others within the wider corpus of Freirean texts. An overview of Freire's published works allows three major periods in his writing career to be identified. It is argued that of these periods, the last (1987–) is crucial in assessing Freire's views on, and contribution to, education, literacy, and politics. Somewhat surprisingly, the rich, multilayered body of work produced in this period is often ignored or downplayed. This, it is suggested, does not merely render readings of Freire incomplete; it also has a bearing on the way commentators interpret *Pedagogy of the Oppressed*. A holistic reading allows a more complex picture both of Freirean theory in general and the place of *Pedagogy of the Oppressed* in that theory in particular, to emerge.

FREIRE'S PUBLISHED WORKS

For the purposes of this discussion, three phases in Freire's writing career are identified: an early period (1965–1975), anchored by the release of *Pedagogy of the Oppressed* in English in 1970; a quieter phase (1976–1986), where the only significant new work was a book based on Freire's experiences as an adult educator in Guinea-Bissau; and a prolific last decade (1987–   ), in which Freire, often in dialogical collaboration with others, wrote at length on the process of teaching, the politics of literacy, the administration of schooling in Brazil, higher education and intellectual life, and the importance of structure, direction, and rigor in liberating education, among other topics. (Several books have been published posthumously, and some of these carry publication dates of later than 1997. For this reason, the last period, while about a decade in length in terms of the commitment of Freire's writing time, remains open. It is possible that other partially completed works will over the next few years be edited and published under Freire's name.)

The Early Works (1965–1975)

When *Pedagogy of the Oppressed* was published in English in 1970 it had a dramatic and almost immediate impact on the educational world. This famous text was the first of Freire's books to find a wide Western audience, but it was not his first published work. Freire started to gather his ideas into book form in the second half of the 1960s, reflecting on his adult literacy work in Brazil and Chile. *Education: The Practice of Freedom* (also published under the title *Education for Critical Consciousness*) was written before *Pedagogy of the Oppressed* but did not come to the attention of most readers in the Western world until the mid-1970s. The two books are, as a number of commentators (e.g., Mackie, 1980b) have noted, quite different in style and focus. *Education: The Practice of Freedom* (Freire, 1976) bears a stronger stamp of liberal ideas, whereas *Pedagogy of the Oppressed* gives evidence of a clear shift to the Left in Freire's thinking. In subsequent works, Freire extended and modified some of the pedagogical arguments introduced in these two early books (and another text, *Cultural Action for Freedom*, first published in 1970 and later released by

Penguin in 1972), while nonetheless retaining a number of key philosophical principles across the entire corpus of his published writings.

The Quieter Years (1976–1986)

The intense period of writing and speaking activity in the early 1970s gave way to a quieter time during the later 1970s and early 1980s. Although Freire was by no means inactive during this period, he assumed something of a lower profile in the international educational scene for almost a decade between the mid-1970s and the mid-1980s. In 1985, *The Politics of Education* (Freire, 1985) was published. This text included a number of essays, most written (but not widely circulated) in the preceding fifteen years, with the addition of a new dialogue between Freire and Donaldo Macedo—who was to become a crucial collaborator, translator and friend over the last ten years of Freire's life—and a lengthy introduction by Henry Giroux. The only other book to appear in this period was *Pedagogy in Process: The Letters to Guinea-Bissau* (Freire, 1978), which, as the name suggests, was largely an account of Freire's approach to adult education in Guinea-Bissau during the mid-1970s. This text was later to attract strong criticism from some commentators, notably the philosopher of education James Walker (1980), who identified an antidialogical basis to Freirean pedagogy. One of Freire's coauthors, Antonio Faundez, also found fault with Freire's stance on the use of the Portuguese language as the medium of instruction for adult literacy learning in Guinea-Bissau (see Freire and Faundez, 1989). Freire's insistence that the local Creole language be employed was regarded as politically naive by some, and, remarkably, utterly misunderstood by even some of the most accomplished Freirean scholars. Kathleen Weiler, for instance, argues—erroneously—that Freire supported the use of the *Portuguese* language in a critical review of several Freirean texts (Weiler, 1996). With the exception of Walker's essay and a few other articles, most of the major criticisms of Freire's work during this period were to emerge at a later stage—when Freire enjoyed what might be termed a "second wind" of publishing productivity.

The Last Decade (1987–)

The publication of *A Pedagogy for Liberation*, coauthored with Ira Shor in 1987, was a pivotal moment in Freire's writing career. This is so in at least three senses. First, it was the beginning of the final—and most prolific—phase of Freire's development as a theorist and practitioner. Second, it marked the beginning of a new way of writing academic texts. It was new, at least, for Freire, though in many senses he had been preparing for it all along. *A Pedagogy for Liberation* was written in the form of a dialogue between Freire and Shor, with both contributors responding to points made by the other in the course of a structured educational conversation. Third, this text was the first of Freire's publications to deal in an extended way with the problem of applying Freirean ideas in First World and contemporary classroom settings. Over the course of a number of well-crafted chapters, Freire and Shor dealt with questions such as: "How can teachers become liberating educators?" "What are the fears and risks of transformation?" "Is there structure and rigor in liberating education?" "Do First-World students need liberating?" "How can liberating educators overcome language differences with the students?" These questions, addressed at greater length in *A Pedagogy for Liberation* than any of Freire's previous books, underpinned several subsequent publications. Shor had already addressed some of them in *Critical Teaching and Everyday Life* (1980), and, like Freire, has extended his ideas in later books (Shor, 1992, 1996).

A second dialogical book—*Literacy: Reading the Word and the World* (Freire and Macedo, 1987)—followed soon after *A Pedagogy for Liberation*. This text, Freire's first full-length elaboration of his literacy theory, was cowriiten with Donaldo Macedo, and over the years has become a key reference point for scholars seeking an alternative to the technocratic models of reading and writing so dominant in Western thought and practice. In addition to chapters on the act of reading, adult literacy and popular libraries, literacy and critical pedagogy, and literacy as a theoretical discourse, the book contains a dialogue on literacy and illiteracy in the United States and further reflections on Freire's initiatives in Guinea-Bissau and São Tomé and Príncipe.[2] *Learning to Question: A Pedagogy of Liberation*, coauthored with Antonio Faundez (Freire and Faundez, 1989), is notable for the tension at one point in the dialogue between the two authors over Freire's approach to education, politics and language in Guinea-Bissau. The book explores the theme of exile in some detail, tackles issues of ideology and power, and advocates a pedagogy of questioning. *We Make the Road by Walking: Conversations on Education and Social Change* (Horton and Freire, 1990), constructed from dialogues between the adult educator Myles Horton and Freire, is similar to *A Pedagogy for Liberation* in the attention it pays to issues facing educators in contemporary First World contexts. Careful editing by Brenda Bell, John Gaventa, and John Peters allows the book to exhibit a tight thematic structure while retaining the warmth and informal tone of the original conversations. The book traverses a wide territory, addressing questions about reading, books, knowledge, democracy, resistance, education, and social transformation, and politics in Brazil and the United States, among other topics. *We Make the Road by Walking* is particularly relevant to the concerns of adult educators, and combines personal accounts of educational experiences with theoretical observations.

Paulo Freire on Higher Education: A Dialogue at the National University of Mexico (Escobar, Fernandez, and Guevara-Niebla, with Freire, 1994) gains its distinctiveness in two senses. First, it is the only book Freire published dealing specifically with higher education (and universities in particular). Second, the text straddles two phases in the development of Freire's thought. The book arose out of a series of dialogues between Freire and a group of Latin American academics in 1984, but did not find its way into print until a decade later. As a result, the book seems oddly out of place among Freire's other later texts. As Colin Lankshear (1994b) observes in his afterword, in many ways the ideas presented in this volume seem to speak to us from another moment in history. *Paulo Freire on Higher Education* revisits a number of themes made familiar by his earlier work—the need to read contexts as well as texts, limits and possibilities in the educational sphere, and the relationship between theory and practice—but also discusses the Nicaraguan revolution, the role of intellectuals in Latin America, and university politics. Although some of the ideas advanced in the dialogue—the importance of tolerance as a revolutionary virtue, for example—resonate with concerns addressed in other books published by Freire in the mid-1990s, the difference between the date of the conversations and the date of publication is readily apparent in the content of the book.

Pedagogy of the City (Freire, 1993a) recalls Freire's experiences as an educational administrator in the municipality of Sao Paulo between 1989 and 1991. Responsible for the educational lives of hundreds of thousands of children in Brazilian schools, Freire paints a vivid picture of some of the difficulties he faced in his position as Secretary of Education during this period. Systematic evaluations of Freire's successes and shortcomings in this role have been published by Torres (1994a) and O'Cadiz, Wong, and Torres (1998). *Pedagogy of the City* combines observations on schooling in Brazil with theoretical material and unfolds through a series of interviews and dialogues, loosely grouped together under two headings: "Education for Liberation in a Contemporary Urban Area" and "Reflections on This Experience with Three Educators." The book does not add significantly to Freirean philosophy, but does contain some interesting passages on teacher training, new technologies, and the decentralization of education.

It is not until *Pedagogy of Hope: Reliving Pedagogy of the Oppressed* (1994) that Freire—in a mature, if relaxed, voice—responds at some length to critics of his earlier work on oppression, liberation, and education. Freire advances an ideal of "unity through diversity," and speaks of the need to address both universals and particulars. Although he does not deal

directly with postmodern texts, Freire nonetheless confronts, in a preliminary way, a number of the deepest questions raised by poststructuralist
and postmodernist authors over the past decade. *Pedagogy of Hope* is
arguably one of Freire's most "readable," and certainly one of his most
deeply personal, texts. It is, together with *Letters to Cristina* (1996) and
Pedagogy of the Heart (Freire, 1997a), the closest we get to an autobiog-
raphy of Freire. Freire provides a somewhat rambling history of events
in his personal and intellectual life, adding to what Taylor (1993), Weiler
(1996), and many others have seen as a certain kind of mythology, and
he does not fully answer his critics. Few of his detractors are mentioned
by name. The arguments advanced by Bowers, Berger, and others find
some comment in the book, but Freire does not quite succeed in providing an extended, robust defense of his views against his harshest critics.
Stylistically, Freire finds a comfortable register in this volume, moving
with ease between different periods in his political and educational development. The book does not have a clear structure or set of guiding
themes or chapter headings. Freire's expressed purpose is to reflect on—
"relive"—*Pedagogy of the Oppressed*, and most parts of the book can be
seen as consistent with this goal.

Some startling revelations emerge through these reflections. We learn,
for example, that for a book that has been so influential, *Pedagogy of the
Oppressed* was drafted in a remarkably short period of time. The first
three chapters, Freire tells us, were written in a matter of weeks. Were
it not for Franz Fanon's *Wretched of the Earth* (1967)—which Freire read
and could not ignore—these three initial chapters would have constituted the whole book. After putting the (three-chapter) manuscript away
in a drawer for some time, Freire, following his encounter with Fanon,
added the important fourth chapter and thus changed the course of the
book's history. It is difficult to imagine how the book might have been
received and engaged over the next quarter of a century without this
final chapter, but it seems certain that the text would not have influenced
as many people as it eventually did. That fourth chapter provides a crucial reference point for many who turn to Freire for theoretical elaboration of principles already discovered through political action. This point
applies, in particular, to indigenous groups involved in "First Nations"
struggles across the globe, and has special relevance to acts of resistance
by the Maori people of New Zealand against policies of colonization (cf.
G. Smith, 1999).

Letters to Cristina: Reflections on My Life and Work (Freire, 1996) acquired
its name from a promise Freire made to his niece many years ago. For
some time, he'd intended to set out some of his key ideas on pedagogy,
philosophy, and politics in the form of a series of letters (to his niece).
This format, he believed, would allow him to mix recollections of personal experiences with theoretical analyses of important concepts and

debates. The book furnishes a deeper glimpse into Freire's early years than any other text, and is the most carefully crafted of the works published in English in the 1990s. *Letters to Cristina* addresses old themes— freedom and authority, the teacher-student relation, and the nature of oppression—in a lucid and concise style in the second half of the book, but also takes up a number of new topics in some detail. There is, for example, a full chapter (letter) devoted to thesis supervision. While avoiding the nostalgia that often accompanies autobiographical accounts, *Letters to Cristina* is notable for its honesty and depth of feeling, as well as rigor. *Pedagogy of the Heart* (Freire, 1997a), in a complimentary fashion, reveals something more of Freire the man. Published posthumously, *Pedagogy of the Heart* is among the most "intimate" of Freire's books. From the pages in this book, Freire emerges as an intensely committed, constantly curious, imperfect being. He speaks, with some obvious discomfort, about his faith, his failures as well as his successes, and his hopes for the future.

Two other books, *Mentoring the Mentor: A Critical Dialogue with Paulo Freire* (Freire, Fraser, Macedo, McKinnon, and Stokes, 1997) and *Teachers as Cultural Workers: Letters to Those Who Dare Teach* (Freire, 1998a) focus on issues of teaching, learning, mentoring, and methods. The former is an edited collection, in which Freire collaborates with James Fraser, Donaldo Macedo, Tanya McKinnon, and William Stokes in gathering a series of critical essays—most from North American authors—on the theory and practice of Freirean education in a variety of formal and informal settings. Freire's chapter in the book confirms his strong opposition to neoliberalism (as the dominant political philosophy of our time), and extends his earlier work by criticizing technocratic approaches to teacher training. *Teachers as Cultural Workers* contains ten "letters" on various themes relating to the process of teaching (e.g., "the first day at school," "the relationship between the educator and the learners," "cultural identity and education," "the question of discipline"), encased between introductory and concluding chapters. The book, published posthumously, provides Freire's most in-depth study of teaching and learning, and speaks directly to teachers facing difficult day-to-day decisions in classrooms and other educational environments. Another small volume, *Politics and Education* (Freire, 1998b), comprising short essays (most written in 1992) on a wide range of educational topics—lifelong education and the city, literacy and citizenship, "unity and diversity," the nature of criticism, education and responsibility, and the Catholic university—was also released in English translation in 1998.

Pedagogy of Freedom: Ethics, Democracy, and Civic Courage (Freire, 1998c), also published posthumously, combines detailed analyses of teaching, learning, research, and the nature of knowing with Freire's observations on the immorality of neoliberalism and global capitalism. The range of pedagogical, epistemological, and political issues addressed is broader than the chapter headings ("Introductory reflections"; "There is no teaching without learning"; "Teaching is not just transferring knowledge"; "Teaching is a human act") suggest. Freire tackles questions about methodological rigor, ethics, and aesthetics; discrimination; cultural identity; common sense; humility and tolerance; freedom and authority; and ideology. There is again a strong focus on the practical dilemmas teachers face as they conduct their daily activities in formal and informal educational settings. Freire discusses not just familiar themes, such as the need to respect the knowledge students bring with them to the classroom, the importance of curiosity in teaching, and the pedagogical significance of dialogue, but also notions of good listening and conscientious decision making, educators' rights, and commitment in teaching. In this book, Freire makes it plain that his acceptance of some postmodern insights (expressed, particularly, in Freire, 1993b, 1994) does not make him a moral relativist. He expresses his support for a "universal human ethic" and reinforces, with examples from Brazil and elsewhere, his abhorrence of the gross inequalities between different social groups under late capitalism. With a foreword by Donaldo Macedo and an excellent introduction by Stanley Aronowitz, this is arguably the best of Freire's later works.[3]

LIFE AFTER *PEDAGOGY OF THE OPPRESSED*

Perhaps the biggest "mistake" in reading Freire is to concentrate on his early works without paying sufficient attention to the many texts in the later phase. Given its extraordinary influence, *Pedagogy of the Oppressed* has, in some ways, become both a blessing and a curse for Freire. It is without doubt his most important single work. In it, he outlines the ontological, epistemological, and ethical basis to his thought, and he sketches an archetypal distinction between two contrasting approaches to education. *Pedagogy of the Oppressed*, in moving leftward from the liberalism of *Education: The Practice of Freedom*, set the political agenda for Freire's subsequent theoretical and practical work. *Pedagogy of the Oppressed* was a landmark publication not just for Paulo Freire, but for educational theory. It was, together with Ivan Illich's *Deschooling Society* (1971), one of the most widely read educational books of the 1970s. It played a part in shaking educational foundations; that is, in prompting teachers—at all levels of the education system—to reconsider assumptions they had long taken for granted.

The strength of the book, I believe, lies in its philosophical depth and radical integration of education with politics. Chapters 1 and 3 of *Pedagogy of the Oppressed* set out Freire's ontological and ethical ideas in comprehensive and lucid detail, and the fourth chapter provides an extensive consideration of the politics of domination at a macro level. The discussion of education is primarily located in chapter 2, and literacy does not figure as prominently as it does in a number of Freire's other texts. The book is often regarded as a bible for adult education, but those looking for specific attention to the particular challenges of working with adults (as opposed to school-age or preschool children) will be better served by some of Freire's other writings. *Pedagogy of the Oppressed* develops the now-famous distinction between "banking education" and "problem-posing education." *A Pedagogy for Liberation* (Freire and Shor, 1987), *Learning to Question* (Freire and Faundez, 1989), *We Make the Road by Walking* (Horton and Freire, 1990), *Pedagogy of Hope* (1994), *Teachers as Cultural Workers* (1998a), and *Pedagogy of Freedom* (1998c) address other crucial educational themes at much greater length. Some of the theoretical areas explored in these books (and others from the last decade of Freire's writing career) include questions about structure and rigor in liberating education, the nature of critical reading and writing, legitimate and oppressive uses of authority in the classroom, the process of study, the role of intellectuals in resisting dominant ideas and practices, dialectical thinking and education, the dynamics of dialogue, the distinction between "facilitating" and "teaching," the bearing language difficulties have on education, the differences between Third World and First World educational settings, and the need for contextualization in pedagogical programs. Although *Pedagogy of the Oppressed* touches on many of these themes, much deeper discussion of them is to be found in the later works.

I would argue, then, that any reasonable assessment of Freire's contribution to the theory and practice of education demands a *holistic* reading of his work. This does not amount to saying that nothing can be gained from reading just one of his books; nor is such a claim meant to imply that there is one "right" way to interpret Freirean ideas. Clearly, people study Freire for a range of reasons and evaluate his work through a variety of different theoretical lenses.[4] The problem, as I argue in chapter 3, occurs when people name themselves "Freireans" and/or profess to practice Freirean principles on the basis of a superficial, fragmented, incomplete, or uncritical reading of his books. This problem is compounded when such people have little knowledge of Freire's biography, his successes and shortcomings as an adult literacy educator, and the contexts within which he worked.

The need for a holistic, thorough, and critical approach applies as much to those who disagree vehemently with Freire as it does to those who enthusiastically endorse his pedagogical practices. Serious distortions not only of Freirean ideas but entire fields of study can result from decontextualized, fragmented, and misguided readings of Freire. Jay and Graff's (1995) misrepresentation of both Freire and the field of critical pedagogy provides an especially telling example of what can go wrong when otherwise reputable theorists attempt to tackle domains of study they clearly know very little about. In construing Freire's educational ideal as "libertarian" (p. 202) and talking of what might happen when the Freirean model is "transplanted" on a North American campus (p. 204), Jay and Graff give ample evidence of having read next to nothing of Freire's work. (For a direct response to Jay and Graff, see Freire and Macedo, 1995.)

A holistic reading of Freire can also have a significant bearing on the way we interpret *Pedagogy of the Oppressed*. There are dangers in ignoring other works even when *Pedagogy of the Oppressed* provides the main focus for a particular discussion. Where other Freirean texts have obvious relevance to an analysis of a theme or issue in *Pedagogy of the Oppressed* we do Freire a disservice in neglecting them. A case in point is Kathleen Weiler's (1991) critique of Freire's theory of oppression, liberation, and education. Although Weiler would not have had many of the Freirean texts from the later period available to her at the time of writing, *A Pedagogy for Liberation* (Freire and Shor, 1987) and *We Make the Road by Walking* (Horton and Freire, 1990) had certainly been published and indeed are cited in Weiler's footnotes. Yet, Weiler refers only fleetingly to these books in her essay. This is despite the fact that she clearly recognizes some of the differences between *Pedagogy of the Oppressed* and later works:

> Freire has repeatedly stated that his pedagogical method cannot simply be transferred to other settings, but that each historical site requires the development of a pedagogy appropriate to that setting. In his most recent work, he has also addressed sexism and racism as systems of oppression that must be considered as seriously as class oppression. Nonetheless, Freire is frequently read without consideration for the context of the specific settings in which his work developed and without these qualifications in mind. His most commonly read text still is his first book to be published in English, *Pedagogy of the Oppressed*. (Weiler, 1991, p. 452)

Having noted this, Weiler then proceeds to virtually ignore what was at the time Freire's "most recent work," making only one other reference to *A Pedagogy for Liberation* and no further references to *We Make the Road by Walking*. No mention of Freire's coauthored book with Antonio Faundez, *Learning to Question* (1989), is made in either the text or the footnotes of Weiler's article. *Pedagogy of the Oppressed* thus remains the principal focus for Weiler's critique, despite her acknowledgment that we do well to contextualize Freire's work. She admits, moreover, that Freire's later work offers something more on questions of oppression than a reading of *Pedagogy of the Oppressed* on its own affords. Rather than engaging the latest work in detail, however, Weiler simply implies—given the lack of references to relevant sections in *A Pedagogy for Liberation, Learning to Question*, and *We Make the Road by Walking*—that any differences between *Pedagogy of the Oppressed* and later books are not worth worrying about. In a discussion dealing with themes of authority and teaching, experience and feeling as sources of knowledge, and questions of difference, this seems odd, given that all of the later works cited above have something more significant to say about each of these topics than *Pedagogy of the Oppressed*. Of course, many other theorists—including the writers to whom Weiler refers—address some or all of these issues in greater detail and in different ways than Freire and his coauthors do. The point is, however, that *Pedagogy of the Oppressed* should not be left to "stand on its own"—as representative of Freire's thought—when subsequent texts convey a more complex view on such topics.

FINAL REMARKS

Freire's contribution to our understanding of education, literacy, and politics cannot be adequately assessed if his written works are decontextualized. *Pedagogy of the Oppressed* represents a defining moment in Freire's theoretical development, and will always stand as his classic text, but there is life (for Freire and his interpreters) beyond this book. Life here refers to both the production of written texts, and lived practices in *contexts*. There are differences between the context to which *Pedagogy of the Oppressed* refers and that within which it was written. Both these contexts differ, in turn, from the contexts within which later Freirean books were produced and from which many of Freire's interpreters have written. Such differences in context play a part in shaping texts and our readings of them. Recognizing and actively fostering a relationship between texts and contexts is, for Freire, an important element in the process of critical reading. Freire's ideas should neither be dismissed outright nor embraced uncritically. A holistic reading of his work allows us to appreciate, critique, and go beyond *Pedagogy of the Oppressed*.

NOTES

1. Cornel West has described the publication of the book as "a world-historical event for counter-hegemonic theorists and activists" (1993, p. xiii).

2. The book has, for example, been highly recommended by academics at the University of Auckland teaching a course on Maori literacy.

3. Another book has recently appeared: *Critical Education in the New Information Age* (Castells, Flecha, Freire, Giroux, Macedo, and Willis,

1999), to which Freire has contributed a chapter, "Education and community involvement." This essay appears in slightly different form in Freire's *Politics and Education* (1998b). A further book to be published posthumously, *Ideology Matters* (Freire and Macedo, 1999), was not available at the time of writing.

4. This is best exemplified by the range of responses to Freire's work in a number of edited collections. Compare, for example, Shor (1987); McLaren and Leonard (1993a); McLaren and Lankshear (1994); Roberts (1999b).

CHAPTER 2

Knowledge, Dialogue, and Humanization: Exploring Freire's Philosophy

This chapter explores elements of Freire's ontology, epistemology, and ethic, with a view to elucidating some of the distinctive features of his philosophy. In developing his philosophical and pedagogical ideas, Freire drew on a wide range of intellectual traditions, including liberalism, marxism, existentialism, radical Catholicism, phenomenology, and aspects of postmodern and poststructuralist thought (Mackie, 1980b; Elias, 1994; Mayo, 1997; Peters, 1999). Although the programs he developed in working with illiterate adults in Brazil and Chile in the 1960s constitute perhaps the most memorable aspect of his work, Freire's practical activities need to be understood in the light of his views on the nature of reality, his conception of what it means to be human, his theory of knowledge, and his ideas on oppression and liberation. These dimensions of Freire's work lie at the heart of this chapter.

FREIRE ON THE NATURE OF REALITY

In his written work, Freire adopts a *dialectical* approach toward understanding the world. This statement has a dual meaning. In one sense, Freire conceives of reality *as* dialectical; in another sense, he *is* (or strives to be) dialectical in his style of social analysis. In other words, Freire attempts to *think* dialectically about a reality which is dialectical. Drawing on ideas from Hegel and Marx, among others, Freire posits a dynamic relation between consciousness and the world (Freire, 1998b, p. 19; Torres, 1994b). He explicitly rejects two positions that ignore the dialectical nature of this relationship: mechanistic objectivism and sol-ipsistic idealism. The former reduces consciousness to a mere "copy" of objective reality; the latter sees consciousness as the creator of (all) reality (Freire, 1972b, p. 53). Objectivist views negate human agency because all human actions become merely a product of material or environmental influences. Mechanistic behaviorism, for example, sees human practice as analogous to the operation of a machine. Human beings exist as ma-terial bodies (with sense organs) who respond to stimuli. For the mech-anistic behaviorist, no human event could be other than it is. A human being could not act other than he or she does in any particular situation, given the combination of stimuli—past and present—to which that hu-man being has been subject. For the extreme idealist, on the other hand, there is no world at all: material reality is simply an illusion, a construc-tion of consciousness. Both stances deny the possibility of reality being transformed through conscious human activity.

According to Freire, all aspects of objective reality are in motion. Ob-jective reality encompasses both the world of nature and socially created material objects, institutions, practices, and phenomena. The world, for Freire, is necessarily unfinished and ever-evolving: "the more I approach critically the object of my observation, the more I am able to perceive that the object of my observation *is not yet because it is becoming*" (Freire and Shor, 1987, p. 82). As reality changes, ideas, conceptions, attitudes, values, beliefs, and so on—in short, all the products of consciousness—shift also. This is not a sequential, lock-step, "cause-and-effect" relation-ship, but a complex process of constant, multilayered interaction between human beings and the world. From Freire's point of view, neither "con-sciousness" nor "world" are comprehensible without the other. Con-sciousnesses are constituted by the world, but without someone to say "this is a world," there *is* no world (cf. Freire, 1997a, p. 32).

Freire, like Marx (1976) and Mao (1968), places particular emphasis on contradictions in the social world. The most important of these in Freire's ethical and political theory is the contradiction between oppressors and the oppressed. Oppressors can only exist *as* oppressors in the presence of their opposite, the oppressed. The two groups stand in an inherently contradictory relationship, irrespective of how either group perceive themselves. The possibility of oppression being negated through an act of (liberating) revolution is always latent if not made manifest.

Thinking dialectically involves seeking out contradictions in social re-ality; it implies a penetration beyond and beneath surface appearances. A dialectical approach demands that social phenomena and problems be understood not in abstract isolation but as part of a totality, and theo-rized in global terms. A true dialectician is always striving to relate one aspect of world to another, and is always seeking to more deeply explain the object of study by contrasting it with that which *it is not*. This is a form of "epistemological encircling": a means of moving closer by gaining a certain kind of distance (Freire, 1997a, p. 92). Thinking dialectically is, for Freire, equivalent to thinking *critically*: it means being constantly open to further questions, and to the possibility—indeed, probability—of current assumptions being revised, repudiated, or overturned. There are obvious similarities here with Giroux's (1981, p. 114) view of the dialectic as "a critical mode of reasoning and behavior, one that represents both a part as well as a critique of conflicts and solutions that define the nature of human existence." In an interview with Carlos Alberto Torres, whom Freire describes as "a man who thinks dialectically and doesn't merely talk of dialectics," Freire gives an example of this orientation toward engaging social problems:

> Today I live the enormous joy of perceiving with every passing day that the strength of education resides precisely in its limitations. The efficiency of education resides in the impossibility of doing everything. The limits of education would bring a naive man or woman to desperation. A dialectical man or woman discovers in the limits of education the raison d'être for his or her efficiency. It is in this way that I feel that today I am an efficient Secretary of Education because I am limited. (Torres and Freire, 1994, p. 106)

FREIRE'S EPISTEMOLOGY

Freire's epistemology can be seen as an extension of his ideas on the dialectical nature of reality. We come to *know* through our interaction with an ever-changing world (Freire, 1976, p. 107). Knowing, for Freire, necessarily implies transformation; it is the task of human subjects encountering a world dynamically in the making. Knowledge arises not from abstract thinking or theorizing, but from human practice. The ordering of moments in the process of knowing is important in understanding Freire's philosophy. Freire is adamant that theory never precedes practice: "First of all I have to act. First of all I have to transform. Secondly I can theorize my actions—but not before" (Freire, 1971a, p. 2). Freire (1972a, p. 50) talks of thinking becoming *authenticated* only when it is "concerned with reality," "generated by action upon the world," and carried out through communication with others. Authentic thinking constitutes an act of knowing. Freire's position here is consistent with the fundamental tenets of dialectical materialism, one of which is that "the production of ideas, of conceptions, of consciousness is at first directly interwoven with the material activity and the material intercourse of men" (Marx and Engels, 1976, p. 42).

Given that all aspects of reality exist in a constant state of change, it follows that we can never know *absolutely*: we can, at best, come *closer* to knowing the *"raison d'être* which explains the object [of study]" (Freire and Shor, 1987, p. 82). Knowing involves searching for the reason for (or behind) the existence of an object or fact (Freire and Macedo, 1987, p. 78). Knowledge, on the Freirean view, is necessarily incomplete: "[K]nowledge always is becoming. That is, if the act of knowing has historicity, then today's knowledge about something is not necessarily the same tomorrow. Knowledge is changed to the extent that reality also moves and changes" (Horton and Freire, 1990, p. 101). Knowing for Freire is a permanent process of discovery—of searching, investigating, inquiring, and probing (cf. Freire, 1985, pp. 1–4; Davis, 1980, p. 66). To know is not to have reached a predetermined destination; rather, it is a manner of "traveling"—a way of being in, and interacting with, the world (through dialogue with others). It is precisely through recognizing that they know little that people strive to know more. Freire speaks of knowing as a *praxis*, implying both a reflective and an active component. Knowing demands a curious, attentive, restless attitude toward, and interaction with, social reality. This cannot be reduced to rational processes alone. In Freire's words: "I know with my entire body, with feelings, with passion, and also with reason" (1997a, p. 30). From Freire's point of view, there can be no "final" act of knowing. Knowledge has historocity: It is always in the process of being. If absolute knowledge could be attained, the possibility of knowing would disappear for there would no longer be any questions to ask or theoretical problems to address. All statements about knowledge and its opposite, ignorance, must be qualified: These terms only make sense when defined in relation to something specific. On the Freirean view, neither knowledge nor ignorance are complete: "No one can know everything, just as no one can be ignorant of everything" (Freire, 1976, p. 117). This insight provides the ground, by implication, for a redefinition of conventional constructs of "the intellectual." As Giroux points out, Freire regards all men and women as intellectuals in the sense that every person constantly interprets and gives meaning to the world (Giroux, 1985, p. xxiii; cf. Gramsci, 1971, pp. 5–23; Lankshear, 1988).

The distinctiveness of Freire's view can be elucidated through a comparison with the Platonic conception of knowledge. Plato (1974) distinguishes true knowledge from mere opinion. Opinion pertains to the visible (physical, practical, material) world; knowledge is confined to the supersensible, intelligible realm (§507). At its lowest level, opinion takes the form of "illusion," by which Plato means simple impressions of the world, or perceptions of objects as they appear in their material form. Given their focus on images and outward appearances, such impressions provide an inherently distorted view of reality (§§509d, 510a). A higher level of opinion is "belief," which is manifest in "commonsense" ideas about "matters both moral and physical, which are a fair practical guide to life but [which] have not been fully thought out" (translator's note, p. 311). Neither illusion nor belief can provide genuine understanding of the nature of reality, because both remain tied to that which can be perceived by the senses. The sensible world deals with particulars, is always changing, and as such is never truly knowable. The world of ideas or forms, by contrast, is unchanging: it is the realm of universals from which the particulars we observe derive. Mathematical (deductive) reason participates in this higher intelligible realm. The pinnacle of pure intelligence, however, is dialectical reason, which Plato describes as follows:

> [I]t treats assumptions not as principles, but as assumptions in the true sense, that is, as starting points and steps in the ascent to something which involves no assumption and is the first principle of everything; when it has grasped that principle it can again descend, by keeping to the consequences that follow from it, to a conclusion. The whole procedure involves nothing in the sensible world, but moves solely through forms to forms, and finishes with forms. (§511b)

The highest level of knowledge, Plato argues, is knowledge of the form of the good (§505a). The good is "the end of all endeavor, the object on which every heart is set" (§505d). The form of the good "gives the objects of knowledge their truth and the knower's mind the power of knowing" (§508e). Attaining knowledge, for Plato, is a matter of remembering or recovering that which existed in the soul before its incarnation in a body. Knowledge has a divine origin: the capacity for pursuing it—that is, recalling what is already there—is "innate in each man's mind" (§518d), though few progress beyond mere opinion to the higher forms of intelligence.

Freire's position is precisely the opposite. True or authentic knowledge for Freire arises not in some realm beyond the sphere of objective reality; to the contrary, knowing is thoroughly grounded in the material world. The origins of knowledge lie not in some form of celestial divination but in the day-to-day transforming moments of human activity. As Freire sees it, knowledge is not recollected through philosophical thought but *created* through reflective action in a social world. Freire, like Plato, wants to go beyond a mere apprehension of appearances, but speaks of searching beneath the surface of the object of study as an intensely practical endeavor. The path to knowledge is not to be found in some form of abstract, inner, individual activity, but in active, communicative relationships with others. Knowing through dialogue does not transcend, but rather is mediated by, the (material) world. For Freire, there is no world of "forms" to be known. Dialectical thinking is elevated above other modes of understanding for Freire, as it is for Plato, but the modes of knowing implied by each theorists' conception of the dialectic are quite distinct. From Plato's perspective, dialectical reason is distinguished by its complete separation from worldly particulars; for Freire, dialectical thinking is defined by its focus on interrelationships between concrete particulars within a social totality. Goodness and knowledge are closely connected for Freire, as they are for Plato. But where Plato speaks of the good as the supreme form from which all particular acts of goodness in the world derive, these acts (i.e., those which are praxical), from Freire's point of view, *are* the supreme good, and it is through them that knowing occurs.

Freire is not an epistemological relativist. As McLaren and Silva (1993) point out, he does not believe all ideas are of equal merit. On the Freirean view, some ways of thinking, some theories, some appraisals of the nature of reality are better than others. As we see shortly, this line of argument applies to Freire's ethic as well: certain ways of living one's life, of acting toward others, of being in the world, are, according to Freire, superior—that is, morally preferable—to others. On the other hand, Freire's theory of knowledge is not absolutist in the Platonic sense: there are no static, unchanging, truths which transcend time and space. Instead, Freire argues that ideas "must be understood contextually as historically and culturally informed discourses that are subject to the mediation of the forces of material and symbolic production" (McLaren and Silva, 1993, p. 55). On the Freirean view, knowledge is *constructed* rather than derived or bequeathed: it is forged within particular social relations, is reflective of (and partially constitutive of) given ideological and political formations, and is always grounded—whether directly or indirectly—in human practice. Certain constructions of reality, though, are better than others: a dialogical and critical reading of the world, for Freire, affords a deeper understanding of the object under investigation than antidialogical or passive stances allow.

As humans, we have the capacity to reflect on the very process of knowing itself, on (our) consciousness and its relationship with the world. We not only can know, but know that we know (Davis, 1980, pp. 58–59). For Freire, the essence of human consciousness is intentionality toward the world. Humans can "stand back" from the immediate reality of their material existence and reflect on it. Freire speaks of this as a crucial moment in human evolution: what Teilhard de Chardin (1959) calls "homonization"—the shift from instinct to thought. Humans have the ability to problematize not only the object of attention but the process through which this problematization takes place. This, then, is a form of "meta-awareness"—an awareness of our conscious efforts to understand ourselves, others, and the world.

HUMANIZATION: FREIRE'S ETHICAL IDEAL

Just as Freire sees knowledge as necessarily incomplete—as always evolving—so he sees human beings as always in a state of "becoming." The human ideal Freire espouses is one of humanization, or "becoming more fully human." One can never, on the Freirean view, become *fully* human—one can, at best, become *more* fully human. Freire sees this calling to "be more" as an expression of human nature making itself in history (1994, pp. 98–99; 1997a, p. 32; 1998b, p. 18). Humans are necessarily imperfect, unfinished, incomplete beings, who exist in and with an ever-changing world (Freire, 1972a, p. 57). To be human, from Freire's point of view, is to be engaged in a permanent process of searching (Freire, 1998c, p. 21). Humanization, which Freire sees as both an ontological and an historical vocation of human beings, is opposed by dehumanization which, although an historical reality, is not an ontological inevitability. Humans pursue their vocation of becoming more fully human when they engage in authentic praxis, through dialogue with others, in a critically conscious way.

The Freirean concept of an ontological vocation can be explained through reference to the ancient Greek notion of human beings having a "function" (cf. Lankshear, 1993, pp. 108–109). Plato (1974) suggests that the "function" of a thing is "that which only it can do or that which it does best . . . everything which has a function [has] its own particular excellence" (§§353a–353b). For every distinctive excellence there is a corresponding defect. Hence, if the function of the eyes is to see, the eyes perform this function well when X has perfect vision but perform their function poorly if X suffers from blindness (§353b). Plato's intent in this line of inquiry is to establish grounds for arguing that a just society is one in which each person performs his or her proper role in accordance with his or her particular function. Different individuals in Plato's ideal society have different functions: philosophers have one function, military experts another, shoemakers yet another, and so on. Aristotle (1976), however, wants to know whether there is a function all human beings have simply through being human: "Just as we can see that eye and hand and foot and every one of our members has some function, should we not assume that in like manner a human being has a function over and above these particular functions?" (§1097b). Aristotle's concern is to discover that which is *uniquely* human. It cannot be the "life" generated by nutrition and manifested in growth, for plants share this with us; nor is it our "sentient" life, for animals possess this quality too. It must, Aristotle concludes, be our capacity for practical *reason* which sets us apart from all other beings or things. The function of humankind, thus, is "an activity of the soul in accordance with, or implying, a rational

principle" (§1098). Whether one reasons well or poorly, the function remains generically the same: *all* human beings are distinguished (from
other beings) by their reason. A function is "performed well when performed in accordance with its proper excellence" (§1098). For Aristotle,
happiness—the "best, the finest, the most pleasurable thing of all"
(§1099)—is the ultimate end to which human actions are directed (§1097).
A good, truly happy, ideal human life is one lived (properly and well)
in accordance with the highest human virtue, namely, reason.

Freire's notion of an ontological vocation can be understood in a similar light. According to Freire, what makes us distinctly human is our
ability to engage in praxis. Praxis is "reflection and action upon the
world in order to transform it" (Freire, 1972a, p. 28). Only human beings
can engage in praxis. Although animals alter aspects of the material
world in the process of adapting to it, their modification of objective
reality is purely instinctive. Human beings, however, have the ability to
consciously and intentionally transform the world. Humans are the only
beings to treat not merely their actions but *themselves* as the object of
reflection (p. 70). Animals are submerged in reality: they cannot stand
back from the world and consider themselves in relation to it. Humans,
by contrast, have the capacity to reflect on the world and to transform
it in accordance with this reflection. Only human beings *work* in the sense
of engaging in *purposeful* activity: consciously directed action on and interaction with the world (Freire, 1974a, p. 141). Animals, for the most
part, merely react to stimuli from the environment; humans, by contrast,
perceive and respond to challenges in the world. These ideas resonate
strongly with Marx's often-cited example of the differences between the
activities, respectively, of architects and bees: "[A] bee would put many
a human architect to shame by the construction of its honeycomb cells.
But what distinguishes the worst architect from the best of bees is that
the architect builds the cell in his mind before he constructs it in wax"
(Marx, 1976, p. 284).

Animals are creatures of contacts; they simply adapt to the world.
Humans, on the other hand, can become both adapted to the world and
integrated with it. Animals are merely *in* the world; humans are both *in*
the world and *with* the world. Animals have no conception of time; they
live in a permanent "today." They cannot "confront life," give meaning
to it, or become committed to it (Freire, 1969, p. 3). Humans, though, are
historical beings, aware of a past and able to conceive of a future. As
responsible beings, humans have an awareness of their own unfinished-
ness (Freire, 1998c, p. 56). Humans, unlike animals, *make* history (and in
so doing confirm their temporality) in consciously transforming the
world around them (Freire, 1972a, pp. 70–73; 1976, pp. 3–5).

For human activity to be praxical there must be a synthesis of reflection and action. Action which is not accompanied by reflection amounts

to nothing more than activism; reflection without concomitant action is mere verbalism (Freire, 1972a, p. 60). Action which is praxical "envelopes the whole being of the actors—their emotions, their feelings, their 'language-thought-reflection'" (Freire, 1970a, p. 1). This does not mean that reflection ought to *always* be followed by action: sometimes, Freire notes, action is not "feasible." Critical reflection is also a form of action (Makins, 1972). The feasibility of action—including educational intervention—in any given situation can only be determined by reflection through communication with others.

To live well, on the Freirean view, is to transform the world through reflective, critical, dialogical action. The vocation of all human beings is to realize this capacity—to live as "social, historical, thinking, communicating, transformative, creative persons" (Freire, 1998c, p. 45)—in the fullest way possible. The pursuit of humanization is a quest to become more profoundly what we already are as humans; that is, beings *of* praxis (Freire, 1970b, p. 16). Not all forms of praxis, though, are humanizing. Freire distinguishes, for instance, between "revolutionary praxis" and "the praxis of the dominant élites," the former being humanizing and the latter dehumanizing (1972a, p. 97). The crucial element fundamental to the first form of praxis but absent in the second is *dialogue*.

DIALOGUE AND SOCIAL TRANSFORMATION

The pursuit of humanization can never, in Freire's view, be an isolated, individualistic activity (Freire and Shor, 1987, p. 109; Horton and Freire, 1990, p. 111). Humans, as communicative beings, enter into relationships with one another, and create a *social* world. "Our being," Freire writes in *Pedagogy for Freedom* (1998c, p. 58), "is a *being with*." In participating in this process, humans simultaneously re-create themselves (cf. Marx, 1970, p. 21; Marx and Engels, 1976, p. 42; Freire, 1972b, pp. 29–30, 51–57). Just as it makes no sense (in Freirean terms) to talk of pursuing one's humanization in isolation from others, so too is it nonsensical to think of having (sole) responsibility for one's dehumanization. We humanize ourselves through dialogue with others. This goes to the heart of what it means to be human for Freire.

Where Descartes (1931, p. 101) theorized self-identity in his famous dictum, "I think, therefore I am," for Freire an "I think" is only comprehensible in the presence of a coexisting "we think." Freire does not deny that individual human beings are unique—that they understand and respond to the world and to others in distinct ways—but argues that it is only through intersubjectivity that individual existence makes sense. The existence of an "I" is only possible because of the concomitant existence of a "not-I," where "not-I" implies both others and world. For Freire, the "we exist" explains the "I exist": "I cannot be," he observes, "if you are not" (Fonseca, 1973, p. 96). The "I exist" does not precede the "we exist" but is fulfilled by it (Freire, 1985, p. 129). Knowing, on the Freirean view, cannot be a purely individual process but is only possible through dialogue—through a relationship with others, whether this is direct (face to face) or indirect (e.g., via texts), mediated by the objective world (cf. Buber, 1958, 1961).

In Freire's moral philosophy, praxis and dialogue are closely related: genuine dialogue represents a form of humanizing praxis. Dialogue is "the encounter between men, mediated by the world, in order to name the world" (Freire, 1972a, p. 61). Naming the world is the process of change itself: the human quest to understand and transform the world, through communication with others. This naming is a continuous process of creating and re-creating; that is, the world, once named, always presents itself afresh as a problem demanding a new naming. Freire claims that humans have a *primordial right* to "speak their word." It is in speaking a "true word" that human beings name the world and thereby transform it. A true word is an authentic, dialogical synthesis of reflection and action. Ultimately, "no one can say a true word alone" (p. 61). To speak a true word is to enter the historical process as a Subject, changing (objective and subjective) reality through consciously directed action, informed by critical discussion with others.

If it is to be humanizing, dialogical communication must involve a "love" of the world and of other human beings. This in turn demands a certain sense of humility. Faith in the ability of others to "name the world," together with trust between participants, and a hope that dehumanization can be overcome, are necessary. Finally, Freire stipulates that critical thinking is vital if dialogue is to become a humanizing praxis (pp. 62–65). When these conditions are satisfied, and where two or more people communicate with one another in seeking to understand a common object of study, there is, Freire argues, a true dialogue and an authentic, humanizing praxis.

THE POLITICS OF LIBERATION

Humanization through critical, dialogical praxis represents the ethical *ideal* for Freire. Frequently, however, the pursuit of humanization by some groups and individuals is impeded by the actions of others. Where this occurs, the situation becomes one of oppression. To prevent someone from engaging in praxis—either through limiting the range of possible actions open to that person, or through inhibiting that person's ability to think critically—is to dehumanize that person. Hence, oppression, as Freire sees it, is dehumanizing. This is what makes us *ethical* beings: our capacity "to intervene, to compare, to judge, to decide, to choose, to desist makes . . . [us] capable of acts of greatness, of dignity, and, at the same time, of the unthinkable in terms of indignity" (Freire, 1998c, p. 53). Fighting against discrimination is an ethical imperative (Freire, 1997a, p. 87). In dehumanizing another, one also—albeit in a different way, and with different implications and consequences—dehumanizes oneself (Freire, 1972a, p. 24; 1996, p. 180). To deny someone else's humanization is also to deny one's own, because, for Freire, humanization is a *dialogical* process. Those who dehumanize others practice a profound form of antidialogue, and thus cannot be engaged in the task of becoming more fully human.

Humanization and dehumanization are both concrete possibilities for human beings, but only humanization is an ontological and historical vocation. The vocation of becoming more fully human is what defines us as human beings; it is the *essence* of being human. Humanization is an historical, as well as ontological, vocation because it calls us to act (on the basis of critical reflection) in the objective world of lived social relations. Dehumanization represents a distortion of this vocation. Freire stresses that dehumanization arises from specific (oppressive) *social* practices: it does not, therefore, constitute a given destiny. If human beings have *created* social structures, living conditions, and modes of thinking and acting that are oppressive, it follows that humans can also change these circumstances.

The task of those who are oppressed is *liberation*. For Freire, liberation is not a psychological process: it is not something that occurs (purely) as a shift in consciousness, or as some form of inner transformation (Brandes, 1971, pp. 6–7). Rather, liberation takes place in the transformative action of human beings on the world, under specific historical and social circumstances. Freire is thoroughly Marxist in his stance here. As Marx and Engels state in *The German Ideology*,

> [I]t is possible to achieve real liberation only in the real world and by real means ... people cannot be liberated as long as they are unable to obtain food and drink, housing and clothing in adequate quality and quantity. "Liberation" is a historical and not a mental act. (1976, p. 44)

For Freire, liberation is a form of critical, dialogical, praxis directed toward overcoming oppression. In earlier works, he makes the claim that the oppressed cannot be liberated by their oppressors, but must liberate both themselves *and* those who oppress them. Paradoxically, only the "weakness" of the oppressed is strong enough to liberate the oppressor (Freire, 1975, p. 17; 1972c, p. 2). Freire believes that faced with a situation in which their pursuit of humanization is impeded, sooner or later the oppressed will begin to resist (Freire, 1972a, p. 21). Conflict between dialectically opposed groups is always possible, even if temporary "settlements" and periods of apparent calm may be reached at certain moments in history. Indeed, conflict can be seen as a fundamental part of social life (Freire, 1998a, p. 45). Freire argues, however, that the oppressed have often been so dominated by their oppressors that they take on the oppressors' view of the world: they see oppression as inevitable. Freire acknowledges that the direct experience of discrimination or exploitation can provide a distinctive understanding of oppression, but also stresses that submersion in an oppressive reality can impair one's perception of oneself and one's relation to others (1972a, p. 22).

Where a distorted perception of reality prevails, there is a danger that the oppressed, in fighting against their oppression, will themselves become oppressors. The model of humanity presented to the oppressed by the oppressors portrays a vision of the oppressor individual as the ideal. Under these circumstances, "to be" (human) is to be like the oppressor (Freire, 1975, p. 16). The psyche of the oppressed person becomes haunted by the "invasive shadow" of the of the oppressor (Freire, 1998c, p. 78). Yet, the oppressed are never entirely engulfed by, or reduced to, the reality of the oppressor. There is an "almost tenuous trace of themselves that makes their creation, their language, and their culture something more than just a copy, makes it a kind of muffled cry of resistance, of the rebel in them" (Freire, 1996, p. 118).

The problem of confronting the ideology of the oppressors is compounded by what Freire, drawing on the work of Fromm (1984), calls the "fear of freedom." The oppressed "are afraid to embrace freedom . . . [whereas] the oppressors are afraid of losing the 'freedom' to oppress" (Freire, 1972a, p. 23). Freire regards freedom as an "indispensable condition for the quest for human completion": Liberation *requires* freedom if it is to be authentic (p. 24). Freedom implies autonomy and responsibility, and must be *won* by the oppressed; it cannot be given to them. Freedom, as Freire understands it, is not unfettered liberty. It takes place within the bounds of human action, intervention and struggle and is always subject to certain constraints (cf. Freire, 1998c, p. 96). Freire speaks of revolutionary action by the oppressed against the conditions that oppress them—and this may include violent struggle—as an act of "love." The violence of the oppressed, though, is "not really violence at all, but a legitimate reaction [to an oppressive situation]" (Freire, 1972c, p. 3). Hunger, racism, sexism, and economic domination within and between countries represent forms of *hidden* or disguised violence (Freire, 1996, p. 185). Sometimes conditions are so intolerably dehumanizing for the oppressed that the violence of revolutionary struggle is justified where it is the only means for overcoming the greater violence of oppression (cf. Fanon, 1967). In later works, however, Freire makes it clear that there are limits to this:

My point of view is that of the "wretched of the earth," of the excluded. I do not accept, however, under any circumstances, acts of terrorism in support of this point of view. Such acts result in the death of the innocent and the spread of insecurity that affects everyone. Terrorism is the negation of what I call a universal human ethic. I am on the side of the Arabs in their struggle for their rights, but I cannot accept the acts of terrorism perpetuated in Munich and elsewhere in favor of those rights. (1998c, p. 22)

Freire warns that the oppressed, having internalized the view of the oppressors, may have little consciousness of themselves as a class. This works against the possibility of effective revolutionary action and serves as a prop for continuing oppression. Freire is socialist to the core in the stress he places on unity, solidarity, and a shared sense of commitment among the oppressed to a better social world. Unity among diverse oppressed groups is essential if their struggles are to be effective; without it, domination via "divide and rule" policies can prevail (Freire, 1996, pp. 180–181; 1997a, p. 86). Solidarity, for Freire, is a reflection of our need, as humans, to be *with* others (Freire, 1998c, p. 72). Echoing the immortal (but now, in postmodern times, somewhat unfashionable) call by Marx and Engels at the end of *The Communist Manifesto* for working people of all countries to unite (Marx and Engels, 1967, p. 121), Freire argues, "the universal solidarity of the working class is far from being achieved, but it is essential and we must struggle for it" (Freire and Faundez, 1989, p. 59). Unity is, Freire insists, all the more important in our current "perverse era of neoliberal philosophy" (1998c, p. 115). While highly critical of the authoritarianism in some socialist regimes, Freire is adamant that capitalism is an inherently unjust mode of production. For him, the work of those committed to liberation lies in bringing the ideals of socialism and democracy together (see Freire, 1996, p. 188).

Liberation, Freire (1972a, p. 25) concludes, is "a childbirth, and a painful one." The struggle for liberation must be ongoing—a permanent process of reflection and action—as social reality changes and new forms of oppression unfold. Although liberation cannot be reduced to merely a process of class transformation, thus denying the individual altogether (Freire, 1996, pp. 159–160), nor can its essentially social character be denied:

I don't believe in self-liberation. Liberation is a social act. . . . Even when you individually feel yourself *most* free, if this feeling is not a *social* feeling, if you are not able to use your *recent* freedom to help others to be free by transforming the totality of society, then

you are exercising only an individualist attitude towards empowerment or freedom. (Freire and Shor, 1987, p. 109)

In any given historical epoch in a given society, there will be a complex array of (often-conflicting) ideas, values, hopes, and challenges
which, in their concrete representations, constitute the *themes* of that epoch (Freire, 1976, p. 5). Critical examination of these themes reveals a set
of *tasks* to be carried out. Freire terms impediments to critical thought
and transforming action "limit-situations." The tasks implied by limit-
situations require "limit-acts" (Freire, 1972a, p. 73). Freire speaks, for example, of the economic dependence of Third World countries on the
First World as a limit-situation: those countries subject to this relationship become "beings for others." In order to become "beings for themselves" (cf. Sartre, 1969), such societies require limit-acts directed
toward revolutionary independence and political sovereignty (cf. Freire,
1970c; 1971b, p. 115).

Freire (1993a, p. 84) maintains that liberation is "the most fundamental
task . . . we have at the end of this century." Overcoming domination or
oppression (Freire uses these terms synonymously) entails negating
those aspects of an oppressive reality which limit the oppressed. Hence,
within a single society where the dominant theme is oppression, there
will be whole range of limit-situations which characterize that oppression. In the Third World countries in which Freire worked, these might
have ranged from the poor living conditions endured by peasants, to the
payment of low wages to workers, to the broader limit-situation of national economic dependency. Although the ultimate task of the oppressed in such situations is liberation, the pursuit of this task calls for
the negation of each of the limit-situations which (together) form an oppressive reality. Freire notes: "[E]pochs are fulfilled to the degree that
their themes are grasped and their tasks solved; and they are superseded
when their themes and tasks no longer correspond to newly emerging
concerns" (1976, p. 5).

In times of transition, as in Brazil during the 1950s and 1960s,
"[c]ontradictions increase between the ways of being, understanding, behaving, and valuing which belong to yesterday and other ways of perceiving and valuing which announce the future" (p. 7). In the Brazilian
case, the movement was from a "closed" society to one in the process of
opening. With this shift, such themes as democracy, popular participation, freedom, property, authority, and education were invested with
new meaning. The transition from one epoch to another is a dynamic
mix of "flux and reflux, advances and retreats," filled with confusion
and uncertainty, but also the hope and anticipation of impending change
(p. 9).

MORAL PRINCIPLES IN FREIRE'S PHILOSOPHY

In extracting key moral principles from Freire's philosophy, three points from the preceding discussion bear repeating:

1. All aspects of reality are constantly changing. This idea, which reflects Freire's dialectical approach toward understanding the world, permeates every dimension of Freire's philosophy. From its starting point in his metaphysic (where Freire speaks of change within and between the objective and subjective dimensions of reality), to his epistemology (where it is assumed that knowledge is never fixed nor absolute), to his ontology and ethic (where he argues that human beings are necessarily incomplete and always in a process of becoming), the principle remains the same: our world—in its myriad material, social, and personal spheres—is a world of change, of interaction, of incompleteness.

2. Freire assumes a certain essence to the human condition. Humans, unlike animals, are conscious, temporal, historical beings. Most importantly, for Freire, all human beings, simply through being human, have an ontological vocation of humanization. In this sense, although Freire acknowledges the educational significance of differences across class, race, and gender lines, there is nevertheless an implicit assertion in his work that there is something about being human which transcends these differences (cf. Weiler, 1991; Freire, 1998c; Freire and Macedo, 1993).

3. Humans interact with objective reality (altering it and modifying themselves in turn) and enter into relationships with others. We live in a *social* world, and any attempt to consider how the world ought to be must take this observation into account. It makes little sense to talk of Freirean ethics purely in terms of certain ideal qualities in, or modes of conduct for, the *individual*: liberation is a dialogical, collective process of struggle.

What, then, can we say about Freire's moral philosophy? In keeping with point 3, above, two related facets of Freire's ethical position must be addressed:

1. At one level, Freire upholds the notion of human beings becoming critical, praxical Subjects, in control—as far as this is possible—of their own destinies as creators of history and culture (and thus of themselves).

2. At another level, Freire's theory points toward a vision of a social world characterized by relations of liberation rather than

oppression—that is, a world where *all* people have the opportunity to engage in humanizing praxis, through dialogue with others.

Given this dual focus, (at least) four key principles in Freire's moral philosophy can be identified:

1. People ought to pursue their ontological vocation of becoming more fully human (through engaging in critical, dialogical praxis).

2. No person or group of people ought to knowingly constrain or prevent another person or group of people from pursuing the ontological vocation; that is to say, no person ought to oppress another.

3. We ought (collectively and dialogically) to consider what kind of world—what social structures, processes, relationships, and so on—would be necessary to enable (all) people in a given social setting to pursue their humanization.

4. All people ought to act to transform existing structures where critical reflection reveals that these structures serve as an impediment to the pursuit of humanization (by any groups within a society): this is the task of liberation.

For those concerned with issues of pedagogy (broadly conceived), a further principle can be added:

5. Educators and others who assume positions of responsibility in the social sphere ought to side with the oppressed in seeking to promote a better (more fully human) world through their activities.

These moral principles are necessarily intertwined in Freirean philosophy, for the pursuit of the ontological vocation by one person inevitably depends on the affording of an opportunity for this pursuit by others (and by the structures, institutions, attitudes, practices, etc. of the world in which one lives). In all cases, the processes involved in pursuing or adhering to Freirean moral principles are continuous and necessarily incomplete: we can, it will be recalled from earlier discussion, only ever become *more* fully human, never *fully* human; similarly, the task of creating a better social world must be renewed each time that world takes on a new face (with a new set of themes and tasks to be confronted).

SUMMARY

To summarize, the moral philosophy of Paulo Freire is built on a dialectical conception of reality and an epistemology in which theory and practice are dynamically related. The ontological and historical vocation of all human beings is humanization, or becoming more fully human. We pursue this ideal when we engage in critical, dialogical praxis. Constraints imposed by one group to the quest for humanization by another group indicate a situation of oppression. An oppressive reality is dehumanizing both for the oppressed and the oppressors. Oppressive social conditions are negated by a praxis of liberation. Given an ever-changing world, humanization is a continuous, unfinished process, with new problems to be addressed as each epoch unfolds.

CHAPTER 3

Ethics, Politics, and Pedagogy:
Freire on Liberating Education

The distinction between "banking education" and "problem-posing education" is one of the best known aspects of Freire's work. The second chapter of Freire's *Pedagogy of the Oppressed* (1972a) has become a classic reference point for scholars and practitioners investigating the nature of liberating education. Given its extraordinary influence, this dimension of Freire's theory merits close attention. It is important, however, that this initial discussion of banking education and problem-posing education be studied alongside Freire's other pedagogical writings.[1] Drawing on Freirean material spanning the last three decades, but concentrating in particular on Freire's later books, the present chapter focuses on the significance of structure, direction, and rigor in liberating education. The propensity among some Western educators to reduce Freirean theory and practice to a "method" or set of methods is criticized, and an alternative view of Freirean education as a distinctive approach to human beings and the social world is advanced.

BANKING EDUCATION AND PROBLEM-POSING EDUCATION: THE CLASSIC ACCOUNT

In chapter 2 of *Pedagogy of the Oppressed*, Freire argues that education is suffering from "narration sickness" (1972a, p. 45). Whether inside or outside schooling settings, the relationship between teacher and students tends to be overwhelmingly monological: The teacher narrates the subject matter to students who are expected to passively receive, memorize, and (if requested) repeat the content of the narration. This is the basis of the "banking" model of education. Teachers "deposit" ideas into students, who become receptacles or "depositories," waiting to be filled with the knowledge the teacher is assumed to possess (p. 45). In the banking system, knowledge is perceived as a "gift" to be bestowed by teachers upon voiceless, patient, ignorant students (p. 46). Banking education is inherently oppressive; it regards students as "adaptable, manageable beings" (p. 47). It is fundamentally antidialogical, and it systematically impedes the development of a critical orientation toward the world. Students are treated as acquiescent "automatons" (p. 48), to be controlled in both thought and action (p. 51). Knowledge becomes static and lifeless, the teacher assumes an authoritarian role, and social reality is trivialized or mythicized. Banking education reflects, reinforces, and perpetuates wider inequalities and injustices, serving the interests of oppressors "who care neither to have the world revealed nor to see it transformed" (p. 47). A paternalistic process of domestication and assimilation is evident (p. 48). The banking approach stifles the creativity— the critical imagination—necessary to address oppressive structures, and poses explicit constraints to liberating praxis. The whole system is thus (from Freire's point of view) thoroughly dehumanizing.

In opposition to banking education, Freire advances a theory of "problem-posing" (or "authentic" or "liberating") education. Problem-posing education begins with the resolution of the "teacher-student contradiction" (p. 53). Teachers become both teachers *and* students (and vice versa): the relationship is one of "teacher-student" with "students-teachers" (p. 53). Dialogue becomes the pivotal pedagogical process. Instead of issuing communiqués, the teacher communicates *with* students, and in so doing learns (and relearns) with them. The relationship between teacher and students, then, is horizontal rather than hierarchical. Participants in the educative situation come to know *through* dialogue, *with* others, *mediated* by the object of study. Where under the banking system ideas are deposited by teachers in a prepackaged, inert form, in liberating education learning takes place through "the posing of the problems of men in their relations with the world" (p. 52). Knowledge is constantly "in the making." It is always in a process of being created as students and teachers seek to unveil—through critical reflection—successive layers of reality. The object of study is not "owned" by anyone; rather, it becomes the focus around which all participants seeking to know gather to reflect and pose problems (cf. p. 54).

Problem-posing education is concerned with "the *emergence* of consciousness and *critical intervention* in reality" (p. 54). Through critical, dialogical investigation, participants begin to understand their world in a depth hitherto unknown to them: that which was once hidden, submerged, or only superficially perceived begins to "stand out" in sharp relief from other elements of awareness (pp. 55–56). Students (and teachers) begin to think holistically and contextually. A new conception of the relationship between "consciousness," "action," and "world" emerges through critical dialogue. Where under the banking system social reality is posited as a fixed inevitability, through problem-posing education students confront, explore, and act purposefully on a dynamic, ever-changing world (p. 56). As participants enter into dialogical relations with others and discover the dialectical interaction between consciousness and the world, they begin to sense that dominant ideas can be challenged and oppressive social formations transformed. Problem-posing education, Freire suggests, is a "revolutionary futurity": it "affirms men as beings who transcend themselves, who move forward and look ahead, for whom looking at the past must only be a means of understanding more clearly what and who they are so that they can more wisely build the future" (p. 57). A pedagogy built on authentic dialogue, conscientization, and revolutionary praxis can never serve the interests of oppressors (pp. 58–59); to the contrary, it is openly supportive of the struggle *against* oppression. Problem-posing education reaffirms human beings as Subjects, furnishes hope that the world can change, and, by its very nature, is necessarily directed toward the goal of humanization.

LIBERATING EDUCATION: A BROADER VIEW

In hindsight, the popularity of this account of banking education and problem-posing education is hardly surprising. Apart from the fact that it is from Freire's most famous book, the attractiveness of its arguments for Western educators is readily apparent. The pedagogical core of problem-posing education—dialogue—carries strong positive connotations, and was seen by many in First World countries as complementary to, or compatible with, emerging "child-centered," "interactive," "problem-solving," and other ostensibly progressive approaches to education during the 1970s and 1980s. The connections between these movements and Freire's educational ideal are, however, often a little dubious if not utterly misleading.

Although child-centered education is sometimes somewhat ill-defined, it tends in many cases to be predominantly individualistic in orientation; Freire, on the other hand, explicitly promotes collective action and structural imagination. Supposedly "new" interactive methods in science education (related in many instances to the move toward constructivist epistemologies in understanding scientific concepts) bear some resemblance to problem-posing education, but lack the overt Freirean imperative to relate classroom knowledge to wider political issues and the ontological vocation of humanization. Problem-solving approaches—whether in mathematics and science education, or "consciousness raising" groups—are in tension with the dynamism of problem-*posing* education (cf. Connolly, 1980, p. 73). Freire avoids talk of problem-solving, for this term suggests there is always a solution to every problem. From Freire's point of view, however, this is not always the case. In one sense, this is a necessary consequence of the political nature of Freirean education: When confronting problems of homelessness, mass illiteracy, poverty, exploitation, and so on, clearly there are no simple solutions. At a deeper level, however, it is in the very act of posing problems that participants pursue their liberation. Beginning to perceive contradictions in ideological positions, institutional structures, and everyday practices is one element in the process of revolutionary change. This critical, problematizing activity is necessarily ongoing and incomplete. As the social world changes, new problems arise, requiring further reflection and action. One does not "find" the solution, then move on to the next problem; rather, the next problem is being created as the present one is being addressed. Often the original problem persists, though in a metamorphosed form.

For teachers and other practitioners searching for a fresh way of organizing classroom life after the rigidity of traditional "rote learning" methods of instruction had become intolerable Freire seemed to have the answer. Dialogue was seen as the key to happier, more fulfilling, more effective learning. Freire's explicit situating of dialogue within the context of an overtly political process of conscientization and a revolutionary mode of praxis was often forgotten in all of this. Dialogue came to be seen as a pedagogical *method*, to be juxtaposed against oppressive monological methods. Yet when the links between dialogue and other key principles in Freire's pedagogy—conscientization, praxis, oppression, liberation, and so on—are ignored or downplayed, the very meaning of problem-posing education is lost. The discussion of dialogue in the second chapter of *Pedagogy of the Oppressed* needs to be read as one part of an integrated whole, and can only be thoroughly comprehended by reference to Freire's other writings. The wider corpus of Freirean texts is also especially helpful in clarifying differences between problem-posing education and a laissez-faire approach to pedagogy. Similarly, Freire's position on "authority" and "authoritarianism," while *implicit* in chapter 2 of *Pedagogy of the Oppressed*, emerges in greater detail elsewhere. In his later publications, Freire explores the role of experience in learning, the teacher-student relationship, the question of what (and how) students ought to read, and issues relating to course planning in some depth. In the discussion that follows, three features of the Freirean educational ideal will be stressed: structure, direction, and rigor.

Education, Ethics, and Politics

Freire sees learning and teaching as essential to human existence. Humans, as unfinished beings, are "programmed" to learn. It is not possible to be human without engaging in certain forms of educational practice. "Education," for Freire, does not apply just to schooling—which, as a mass movement, is a relatively recent historical phenomenon—but to the whole of life (Freire, 1998b, pp. 25–26). To live is to decide, to opt, to choose, to struggle. This confirms our existence as ethical and political beings, and signifies the crucial importance of education in social and individual formation (Freire, 1998c, p. 53).

Freire never tired of repeating that education cannot be neutral (see, for example, Freire, 1971a, pp. 1–2; 1972b, pp. 173–174; 1979, p. 28; 1987, pp. 211–212; 1998c, pp. 92–93). His recognition of the political nature of all pedagogical activity is arguably one of his greatest contributions to the field of education (Mayo, 1997, p. 365). Freire reminds us that learning never takes place in a vacuum. Whether in formal or informal settings, learning always builds in some way on the past and is necessarily shaped by the social structures and relations of the present. The sociopolitical context sets limits on what can be achieved by educators, but also leaves spaces for resistance (cf. Freire, 1998c, p. 110). Individual teachers or coordinators cannot but bring certain attitudes, values, beliefs, and predispositions to bear on the educative process. Whether recognized and acknowledged or not, the assumptions educators begin with structure and shape their pedagogical activities. Every decision, policy, or practice in an educational setting implies a particular conception of human beings and the world and a specific ethical position (cf. Freire, 1971a, p. 2).

Teachers do not need to have explicitly asked, "What *ought* I to do?" or "What political views do I support?" for their educational activities to be non-neutral; a certain ethical stance is already assumed in any consciously directed, deliberate action in an educative setting. Declaring oneself "neutral" is, Freire claims, a profoundly political statement. Those who purport to be "apolitical" often provide, either wittingly and unintentionally, support for the status quo. An educator, then, is always, in effect, "taking a stand," whether openly or implicitly. Freire observes:

This is a great discovery, education is politics! After that, when a teacher discovers that he or she is a politician, too, the teacher has to ask, What kind of politics am I doing in the classroom? That is, In favor of whom am I being a teacher? By asking in favor of whom am I educating, the teacher must also ask against whom am I educating. (Freire and Shor, 1987, p. 46)

Shor notes that for Freire the entire fabric of educational activity is political. This is revealed in myriad features of educational life, including the selection of subjects for a syllabus; the means employed in deciding on course content; the form of communication between teachers and students; the type of tests and grading policies used; the physical structure of classrooms; the attitudes towards different kinds of speech; the equality or lack of it in funding levels; and the links between educational institutions and the business community (Shor, 1993, p. 27). Even seemingly insignificant moments in the processes of teaching and learning—a brief period of silence, a smile, a gesture, a request to leave the room, the manner in which a question is asked—have political significance (cf. Freire, 1998c, p. 89).

Freire was always explicit in declaring his ethical and political position: his concern was to work toward the liberation of the oppressed. Of course, not all teachers, policy makers, and politicians share this goal. Freire believes, however—given his conception of humanization—that all teachers who are *against* the kind of dehumanization fostered through banking education ought to "side with" the oppressed in pursuit of a better social world. Taking a side—asking who one is working with and for, and who and what one is against—is a necessary part of the teaching process (Freire, 1994, p. 109; 1997a, p. 40). Freire describes his own stance as a teacher in the following terms:

> I am a teacher who stands up for what is right against what is indecent, who is in favor of freedom against authoritarianism, who is a supporter of authority against freedom with no limits, and who is a defender of democracy against the dictatorship of right or left. I am a teacher who favors the permanent struggle against every form of bigotry and against the economic domination of individuals and social classes. I am a teacher who rejects the present system of capitalism, responsible for the aberration of misery in the midst of plenty. I am a teacher full of the spirit of hope, in spite of all signs to the contrary. I am a teacher who refuses the disillusionment that consumes and immobilizes. I am a teacher proud of the beauty of my teaching practice, fragile beauty that may disappear if I do not care for the struggle and knowledge that I ought to teach. (1998c, pp. 94–95)

Teachers who do not themselves come from the ranks of the oppressed must be "reborn" as educators and join with the oppressed in their struggle against dehumanization. Freire speaks of this process as a form of "Easter experience" (1985, p. 123), and adopts from Amilcar Cabral (1980, p. 136) the notion of teachers from bourgeois backgrounds committing "class suicide." This implies *renouncing* the oppressive elements of one's class of origin while simultaneously *announcing* one's commitment to the liberation of the oppressed through dialogue, the problematization of social reality, and political transformation.[2]

Structure and Direction in the Pedagogical Process

Freire does not advocate an "anything goes" style of pedagogy. Liberating education, contrary to popular misconception, is structured, purposeful, directive, and rigorous. In later works, Freire distinguishes between three approaches to education: the authoritarian (or manipulative, or domesticating), the laissez-faire (or spontaneous), and the liberating (or radical democratic). The first and third of these correspond, in general terms, to banking education and problem-posing education, respectively. Freire argues that (liberating) teachers have a responsibility *as teachers* to be directive. The liberating teacher does not "wash his or her hands of the students" (Freire and Shor, 1987, p. 171), leaving them to structure and direct educative situations as they see fit. To hand all decisions regarding reading material, teaching style, and curriculum content over to students is not to promote freedom but to grant license. Although Freire retains the notion of all participants in a problem-posing dialogue being both teachers and students, this does not mean that teachers and students assume exactly the *same* role in the educative process. As Freire puts it in *Pedagogy of Hope*, "it is a *difference* between them that makes them precisely students or teachers. Were they simply identical, each could be the other" (1994, p. 117). The liberating teacher gives structure and direction to learning, while encouraging and enhancing academic rigor. The teacher has a responsibility to provide constructive, critical feedback on written work, and should always have "a plan, a program, [and] a goal for the study" (Freire and Shor, 1987, p. 172). The teacher's role is to direct in the sense of *guiding* (but not forcing) students through a course of study.

The term "facilitator" (rather than teacher) is often used by adult educators who espouse a commitment to Freirean principles. This notion seems to capture the directive essence of liberating education: the educator's responsibility rests precisely in his or her duty to *furnish the conditions* for effective (by which Freire means critical, dialogical, and praxical) learning to take place. The term must be employed with care, however, if it is to accurately convey Freire's intentions. In his book with Myles Horton, Freire states that the educator "cannot be a mere facilitator" (Horton and Freire, 1990, p. 180). This point is given more extended and explicit attention in Freire's subsequent publications. For example, in a dialogue with Donaldo Macedo, Freire notes:

When teachers call themselves facilitators and not teachers, they become involved in a distortion of reality. To begin with, in de-emphasizing the teacher's power by claiming to be a facilitator, one is being less than truthful to the extent that the teacher turned fa-cilitator maintains the power institutionally created in the position. That is, while facilitators may veil their power, at any moment they can exercise power as they wish. (Freire and Macedo, 1995, p. 378)

Freire is adamant: "I consider myself a teacher and always a teacher. I have never pretended to be a facilitator. What I want to make clear also is in being a teacher, I always teach to facilitate. I cannot accept the notion of a facilitator who facilitates so as not to teach" (p. 378). Clearly, then, if being a facilitator means minimizing the educator's involvement to the point where he or she is no longer an essential *participant* in the dialogical process, but merely a bystander, Freire would have opposed the term (and its embodiment in practice). The educator's active involve-ment in dialogical investigation with students is essential. If the term is used in the stronger sense—that is, to indicate a move away from the traditional, banking idea of teaching—Freire might have had no objec-tion to it. As the passages quoted earlier indicate, however, a preferable stance would be to retain the term "teacher" while at the same time rendering problematic certain practices which parade (falsely, in Freire's opinion) under the banner of teaching.

Freire insists that teachers ought not to avoid bringing their own po-litical beliefs to bear on their educational practice. Teachers should, he says, disclose their intentions and discuss their dreams with students. This implies being open about what one regards as ethically desirable and ethically undesirable. It also suggests that teachers not only have a right but a responsibility to respond honestly when confronted with stu-dent views contrary to their own. "My role as a teacher," Freire says, "is to assent the students' right to compare, to choose, to rupture, to decide" (1998c, p. 68). This does not mean, however, that one should *impose* one's views on students. Freire notes that although students in his classes were aware of his membership of the Brazilian Worker's Party, it would have been unacceptable for him to attempt to change the academic policy of the university to reflect party policy (Escobar et al., 1994, p. 138). He respected those who did not share his political affiliations, and he be-lieved students should never be compelled or coerced to accept the teacher's position. The teacher's ideas, along with all others, should al-ways be open to question. Freire argues that educators have a duty to teach "what seems to them to be fundamental to the space-time in which they find themselves" (1994, p. 130), but cautions against the possibility of one dominant view shutting out all others. This point applies to *all* participants in an educative situation. Whether one is a teacher or a student, no one, from a Freirean point of view, has the right to insist that their understanding of reality is the only acceptable, legitimate, or defensible one. More than this, though, teachers have a responsibility to actively promote consideration of alternative views: to stimulate contrary discourses and invite critical appraisals of their own views (p. 78). Providing the necessary resources for investigating competing perspectives on controversial issues—via lectures, recommended readings, the posing of new problems and asking of new questions—thus becomes important in maintaining the sort of healthy debate Freire encourages.

Freire's discussion of the differences between authoritative and authoritarian approaches to education in later works is instructive here. A democratic teacher, Freire argues, "can never stop being an authority or having authority" (Freire and Shor, 1987, p. 91). This authority derives from the educator's knowledge of his or her subject, and from the responsibility the educator has for coordinating, structuring, and facilitating the educative process. The teacher's authority is necessary for freedom to develop (Freire, 1997a, p. 90). This, for Freire, is only an apparent paradox. Where teachers renounce or deny their authority, freedom becomes license; where they forget the freedom of students altogether, authority becomes authoritarianism (see Freire, 1987, p. 212; 1997a, p. 90). The differentiation between "freedom" and "license" here is not a conceptual distinction but a substantive (normative) one. The key to understanding Freire's position lies in the *purpose* of exercising authority; namely, to promote the appropriate conditions for allowing others to liberate themselves. As Freire puts it in *Letters to Cristina* (1996, p. 150), "authority is an invention of freedom so that freedom may continue to be." If authority is completely relinquished, the structure, direction, and focus necessary for rigorous dialogical reflection on a common object of study is missing.

For Freire there is a close connection between authoritarianism and manipulation. A manipulative approach to pedagogy is one in which students are expected to believe X or Y without question, or irrespective of the evidence in favor of X or Y. One dimension of manipulation is the systematic impeding of a curious, interested, creative, questioning orientation toward the world. For Freire, asking questions is an essential part of the learning process. The liberating educator welcomes questions as a sign of the students' critical engagement with the object of study; the authoritarian teacher tends to regard questions as an attack on his or her professional authority (Freire and Faundez, 1989, p. 35). The defensiveness of the authoritarian teacher when faced with challenging questions springs from a fear of the answers such questions might give rise to (p. 36). The manipulative teacher has no intention of unveiling reality, or of penetrating surface appearances. Manipulation denies, distorts, and mythicizes reality. It represents an attempt to turn the world into something it is not and to enforce compliance with this falsification. This process can be deceptively subtle: "We can be authoritarian in sweet, manipulating and even sentimental ways, cajoling students with walks through flowery roads, and already you know what points you picked for the students to know" (Freire and Shor, 1987, p. 91).

Freire speaks of an "inductive moment" in the educative process. This is the moment, he says, "where the educator cannot wait for the students to initiate their own forward progress into an idea or an understanding, and the teacher must do it" (p. 157). Should students spontaneously "put all the knowing together" (p. 158), so much the better, but where this does not occur the educator ought to intervene and assist in moving critical discussion forward. An authoritarian teacher attempts to retain total control over the students' learning by "monopolizing" the inductive process, whereas a liberating teacher *starts* the process when necessary but always with a view to transcending the inductive moment to allow students to continue critical investigation themselves (pp. 157–158). The teacher's role, thus, is to step in—to initiate, redirect, or give a focus to, dialogue and study—with the express purpose of creating the possibility for *others* to give direction to the educative process. Paradoxically, then, deliberate assistance (in keeping dialogue moving in a critical direction) at *certain* points is necessary if these intervening moments are to be minimized. To put this another way: "It's impossible for me to help someone without teaching him or her something with which they can start to do by themselves" (Horton and Freire, 1990, p. 193).

If educational dialogue is to be liberating, it requires a clear, though not *rigid*, structure. Freire does not advise teachers to adhere to a program of study dogmatically, or simply for the sake of following a prescribed syllabus. The purpose of structure—the provision of a framework within which meaningful, directed dialogue can occur—should always be kept in mind. Slavish devotion to a set plan or course outline can be counterproductive: important opportunities for deeper interrogation of the object of study can be missed, and student enthusiasm can be dampened. Without some form of structure, however, the goal of liberating education can be similarly compromised. Dialogue can lapse into idle chatter and opportunities for collective critical inquiry can be lost. Students may enroll in a course for different reasons, and benefit in different ways from their participation, but there need to be some learning objectives common to all.

Dialogue with a Purpose

The wider purpose of liberating education is, as the name suggests, *liberation*, through the posing and addressing of problems. This involves, in part, the formation of dialogical settings devoted to questions of oppression. Each educational program has, or ought to have, more specific purposes: for example, learning to read and write, acquiring knowledge in a given subject, discovering how to perform particular tasks, and so on. Moreover, in any liberating educative effort, the concern is to address *this* oppressive situation, or *that* one, not some abstract notion of "oppression in general."[3] The purposeful character of liberating education also relates to the Freirean concept of an ontological vocation: the "purpose" of all human lives, simply through *being* human, is humanization, and all liberating educative efforts are ultimately directed toward this end.

Freire argues that if dialogue is to be politically transformative, it "implies responsibility, directiveness, determination, discipline, [and] objectives" (Freire and Shor, 1987, p. 102). Dialogue does *not* signify the necessary abandonment of existing knowledge. Ideas are constantly *re-examined* in a dialogical setting, but this does not mean there is no stability or continuity in what participants know over time. Freire notes:

> [B]y discussing dialogue every day with students, I am not changing every day my understanding of dialogue. We arrive at the level of some certainty, some scientific certainty of some objects, which we can count on. What dialogue-educators know, nevertheless, is that science has historicity. This means that all new knowledge comes up when other knowledge becomes old, and no longer answers the needs of the new moment, no longer answers the new questions being asked. Because of that, all new knowledge when it appears waits for its own overcoming by the next new knowledge which is inevitable. (pp. 101–102)

Teachers, Freire stresses, should not withhold what they already know of their subject area from students; indeed, they have a duty to share this knowledge, just as students have a responsibility to *engage* the ideas presented by the teacher. Students should not be compelled to "speak up" in problem-posing education; nor should they be permitted to subvert the dialogical process for other students who wish to make a verbal contribution (pp. 102–103). Silence has an important role to play in communicative relationships. Silence affords participants in a dialogue the space to truly listen to what others have to say. It allows one to appreciate questions and doubts, and to "enter into the internal rhythm of the speaker's thought and experience that rhythm as language" (Freire, 1998c, p. 104). Those genuinely committed to the experience of dialogical communication, and not merely the transmission of information, must, at times, control their urge to speak, aware that others share the same right (and duty) to express their ideas.

All contributions to an educative dialogue should be treated with re-

spect. This principle springs from Freire's conviction that no one is ignorant of everything, just as no one knows everything: all participants
are capable of contributing helpfully to the educative engagement. At a
deeper level, respect for others—in the sense of listening to, and reflecting on, what they have to say—follows simply from the fact that they
are fellow human beings. All human beings have the same ontological
vocation, an essential dimension of which is the formation of dialogical
relationships with others. *All* human beings, then, have a "calling" to
engage in dialogue: dialogue is a fundamental part of being human. The
refusal to listen to others who are different, or hold views antagonistic
to one's own, constitutes an act of oppression. There are no "stupid"
questions or final answers, though some questions and answers may be
more naïve than others. The educator's role is not to squash the inquis-
itiveness of students, or to impede the "inner movement of the act of
discovery." Instead, even when a question seems to be poorly articulated
or "wrongly formulated," the teacher should not ridicule the student but
assist the student to "rephrase the question so that he or she can thereby
learn to ask better questions" (Freire and Faundez, 1989, p. 37).

This does not mean that all contributions—whether in the form of
questions, comments, or responses—should be accepted uncritically. *All*
views—whether embedded in texts, advanced by the teacher, or developed by students—ought to be open to question in a liberating educative
situation. The teacher plays an important role in structuring the critical
process here. He or she must strive to foster respectful rather than destructive criticism. For Freire, a critical attitude is necessarily respectful.
To critically engage the ideas of another implies the existence of something *worthy* of engagement. Destructive criticism reflects, or is compatible with, an authoritarian attitude where the object is to crush the
creative process. In a liberating educational environment, criticism is
coupled with listening and reflection; in an authoritarian situation, teachers and students merely *react* to the views of others. The liberating
teacher has a directive responsibility to ensure dialogue does not lapse
into either an arena for abusive attacks or an artificially tolerant atmos-
phere where all views are accepted unconditionally. Freire believes that
in examining any object of study some ideas are better than others, but
he is always open to the possibility that his reading of reality might be
wrong.

Liberating Education: A Serious Endeavor

Liberating education demands—of both teachers and students—the
highest standards of academic rigor. Freire is concerned to counter the
myth that authoritarian education is somehow more rigorous than liberating education (Freire and Faundez, 1989, p. 33). From his point of

view, the tables should be turned here. Intellectual rigor, as Freire conceives of it, is absolutely fundamental—indeed, indispensable—to problem-posing education, while banking education systematically impedes rigor. Teachers, Freire argues, must be thoroughly conversant with the literature pertinent to their domain of study, and must seek to continuously "relearn" their subject. "Reading" for Freire implies the fullest possible engagement with texts, not simply a skimming of content matter (see Roberts, 1993, 1996a, 1998d). Studying for Freire is an inherently difficult and demanding, but also potentially joyous, process (Freire, 1987, p. 213). The joy of study arises precisely from the attempt to apprehend the object of study critically. As Freire observes in one of his last works, joy and rigor need not be viewed as mutually exclusive terms (Freire, 1998a, p. 4). Joy, Freire reminds us, "does not come only at the moment of finding what we sought. It comes also in the search itself" (1998c, p. 125). Study requires discipline, though this does not imply a *disciplinarian* stance on the part of the teacher. Rather, it is the self-discipline and collective effort of teachers and students investigating the object of study through purposeful, directive, structured, *critical* dialogue to which Freire refers. Study is *work*. It demands great effort and a mustering of intellectual energies such that learners transcend mere awareness and penetrate beneath the surface of the subject or object under investigation. In this sense, studying represents an extraordinary or *exceptional* state: a mode of being beyond (or at least in contradistinction to) that which typifies everyday conscious activity. In the process of studying, Freire tells us, we encounter "pain, pleasure, victory, defeat, doubt, and happiness" (1998a, p. 28).

Liberating education is thus a profoundly *serious* endeavor. This is in keeping with the seriousness of the situation the oppressed find themselves in. Teaching, for Freire, ought never to be reduced to a "feel-good" process. This does not mean that the liberating classroom should be somber or devoid of humor. In *A Pedagogy for Liberation*, Freire draws a distinction between humor and just laughing:

> A humorist is not just a smile-maker, someone who makes people laugh. No! Even sometimes, good humor leads you *not* to smile or laugh. But, on the contrary, good humor does not make you laugh as much as it makes you seriously think about the material. Humor is Chaplin. He unveiled all the issues he tried to describe, to live with in the cinema. In the shows, he revealed what was behind the situations. (Freire and Shor, 1987, p. 162)

Problem-posing education is not a theater for superficiality, nor does it represent a mode of entertainment (p. 214). Nonetheless, where opportunities exist to incorporate humor into dialogue as a means for enhancing serious engagement with the subject at hand rather than trivializing it, educationists should make the most of these. As Shor notes, "Humor is not a mechanical skill you add to dialogical methods like icing on a cake. It has to be part of our character and the learning process" (p. 162).

Freire is careful to point out that his criticism of authoritarian education is not directed at individual teachers; rather, his concern is with the *system* of banking education, the attitudes that underpin it, and the wider social relations in which it is enmeshed. In his discussion of banking education and problem-posing education in *Pedagogy of the Oppressed*, Freire raises the possibility of teachers adopting a banking approach unknowingly. There are, he says, "innumerable well-intentioned bank-clerk teachers who do not realize that they are serving only to dehumanize" (1972a, p. 48). Indeed, one of his most important messages is that we need to break away from individualistic thinking and begin to problematize reality in holistic, structural terms. He advocates *collective* action against oppressive social formations (of which banking education is one example). Freire speaks of the oppressive effects of "divide and rule" policies, and highlights the dangers associated with splintered, disconnected, overly localized struggles (see Freire, 1972a, 1994, 1997a, 1998c).

If teachers uphold the liberating ideal advanced by Freire, they are, he argues, worthy of our deepest respect. Many educators regard teaching as a vocation (Freire, 1998c, p. 126) and persist with their work in the face of enormous obstacles. The dignity and importance of teaching should be acknowledged by teachers themselves (Freire, 1998a, p. 34) and by members of the wider community. Such recognition, Freire insisted in later works, should include better salaries and conditions for teachers (see Freire, 1996, 1998a, 1998c). The teacher in Freirean education is invested with awesome responsibilities, and must be supremely committed to dialogue, the act of knowing, and social transformation. Freire's words in *Teachers as Cultural Workers* are apposite here:

> [T]he task of the teacher, who is also a learner, is both joyful and rigorous. It demands seriousness and scientific, physical, emotional, and affective preparation. It is a task that requires that those who commit themselves to teaching develop a certain love not only of others but also of the very process implied in teaching. It is impossible to teach without the courage to love, without the courage to try a thousand times before giving up. (Freire, 1998a, p. 3)

Freire identifies a number of qualities (attributes or virtues) necessary for progressive teachers. These include humility, a generous loving heart, respect for others, tolerance, courage, decisiveness, competence, verbal parsimony, openness to what is new, perseverance in the process of struggle, a spirit of hope, and an ability to say "*yes* to life" (Freire, 1998a, pp. 39–45; 1998c, p. 108). Teaching, for Freire, is a multifaceted process, involving a complex combination of rational, emotive, active, and even spiritual processes. "The beauty of the practice of teaching," Freire tells us, "is made up of a passion for integrity that unites teacher and student" (1998c, p. 88). *Caring* for students is essential to the activity of teaching. Teachers should seek to uphold the highest critical standards, but this does not mean they must hide their feelings or become cold and distant (p. 125). For the characteristics of good teaching to flourish, certain rights for educators—freedom in teaching, opportunities for criticizing the authorities without fear of retaliation, and paid sabbaticals, for example—need to be protected (Freire, 1998a, pp. 45–46). Good teachers are not *born* with qualities needed to do their jobs well; instead, such virtues are "acquired gradually through practice" and demand a political context in which the educator's role is recognized as crucial (p. 39).

NOT "A METHOD"

I want to suggest in this section that Freire's pedagogy cannot be reduced to a set of methods, techniques, or skills (cf. Aronowitz, 1993; Macedo, 1994; Bartolome, 1994; Brady, 1994). Liberating education, I maintain, represents a particular approach to human beings and a specific orientation to the social world, from which general principles—not universally applicable methods—for teaching and learning can be generated. As I argued in the Introduction and chapter 1, understanding the pivotal dimensions of Freire's approach demands a holistic reading of his work, and an antitechnocratic stance on complex educational issues and problems. In adopting this view, I take as my starting point Donaldo Macedo's appraisal of the U.S. education scene in a dialogue with Freire published in 1995. Macedo observes:

> Part of the reason why many teachers who claim to be Freire-inspired end up promoting a laissez-faire, feel-good pedagogy is because many are only exposed to, or interpret, your leading ideas at the level of cliché. By this I mean that many professors who claim to be Freire-inspired present to their students a watered-down translation of your philosophical positions in the form of a lock-step methodology. Seldom do these professors require their students to read your work as a primary source and, in cases where they do read, let's say, *Pedagogy of the Oppressed*, they often have very little knowledge of other books that you have published. (Freire and Macedo, 1995, p. 380)

Noting the puzzlement among students who are frequently told about Freire but never required to engage his work, Macedo cites the case of a teacher who began a workshop by proclaiming, "My project is Freirean inspired. I'll be talking about Freire even though I haven't read his books yet" (p. 381). This represents, on one level, a bizarre confession, and a worrying state of affairs from an educational point of view. It is less than surprising, however, when understood as one manifestation of a form of reductionism that appears to be rampant not only in North America but also many other parts of the Western world in contemporary times.

Freire never denied the necessity of learning how to perform certain tasks, or of developing the requisite skills, in given fields of study. Doctors obviously need to learn surgical techniques; pilots must learn how to operate complicated instrument panels; and logicians cannot analyze arguments without knowing the fundamentals of syllogistic and other forms of reasoning. Freire would also have been quite happy to admit that in *teaching* students in these and other subject areas, educators must employ particular methods and draw upon certain skills. If the approach to teaching and learning about a subject is to be liberating, though, it is not the methods, skills, and techniques that define it as such; rather, these things *flow from* a specific ethical and political stance. The essence of banking education is not monological teaching methods but a distinct orientation toward human beings and the world. People under the banking system are regarded as adaptable, manageable objects to be manipulated into the existing (oppressive) social order. Monological and authoritarian methods reflect, reinforce, and help perpetuate this view of the world. Problem-posing education begins from different assumptions: humans, for the liberating educator, are praxical beings—Subjects who, as Freire would put it, "make" history and culture—who ought to be given maximal opportunities to transform the world through reflective action. Methods such as encouraging students to ask questions in class, setting problems to be pursued rather than simply giving answers, allowing time for discussion, and promoting reflection on personal experiences are what might reasonably be expected from a teacher committed to the Freirean view of humanization through praxis. These techniques do not themselves demonstrate the character of liberating education.

If it is an approach or an orientation toward human beings and the world with which we are dealing, then specific "how to" questions can only be addressed in context. That is to say, the best methods in one situation may not be the best methods in another. Teachers not only must take into account the social and political context within which learning occurs but also the experiences and existing forms of knowledge among participants. To reduce liberating education to a methodology, or a set of classroom techniques, is to *de*contextualize it.

Methods ostensibly transcend culture and history. Surgical procedures are the same irrespective of the hospital or country they are performed in; certain methods of mathematical proof remain consistent over time; various quantitative systems of research can be duplicated in any number of different studies; syllogistic logic is the same for contemporary analytic philosophers as it was for Aristotle; and so on. In some spheres of human activity, it is assumed that methods must be duplicated in the same way regardless of the context. In such cases, it is believed that any deviation from the precise techniques or practices associated with a particular method will reduce its effectiveness. Certain methods of sports coaching, giving birth, and teaching skills to youngsters fall into this category.

If Freire's work is conceived purely or primarily in methodological terms, one implication is that his approach to literacy education in the Third World should be readily "transportable" to the First World as a "prepackaged" set of clearly defined techniques. An avowedly Freirean educator might concede that specific details of "the method" would have to be changed (e.g., aspects of the syllabic recombination process, in the light of the differences between Portuguese and English), but believe that apart from features clearly ruled out in particular contexts Freire's techniques should adopted "to the letter."

Freire was vigorously opposed to this line of thinking, and in later works (1997b, 1998a) was disturbed to see it (re)emerging, under neoliberal political conditions, in technocratic, prepackaged approaches to teacher education. From a Freirean standpoint, every educational situation presents a *distinct* challenge to be addressed. The first question an educator ought to ask is not "What methods should I use?" but "What human ideals do I (or we) wish to promote?" From this starting point, more specific questions follow: "What are the limits and possibilities in seeking these ideals within *this* situation (at this time, in this place, subject to these political constraints, given these social relations, within this structural framework, etc.)?" and "What overall goals and strategies are appropriate in light of the ideal and the situation?" Only after these concerns have been addressed (that is, theorized—critically and dialogically) can the question "What methods would be best?" be authentically answered. Of course, this is not meant to imply some sort of lock-step, rigid, sequential procedure: the whole process of deciding what ought to be done in any educational setting should be thoroughly dialectical. But Freire is adamant that the first priority for an educator is to confront questions about human beings and the world, after which methodological problems can be addressed.

This suggests an important distinction for those commenting on or attempting to apply Freirean ideas. In his literacy education work in Brazil, Chile, and other Third World countries, Freire adopted certain procedures. He encouraged discussion and active participation rather than silent compliance and the mechanical repetition of words from the teacher; he used pictures depicting aspects of everyday life as a focus for dialogue and critical engagement; he produced discovery cards with words broken down into syllabic families; and so on (see chapter 4). It seems perfectly consistent with Freire's position to talk of these as "methods"—used in specific programs, at particular times, within several different social contexts, and developed in accordance with a substantive and overt ethical and political stance. It is quite another matter, however, to speak of Freire's whole approach to pedagogy as "a method." This is blatantly distortive. It is possible to develop pedagogical *principles* from a holistic reading of Freire's books (cf. Freire, 1996, p. 127) but these principles suggest, at most, parameters within which methodological decisions can be made. Principles are not equivalent to or synonymous with methods; nor does a *set* of principles amount, in total, to *a* method. If this distinction is legitimate, the dangers of referring to "*the* Freirean method," "Freirean methodology," or even "Freirean *methods*" (if such a phrase is employed in a decontextualized way) should be readily apparent. This sort of language directs attention away from the very dimensions Freire regards as most significant in any pedagogy: a conception of human beings and the nature of reality, an epistemological theory, an ethical position, and a political stance—from which broad (not fixed) underlying principles are derived.

A NOTE OF CAUTION

In opposing the domestication of Freirean pedagogy, a note of caution must be added. Care must be taken if excessive generalizations about educational movements in the Western world are to be avoided, and acknowledgment must be made of the considerable gains made by those who have successfully adapted Freirean (and other) ideas to suit different educative situations. Let me return to the example of child-centered education in elaborating this point. My comments earlier in the chapter were not meant to suggest that Freire's work has been misappropriated by *all* supporters of "child-centered" education (or by all devotees of "interactive" science education). It could be argued, of course, that advocates of child-centered methods of teaching and learning *should*, if they are to adhere to Freire's own advice, refashion Freirean ideas, appropriating those elements which prove helpful for their own context(s). It might be suggested that child-centered learning, under the influence of Freire and other progressive thinkers, has provided a highly effective vehicle for moving away from an oppressive banking system toward a more liberating approach to education for young people: one that was expedient and appropriate for the situations in which it was developed. Something of the utopian vision in Freire's writings may have been lost in this process of adapting his ideas to suit different circumstances, but significant pedagogical improvements have nevertheless been made, and debate about substantive educational issues has been enhanced. Child-centered learning arguably addresses the oppression of children by attempting to move away from an education system that destructively labels some children as "failures" (and others as "successes") at an early age to one where children are valued for their particular skills and abilities. Moreover, even if the focus in child-centered education is on the individual, in encouraging children to maximize their potential as learners, there are clear gains for a society as a whole. Child-centered education, in short, values children for their own worth as human beings—a stance fully commensurate with Freire's ethical position—and stresses horizontal, rather than hierarchical, relationships between participants in the educative process. Accordingly, child-centered systems often emphasize project-based learning, where the teacher does, in an important way, act as a "facilitator" of the child's learning. Such an approach is certainly "political," as all systems of education are, and, although perhaps less "radical" than Freire's work with Brazilian and Chilean adults, is clearly worthwhile.[4]

This line of argument turns on two related issues. One issue relates to the process of applying Freirean ideas; the other deals with what has been achieved by educators *other* than Freire. With regard to the first issue, in applying any theorist's ideas a complex process of interpretation and negotiation is always involved. When we come across a thinker for the first time, we must, as Freire himself constantly reminded us, always relate the new ideas we encounter to something within the realm of our existing knowledge or previous experience. This, for Freire, is an epistemological necessity in the learning process. We cannot make sense of anything outside of some sort of cognitive framework, which presupposes the existence of certain attitudes, beliefs, values, practices, and so on, formed within particular contexts and discursive arenas. If we see some merit in that thinker's theory, a certain form of adaptation is necessarily required from the moment we first confront the author's text(s). The ideas we encounter are always "filtered" through the process of reading (or listening, or firsthand observation) and interpretation. In this sense, then, our application of a theorist's ideas is always partial and incomplete. There is no "pure," complete reading of Freire's work. This does not mean, however, that some readings, interpretive positions, and modes of understanding may not be better than others. In the Introduction I argued that if we are to be true to the ideals Freire espouses, a holistic, contextualized, antireductionist, and critical approach to his work is clearly superior to a fragmented, decontextualized, technocratic, or passive reading. The objective, in Freirean terms, is to come *closer* to the raison d'être or essence that explains the object of study, while none-theless being aware that one can never know the object of one's inves-tigation absolutely or completely (cf. Freire and Shor, 1987, p. 82).

At stake here is the question of what we hope to achieve or do, and how we *name* what we have achieved or done, in reading Freire. As educationists, we consult the work of numerous theorists in forming and applying our ideas in various professional and personal domains (in classrooms, homes, factories, prisons, etc.). Obviously, few people have time to read all the published writings of every major theorist encoun-tered in the course of their studies. Reading is typically a selective proc-ess, demanding considerable sifting and sorting through voluminous collections of theoretical material. It is impossible, moreover, to defini-tively assess the precise extent to which, and ways in which, one has been influenced by particular thinkers. But to say that Freire has been an influence over child-centered education is not equivalent to declaring that the child-centered education movement, or even specific child-centered classrooms, are *Freirean* in their approach to learning. The latter involves a form of *naming* of one's ethical, epistemological, and educa-tional position, which, if it is to be authentic (in the Freirean sense), ought to involve rigorous scholarly engagement with a wide range of Freirean texts. Freire may have been an influence in the development of many worthwhile educational programs, but it does not follow from this that all these initiatives are examples of Freirean liberating education. The distinctive strengths of many such programs might be more accurately attributed to the influence of other thinkers, or to an original synthesis of *many* theories. Child-centered educators have arguably been success-ful, at least in part, because they have managed to integrate a diverse range of educational ideas into a coherent, but not rigid, philosophy of the learning and teaching process.

CONCLUDING COMMENTS

Freire's focus in chapter 2 of *Pedagogy of the Oppressed* is on two ped-agogical approaches: banking education and problem-posing education. The distinction between two clearly opposing forms of education has an immediate appeal: it permits definite lines to be drawn between that which is liberating and that which is oppressive, and allows educators to declare their own intentions and allegiances with unwavering convic-tion. A teacher is *either* humanizing *or* dehumanizing in his or her ped-agogical stance. Binary oppositions of this kind have been problematized in recent times by postmodernists, and Freire's proclivity to using them as a major theoretical device leaves him especially vulnerable to criticism (see Giroux, 1993). Although Freire's written works are replete with di-chotomous theoretical constructs ("active" versus "passive"; "integrated" verses "adapted"; "liberation" versus "oppression"; "humanization" versus "dehumanization", etc.), his later writings suggest there is no *single* antithesis to "liberating education." For Freire, liberating education stands opposed to *two* pedagogical approaches: one authoritarian, the other laissez-faire. At one end of the scale, the teacher is granted total authority and exercises this in a disciplinarian and oppressive manner; at the other pole, the teacher relinquishes (or is stripped of) *any* authority, and students do as they please. Both are in tension with the ideal of humanization. Authoritarian education is blatantly antidialogical, whereas laissez-faire approaches diminish the *purposeful* character of education and human struggle.

There can be little doubt that Freire's account of banking education and problem-posing education in the second chapter of *Pedagogy of the Oppressed* represents one of the best, and certainly one of most influential, concise statements of liberating education from the past three decades. Freire did not subsequently contradict or renounce any of the major principles discussed in that chapter, but he did *extend* and clarify many points from this classic early piece in later publications. In particular, and partly in response to repeated misreadings of his works, he stressed the importance of structure, direction, and rigor in his educational ideal. To be a liberating educator implies a certain clarity and conviction in one's ethical and political position, coupled with thorough preparation and a willingness to work dialogically with others. The problems to be addressed in liberating educational settings must be continuously confronted afresh as the world—in its myriad social, cultural, and political dimensions—ever evolves.

NOTES

1. Discussion of Freire's educational theory in this chapter is by largely confined to issues of pedagogy. Freire tends to use the terms "education" and "pedagogy" synonymously, though in almost all cases his references to the latter have or imply some connection with the theory and practice of teaching and learning. Even if teaching and learning are employed in the widest sense here (i.e., not restricted to schooling or institutional settings), there is arguably more to education than this. It is assumed throughout that it is *adults* with whom we are dealing when references are made to "students." The terms "educator" and "teacher" are used interchangeably.

2. This notion becomes highly problematic if it is recognized that teachers often occupy contradictory social positions, oppressed in some senses but privileged in others (see Weiler, 1991). One way of responding to this is to see "class suicide" as an ideal teachers might strive for but not necessarily be able to attain (Mayo, 1993, p. 19).

3. Although all of the programs with which Freire was involved had different problems to be confronted, thematized, and acted on, Freire's tendency, in some writings, toward abstract and universalist pronouncements in his *theorizing* about oppression and liberation has drawn sharp criticism. This issue is addressed in chapter 6.

4. For an in-depth discussion of arguments for and against child-centered education, see Darling (1994).

CHAPTER 4

Freirean Adult Literacy Education

Freire's approach to adult literacy education is intimately linked to his wider philosophical position and his pedagogical theory. In this chapter, which is largely descriptive in character, I give an account of some of the key features of Freire's literacy initiatives in Brazil during the early 1960s. Mention is also made of Freire's contributions to several other literacy and adult education programs in the Third World. The next chapter shows how ideas originally developed through these experiences in the field were refined and extended in Freire's theoretical work on literacy.[1]

FREIRE'S LITERACY WORK IN BRAZIL

Freire describes his literacy work with Brazilian adults in some detail in *Education: The Practice of Freedom* (1976, pp. 41–84). His appointment in 1963 as director of the National Literacy Program was preceded by more than fifteen years of experience in the field of adult education, in both urban and rural areas. He recalls that while he experimented with many different pedagogical methods and means of communication during this formative period, his one overriding conviction remained the same: "[O]nly by working with people [says Freire] could I achieve anything authentic on their behalf" (p. 41). The sponsorship by Miguel Arraes of an adult literacy program in Recife in 1962 provided Freire with the platform to launch his now-famous "culture circles" (Mackie, 1980a, p. 4). In the culture circles, illiterate adults were invited to participate in a process of critical reflection on the social conditions in which they found themselves. Freire abandoned many elements of traditional teaching in the project, replacing lectures with dialogue, the teacher with a coordinator, and the term "pupils" with "group participants" (Freire, 1976, p. 42). Encouraged by Freire's achievements in the Recife program, President Joao Goulart appointed Freire director of the National Literacy Program. Although the campaign was brought to a premature end with the military coup d'etat in 1964, the approach Freire adopted in Brazil was later to be reworked and applied (by Freire and others) in several Third World countries from the 1960s to the 1980s.

Freire's literacy work in Brazil comprised three related stages: (1) an investigation of the social situation of the adult illiterates, and the preparation of materials and agendas; (2) an introduction to the concept of culture through the analysis of a series of pictorial representations of aspects of Brazilian life; and (3) the use of a small number of "generative" words for assisting in the process of reading and writing.[2] These are discussed in turn.

Investigative and Preparatory Work

Freire identifies five phases in this stage of the program. In phase one, adult literacy workers researched the vocabulary of the people with whom they were working. From informal interviews, and in some cases from periods spent actually living and working with families in rural and urban communities, lists of "charged" words were built up. Investigators, Freire comments, were to search for words which were infused with emotion and meaning for the adult illiterates. The words were chosen on the basis of their centrality in the daily lives of those in the community, and were laden with "longings, frustrations, disbeliefs, hopes, and an impetus to participate" (Freire, 1976, p. 49). Freire is careful to point out that the words selected in this early phase emerged from the adult illiterates themselves, and did not merely reflect the literacy workers" predispositions about what was important as far as a reading vocabulary was concerned (p. 50).

Once the process of informal interviewing and investigation had been completed, fifteen to eighteen "generative" words were selected for each area covered by the campaign. This was the second phase of the preliminary work. Words were generative in two senses. First, they were imbued with existential meaning—that is, they corresponded to the most fundamental concerns, ideas and practices of the adult illiterates' lives— and were thus pregnant with possibilities for discussion of daily life in political, social, and cultural context. In this sense, then, the adopted words generated reflection on lived, everyday reality, and offered the potential for a deeper, more critical understanding of that reality. Words were also selected on the basis of their phonemic richness; specifically, an effort was made to find words that could be broken down into syllables, combined with vowels, and reformed to generate new words. Freire further stipulated that "the words chosen should correspond to the phonetic difficulties of the language, [and should be] placed in a sequence moving gradually from words of less to those of greater difficulty" (p. 51).

Phase Three was the creation of "codifications." These were pictorial representations of generative words. Frequently, the pictures would encapsulate situations from the daily lives of the participants. Generative words were embedded in the codifications, and graduated in terms of their phonetic complexity. A generative word might embrace the entire situation depicted in the picture, or it might be relevant to only one aspect of the situation (pp. 51–52).

The fourth and fifth phases of the investigative and preliminary stage of the program consisted in the explication of "agendas" (i.e., the style, methods, and content of the program) for culture circle coordinators, and the production of discovery cards with the breakdown of generative words into phonemic families (pp. 52–53). Six hundred coordinators were requested at the start of the program, and more than 30,000 applications were received. A two-page test was administered in a football stadium, and coordinators were selected on the basis of their answers to questions such as these: "Brazil is largely a marginal society. How shall we get out of this situation?"; "What do you think of the condition of education in Brazil at the present moment?"; "Why did you decide to apply for this job?" (see Fonseca, 1973, p. 95). Freire observes that as far as informing coordinators of the nature of the program was concerned, the difficulty lay not with instruction in the technical aspects of the method employed for teaching reading and writing, but with the inculcation of a particular orientation toward the learning process. Coordinators were called to abandon traditional narrative, "banking" approaches to education in favor of a pedagogical system based on the principle of dialogue (Freire, 1976, p. 52).

An Introduction to the Concept of Culture

After all the initial preparations had been put in place—the existential situation of the participants explored, generative words selected, posters or slides of codifications made, and coordinators given their agendas— the next stage in the program could commence. In Brazil, this second stage—an exploration of ideas about nature, culture, work, and human relationships—occupied up to eight sessions of the overall program. (Literacy groups met for one hour each week-night for a period of up to eight weeks [Brown, 1974, p. 32].) The conditions which prompted the introduction of this second stage in the Brazilian program are neatly captured by Bee (1980):

> The task of motivating the Brazilian people was a difficult one. They were apathetic, downtrodden, and fatalistic in their attitudes. In order to change this demoralizing situation into something more positive and responsive Freire and his team needed to convince the people of their own worth, to show them that no matter how de-nuded of dignity they considered themselves to be, they were in fact makers of culture, of history, and subjects in life, not merely objects of manipulation. (p. 40)

Toward this end, Freire commissioned the services of the Brazilian artist Francisco Brenand in putting together a series of pictures designed to introduce the notion of "culture." The pictures were made into slides and projected on to the walls of houses where culture circles met. (Where it was not possible to use the wall of a house, the reverse side of a blackboard was used.) There were ten pictures in the original sequence, each intended to initiate dialogue based around a particular theme.[3] These visual representations were deliberately ordered, such that later pictures and their respective themes built on ideas discussed in earlier pictures.

The first picture showed a peasant man standing beside a well and a tree, holding a hoe and book, with a pig in the foreground and a house in the background. All aspects of the picture (apart, perhaps, from the book) were familiar to those participating in the program. Coordinators were instructed to begin by asking, "What do you see in the picture?" Once the various aspects of the scene had been identified, participants were asked such questions as these: "Who made the well?"; "What materials did he use?"; "Who made the tree?"; "How is the tree different from the well?"; and so on (Brown, 1974, p. 26). From this problematization of the reality depicted in the picture, adults in the program began to distinguish between nature and culture, between objects that exist in the natural world and those created by human beings. The second picture depicted a man and woman standing together, surrounded by a variety of farm animals. Discussion in this case centered around the differences between animals and human beings. Participants worked toward the notion that humans are beings of communication, capable of entering into dialogue with one another, mediated by the world of nature (Brown, 1974, p. 26; Freire, 1976, p. 65).

The third, fourth, and fifth pictures, taken as a group, each represented different variations around the theme of hunting. The third and fourth pictures showed a child using a bow and arrow and a man using a gun. A contrast was drawn between the two different types of hunting, the former (i.e., making and using a bow and arrow) being passed on as a skill from father to son without the aid of writing, the latter (shooting) involving a tool so complex that written instructions were necessary for its construction (Brown, 1974, p. 26). After ideas about the differences between oral and literate culture, the transformation of materials from nature to culture, and the implications of education for technological development had been thoroughly investigated, participants were presented with a picture of a cat preying on mice in order to sharpen earlier distinctions between humans and animals. Dialogue focused on the concept of humans as conscious, reflective, knowing beings. Seen as a whole, the collection of representations in pictures 3, 4, and 5 "produced a wealth of observations about men and animals, about creative power, freedom, intelligence, instinct, education, and training" (Freire, 1976, p. 71).

The sixth and seventh pictures were also closely related, picture 6 illustrating two people at work making clay pots, and picture 7 displaying a finished clay pot being used as a vase. In the vase were flowers, and on the vase was a picture of flowers. With the sixth picture, the theme of transforming the products of nature through work was discussed. The introduction of the seventh picture served as a bridge between earlier pictures and the final three that followed. Participants, for the first time, saw a graphic representation of an object—the flower on the vase—demonstrating the transformation of nature into a symbol (Brown, 1974, p. 29). This idea was extended in the eighth picture, which showed a book, opened to a page with a particular arrangement of written symbols. After the coordinator had read what was shown on the page of the book, members of the group quickly recognized it as a poem, and the ensuing discussion revolved around the different expressions of culture exemplified by the vase and the poem. Participants were also encouraged to debate issues raised in the poem itself (Freire, 1976, p. 77).[4]

The ninth picture depicted two cowboys from separate regions in Brazil. Participants talked about the differences in their (i.e., the cowboys') clothing and possible behavior. They also discussed the way in which traditions initially develop in response to a need, but sometimes persist after the need has passed (p. 79). Finally, in the tenth situation, members of the group saw themselves portrayed in visual form. The picture showed a group of peasants assembled in a culture circle, with the coordinator at the front of the room pointing to one of the earlier pictures. This was an important moment in the process of self-reflection, and the first step along the road to critical consciousness. The group conversation concentrated on such themes as "culture as a systematic acquisition of knowledge" and "the democratization of culture" (p. 81).

By the time this stage of the program had been completed, Freire attests that participants were highly motivated to continue learning. He

summarizes his thoughts on the significance of this part of the literacy
process thus:

> Literacy makes sense only in these terms, as the consequence of
> men's beginning to reflect about their own capacity for reflection,
> about the world, about their position in the world, about the en-
> counter of consciousness—about literacy itself, which thereby
> ceases to be something external and becomes a part of them, comes
> as a creation from within them. (p. 81)

The intellectual advances demanded of participants in examining the
series of pictures can be described as follows. In broad terms, the movement is from lesser to greater complexity, from the more familiar to the
less familiar, and from the concrete to the more abstract, as the sequence
progresses. The representations deal with themes which correspond to
fundamental tenets in Freire's ontology, metaphysic, and epistemology.
The discussion moves from "nature" to "culture," and from the "unlet-
tered" to the "lettered" world. The notion that men and women are beings of relationships who transform the world is constantly reinforced.
Initially, transformation is related to "work." This arises logically from
a consideration of familiar daily tasks and activities. In the middle pictures, participants are required to draw some sharper distinctions between humans and animals. In the last representation, participants deal
more directly with political transformation—with the prospect of building more democratic social structures. As participants move through the
sequence, then, they are increasingly encouraged to "step back" from
their daily reality, to examine the familiar and the concrete in a new
light, to reconsider their relationships with others and with the world.
The rhythm of the sequence mirrors the movement of the program as a
whole. The starting point in both cases is the existential situation of the
participants, which then becomes the focus for close investigation, leading to a simultaneous reading of words and "rereading" of the social
world.[5]

Syllabic Combinations Through Generative Words

For the first two stages of the program, no direct attempt at teaching
participants how to read and write in the traditional sense of encoding
and decoding print symbols (i.e., forming and interpreting letters, words,
and sentences) was made. The goals were to learn as much as possible
about the world(s) of the illiterates and to foster discussion of anthro-
pological, social, and political issues. As the more conventional expectations of a literacy program started to be addressed, the learning of
syllabic combinations continued to be integrated with an exploration

of contexts from which generative words emerged. After a group had exhausted analysis of the codified situation encapsulating the first generative word, the word itself was introduced. Participants were encouraged to visualize (but not to memorize) the word, and with the aid of the codification, to establish the semantic link between the generative word and its object of reference (Taylor, 1993, pp. 52–53). The word was then displayed without the accompanying codification and broken down into its component syllables. The syllables of the word, once recognized by the members of the group, could be paired up with vowels and recombined with other syllables to make new words. This technique, as Sanders (1972, p. 591) notes, was greatly aided by the fact that Portuguese is a syllabic language, with "little variation in vocalic sounds and a minimum of consonantal combinations." Although different generative words were chosen for each area covered by the program, the first word was always trisyllabic, with each of the three syllables consisting of one consonant and one vowel (Brown, 1974, p. 30).

The purpose of beginning this way is made apparent in Freire's often-cited example of the generative word, *tijolo*. This word—which in English means brick—was the first generative word used in a culture circle in Cajueiro Seco, a slum area in Recife (p. 31). After the word had been thoroughly discussed in its codified setting, it was introduced on its own and its syllables *ti, jo,* and *lo*, were read aloud by the coordinator of the group. The first syllable was then presented in a sequence of consonant-vowel combinations, in the following manner: ta-te-*ti*-to-tu. Although participants recognized only *ti* in the first instance, they quickly moved to the observation that "while all the syllables begin the same, they end differently" (Freire, 1976, p. 54). In this way, the basic vowel sounds were rapidly grasped, and the coordinator could proceed with the introduction of the other two syllables in the generative word, building up this sort of pattern on the discovery card:

ta-te-ti-to-tu
ja-je-ji-jo-ju
la-le-li-lo-lu

After sounding out each of the syllables, participants were given the opportunity to form new words from the "pieces" depicted on the discovery card. Hence, the possibility emerges of illiterates creating words such as *tatu* (armadillo), *luta* (struggle), *loja* (store), *juta* (jute), and *lote* (lot). Freire was not concerned if participants formed combinations of syllables which were not actual words; it was the discovery of the mechanism of phonemic combination—and the "naming" of words as an active, creative process—that was important. More important still, though, was the discussion that surrounded the introduction of each generative word. In the case of the word *tijolo*, the theme of urban reform became the subject of debate; with the generative word *favela* (slum), groups deliberated on problems relating to housing, health, food, and education; *terreno*, the Portuguese word for land, stimulated discussion around such subjects as irrigation, natural resources, and economic domination.[6]

Results and Repercussions

Freire and his coworkers found that fifteen to eighteen carefully selected generative words for each group were sufficient to bring formerly illiterate adults to the point where they were "reading newspapers, writing notes and simple letters, and discussing problems of local and national interest" in six weeks to two months (p. 53). It was hoped that this achievement could be consolidated, and political transformation intensified, with a postliteracy stage. Freire regarded the postliteracy phase as crucial in any program of education and national reconstruction. While the literacy work concentrates on generative *words*, a key element in the postliteracy stage is generative *themes*. These themes, he suggests, should be drawn from the problems, issues, struggles, conflicts, and politics of national, regional, and local life. Through critical exploration of these issues, the limit-situations confronting participants are identified and, when necessary and possible, negated with limit-acts. However, plans for the establishment of 20,000 culture circles across Brazil in 1964 were crushed by the military coup, and Freire was forced to extend his adult literacy efforts elsewhere.

The attitude of the Brazilian government toward Freire after his forced exile is clearly (if implicitly) revealed in an article published in the *Journal of Reading* in the mid-1970s. In this piece, Arlindo Lopes-Correa (1976), the then-president of MOBRAL (the Brazilian Literacy Movement), outlines the methods used by the Brazilian government to overcome functional adult illiteracy. In a remarkable act of plagiarism, Lopes-Correa runs through a literacy process involving generative words, syllabic families, discovery tables, and pictorial codifications without once mentioning Freire's name. (The author of the article even uses Freire's classic example of the breakdown of the generative word *tijolo*.) Freire's work is not listed in the bibliography. References to conscientization and praxis have been removed, and Freire's call for literacy to be a means through which illiterates attain a deepening political awareness is replaced by the expressed hope that "pupils"—a term Freire avoided as far as possible—develop "an interest in continued self-learning through reading" (p. 534). The "technical" aspects of Freire's literacy method have been appropriated almost to the letter (with their source of origin left unacknowledged), but the radical, critical force of Freire's work has been placed to one side.[7]

Further evidence of the treatment afforded Freire by Brazilian authorities more than a decade after the military coup can be gleaned from comments made in one of a series of conversations at the University of Massachusetts and Harvard University in the 1980s. Freire reveals that the well-known "Declaration of Persepolis" (1976)—a concise statement of aims for adult literacy work formed at the conclusion of a conference with representatives from across the globe—was signed by all participating countries *except* Brazil. The Brazilian delegates protested Freire's presence and left the meeting (Bruss and Macedo, 1985, p. 14).

FREIRE'S INVOLVEMENT IN OTHER LITERACY PROGRAMS

A comprehensive account of Freire's post-1964 literacy endeavors is beyond the scope of this chapter. It is important, however, to mention some of the other major adult literacy programs with which he has been involved, and to note some of the similarities and differences between these programs and the Brazilian campaign.

After a short stay in Bolivia following the Brazilian coup, Freire spent five years working in Chile. His involvement with the Chilean Agrarian Reform Corporation, notwithstanding some resistance from sections within the Frei government of the time (Mackie, 1980a, p. 5), was extensive, and Freire was able to extend both his theory and practice of adult literacy education considerably. There were some differences, though, between Freire's Brazilian program and his work in Chile. Lloyd (1972) notes that although many of the coordinators in Brazilian culture circles were students, the program in Chile had to rely on paid instructors, many of whom were primary-school teachers who experienced some difficulties in changing from traditional (monological) teaching methods to a dialogical approach to education: "Despite training in dialogue and the Freirean method, paternalistic attitudes and patterns persist[ed]" (p. 12). After overcoming the political and pedagogical hurdles, Freire's system became an official program of the government, and Chile was recognized by UNESCO as one of the five nations most effective in overcoming illiteracy (p. 11). Freire incorporated discussion of the concept of culture into the "generative words" stage of the program in Chile, instead of devoting a series of separate sessions to this task. This was because "the Chilean, unlike the Brazilian who liked discussion about himself as a creative, cultural being, tended to lose interest if he did not begin to learn immediately" (Sanders, 1972, p. 593). The generative words and codifications, of course, were different in the Brazilian and Chilean campaigns, but the fundamental techniques for learning how to form words (through syllabic combination) were the same.

Freire was briefly involved with adult education work in Tanzania in the early 1970s, but his chief commitments in the decade following his departure from Chile were to literacy programs in São Tomé and Príncipe, and Guinea-Bissau. Both of these programs have attracted a measure of criticism, as well as favorable evaluation; Freire's work in Guinea-Bissau, in particular, was fraught with operational difficulties. The major problem that emerged was a difference in opinion between Freire and the government of Guinea-Bissau (for whom he was working) over the issue of the Portuguese language. Freire felt that the country could never lift the yoke of colonial oppression completely while it continued to favor the language of the colonizers over the local Creole language as the only medium of instruction. The government insisted that Portuguese remain the official language, and an impasse was reached. In his own appraisal of his achievements in Guinea-Bissau, Freire concedes that the degree of technical competence with print attained by adults in the program was not high, but argues that emergence of a new form of political awareness among participants outweighed this. He attributes the "failure" of the campaign to promote an adequate command over the alphabet to the persistence of the authorities in wanting to uphold the Portuguese language (Freire and Macedo, 1987, pp. 114–115).[8]

In São Tomé and Príncipe, Freire made a significant break from earlier practices in supporting the use of a primer for literacy learning. From his earliest experiences with adult illiteracy in Brazil, Freire had steered clear of primers, basing his mistrust on the belief that they "set up a certain grouping of graphic signs as a gift and cast the illiterate in the role of the *object* rather than the *Subject* of his learning" (Freire, 1976, p. 49). Adult education efforts in São Tomé and Príncipe were organized around books called "Popular Culture Notebooks." The first primer in the series—"Practice to Learn"—was employed in the literacy phase. Additional material was introduced in the postliteracy stage (Freire and Macedo, 1987, pp. 64–65). "Practice to Learn" was a workbook with sets of words and sentences for illiterates to tackle, coupled with codifications and themes for discussion. The primary notion presented in the early part of the book was the idea that people learn through (social) practice. As learners worked their way through the book, they were introduced to progressively more complex themes and ideas relating to national independence, work, knowledge, exploitation, and colonialism. Learners were given opportunities to write words and sentences of their own in each part of the workbook.

The program was, in Freire's terms, successful, though not without its difficulties. Most of these were tied to wider problems in the overall process of national reconstruction following the country's independence in 1975. Freire mentions obstacles such as the following: international fluctuations in the price for cacao (the main product of São Tomé and Príncipe); a lack of "national cadres" able to deal with the tasks of post-colonial rebuilding of the country; and a shortage of trained personnel and material resources for adult literacy work (1981, p. 30). The campaign in São Tomé and Príncipe has been criticized by Gee (1988) for the contradictions it embraced between, on the one hand, wanting to encourage people to become independent thinkers and yet, on the other hand, telling them what it means to "think correctly".[9] All in all, though, Freire's work in São Tomé and Príncipe has not been marked by the same controversy that accompanied the program in Guinea-Bissau, perhaps largely because, as Freire himself points out, he and his wife Elza found themselves absolutely at one with the government in its articulation of national goals (see Freire and Macedo, 1987, p. 64).

NOTES

1. For discussion of Freire's adult literacy work, see Freire (1972a, pp. 81–95; 1972b, pp. 29–47; 1976, pp. 41–84; 1978, pp. 5–68; 1981; 1985, pp. 7–18, 21–27); Freire and Macedo (1987, chs. 4 and 5); Horton and Freire (1990, pp. 83–95); Brown (1974); Sanders (1972); Lloyd (1972); Bee (1980).

2. It is tempting to call the third stage the "actual literacy training" (Sanders, 1972, p. 593), because it was only at this point in the program that participants learned the "mechanics" of reading and writing—that is, the formation of words and sentences. But giving in to this temptation represents a serious mistake, for literacy, as it is conceived by Freire, consists in much more than simply the mastering of the medium of print: the preceding or coexisting analyses of nature, culture, work, human relationships, and so on and the attendant posing of problems pertaining to local and national politics are as much a part of what it means to become "literate" in Freirean terms as the learning of letters and words. (See chapter 5.)

3. The originals were taken from Freire. The pictorial situations published in *Education: The Practice of Freedom* were produced by another Brazilian artist, Vincente de Abreu (Freire, 1976, p. 61). Cynthia Brown was able to obtain eight of the original sequence of ten pictures, all (eight) of which are reproduced in her article, "Literacy in 30 Hours: Paulo Freire's Process in Northeast Brazil." Figures 5 and 8 in the collection shown by Brown are from the de Abreu set. (See Brown, 1974, pp. 27–28.)

4. The text shown in the picture was, of course, in Portuguese. The poem is about the dangers of the atomic bomb (see Brown, 1974, p. 29).

5. For a detailed discussion of this stage of the program, see Taylor

(1993, ch. 5). The notion of "reading the word and the world" figures prominently in Freire's later theoretical work on literacy, and will be investigated in chapter 5.

6. For an in-depth analysis of Freire's approach to codification and decodification, see JanMohamed (1994).

7. This is not an isolated example. Other post-1964 work on literacy in Brazil also renders Freire invisible. There is one citation of Freire's work, but no discussion of it, in Chesterfield and Schutz (1978). Another article (Moreira, 1985) does not even mention Freire.

8. For an excellent discussion of this issue, see Mayo (1995).

9. The notion of "correctness" reappears in a number of Freire's later writings (see, for example, Freire, 1993a, 1994, 1998c). Elsewhere (Roberts, 1999a) I have argued that "correct thinking" is, for Freire, equivalent to "*critical* thinking."

CHAPTER 5

Extending Literate Horizons: Freire and the Multidimensional Word

This chapter begins with a brief consideration of the relationship between politics, experience, and literacy in Freire's work. Attention then shifts to the pivotal importance of dialogue in Freirean programs of adult literacy education. This preliminary discussion gives rise, in the third section, to a more detailed analysis of the multifaceted "word"—comprising spoken, written, and active dimensions—as the defining characteristic of Freire's approach to literacy. The final section sketches the parameters for an expansive concept of *critical* literacy, premised on the Freirean conception of humans as reflective, dialogical, praxical beings, and squarely grounded in an ethic and pedagogy of hope.

POLITICS, EXPERIENCE, AND LITERACY

Literacy is typically regarded as unquestionably worthwhile. Claims about the benefits of literacy—and the undesirability of illiteracy—must, however, be made with caution (see Street, 1984; Lankshear with Lawler, 1987; Graff, 1987; Roberts, 1997b). Freire anticipated later critiques of popular assumptions about the value and consequences of literacy in some of earliest writings. In *Cultural Action for Freedom* (1972b), for example, he criticizes the "digestive" concept of knowledge embedded in many adult literacy education programs. Illiterates, he points out, are sometimes regarded as "undernourished," "poisoned," or "diseased" beings, in need of the "cure" of literacy. A mere depositing of (written) words where none existed before supposedly provides the "bread of the

spirit" to be "eaten" and "digested" by illiterates (pp. 23–24). This conception of illiteracy fuels a (paternalistic) humanitarianism in literacy
campaigns: the words of the lettered coordinators or teachers are to be
brought and gifted to those in need to save them from the deprivation(s)
of wordlessness. Yet, as Freire observes, "[m]erely teaching men to read
and write does not work miracles; if there are not enough jobs for men
able to work, teaching more men to read and write will not create them"
(p. 24).

Illiteracy, Freire recognized from the beginning, is a reflection or a
manifestation—but not the *cause*—of wider structural inequalities. Keeping significant sections of the population in a state of illiteracy, while
granting full access to the written word for a privileged few, can be seen
as an act of violence. The rights of full citizenship are freq ently denied
those who are illiterate (Freire, 1998a, p. 2). Freire speaks of adult illiterates as "beings for another"—dominated people within an oppressive
social order. The solution to this situation does not lie in more deeply
immersing illiterates within the structures that oppress them, but in
transformation of the conditions of oppression. Literacy is, potentially at
least, one element in the struggle to overcome oppressive social conditions.

For Freire, literacy must be understood contextually. Any attempt at
setting up a literacy program must (if it is to be humanizing) involve an
examination of the culture of the region within which literacy educators
are working. A literacy initiative will never be successful, Freire contends, unless it recognizes the nature of daily life—and the social structures which, in (large) part, determine the limits and constraints of
everyday activities—for participants in the program. This is why Freire
insisted from the beginning that the preliminary stage of his practical
literacy work in Brazil—the investigation of local themes, practices, and
conditions—was so important.

Literacy, for Freire, is always a *political* phenomenon. This is so from
the moment at which a person is invited (or compelled, as in compulsory
reading at school) to learn to read the written word. The decision to
encourage someone to become literate is a political one, just as the denial
of literacy is also a political decision. (Witness the direct correlation between illiteracy and being denied the vote in Brazil in the 1950s and
early 1960s.) But, more than this, the *way* that someone becomes literate
and practices reading and writing thereafter is undeniably a question of
politics. In his earlier writings, Freire suggests that the options are to
either institute a form of literacy pedagogy that aims to domesticate and
adapt people to accept an oppressive set of social circumstances, or to
foster forms of reading and writing that seek to challenge these conditions (see Freire, 1972a, chs. 2–3; 1972b, pp. 21–47; 1976, pp. 41–58, 134–

162). In later books, this binary, either-or logic gives way to a more complex position in which literate activities are seen to take a wider variety of forms (compare, Freire and Macedo, 1987; Freire, 1994, 1998a, 1998b, 1998c).

Freire argues that the words which form the beginning of any literacy program must be based on the experience(s)—the lived reality—of participants. Freire's literacy work in Brazil provides a classic illustration of this principle. As noted in the previous chapter, a series of generative ("charged," emotive) words corresponding to aspects of everyday life in Brazil provided the foundation for the program. Freire argues that the same principle should apply at all levels in the educational spectrum, whether it is adults or children with whom one is working. The first words for any person learning to read and write must be their words: words from *their* world (cf. Freire, 1983).

This does not mean that personal experience should represent the endpoint of a literacy program. Education, Freire was always quick to say, ought to challenge people to go *beyond* their current understanding of the world (whether this is through reading and writing, or any other form of social practice), by challenging them, demanding something more of them in their thinking than they have been accustomed to, and extending their existing critical capacities (cf. Freire, 1996, pp. 128–129). Freire's point is that each person has unique access to at least one domain of knowledge—the reality of their lived experience. No one knows *my* world—my perceptions, feelings, longings, sufferings, activities, and so on—quite the way I do. A literacy program (indeed, any educational program) cannot succeed if learners are unable to relate in *some* way to what educators or coordinators are saying. The stronger the connection with existing knowledge and experience, the better (other things being equal) learners will be able to proceed with further learning by building on this base.

Freire would have regarded a literacy campaign that left participants with no better understanding of the world at the end of the program than that which they had when they started as a failure. The notion of change is vital in Freirean education (see chapter 7). But in the process of being challenged to go beyond "where we are now," it is necessary to constantly relate back to the "old" (or the existing) to understand what is being encountered in the "new." In fact, a crucial element of Freire's literacy work was the *reinterpretation* of existing conceptions of reality in the light of new experiences. When Freire discusses "experience," he is referring to the whole web of practices, relationships, activities, and interactions with material phenomena from which a person's understanding of their world derives. This form of understanding provides an indispensable route through which to meet new ideas, but it should not be accepted uncritically as the final or most accurate reading of reality (compare, Horton and Freire, 1990, p. 98; McLaren and Silva, 1991, pp. 38–40).

THE IMPORTANCE OF DIALOGUE

The crucial bridge between existing and new forms of knowledge and experience in any educational endeavor (a literacy program being one example) is dialogue. Dialogue provides a "way into" the world of the illiterate (or the world of any learner in an educative situation) for teachers or coordinators; indeed, there is no other way of properly "tapping" the unique world of each learner's knowledge and experience apart from dialogue. Equally, and this point is often forgotten, dialogue is the means through which learners can enter the (lettered, literate) world of the coordinator. The purpose of dialogue in a literacy program not only is to facilitate the acquisition of reading and writing abilities, but also to promote a critical comprehension, and transformation, of the participants' social world. As Freire sees it, dialogue is intrinsic to the literacy process. Learning to read and write implies a relationship between two or more people. It is inconceivable, from a Freirean standpoint, to talk of becoming or being literate alone. This idea springs from Freire's recognition that language is necessarily social and shared. (Wittgenstein's point about private language being impossible is apposite here.) This is the *starting point* for Freire's notion of dialogue, but it does not reveal the particular form Freire believes dialogue should take in educational settings.

Freire talks of intersubjectivity, or intercommunication, as a fundamental human characteristic (1976, p. 134). The human world, for Freire, could not exist without communication. No human being can think, act, or *be* alone. This point has profound implications for the way education and literacy are conceived. Freire states:

At the moment in which educators carry out their research, when as cognitive Subjects they stand face to face with a knowable object, they are only apparently alone. Not only do they establish a mysterious, invisible dialogue with those who carried out the same act of knowing before them, but they engage in a dialogue with themselves too. Place [*sic*] face to face before themselves they investigate and question themselves. The more they ask questions the more they feel that their curiosity about the object of their knowledge is not decreasing. It only diminishes if it is isolated from human beings and the world. (p. 148)

The immediate *physical* presence of other human beings is thus not a prerequisite for all forms of dialogue. Hence it becomes possible to speak of a dialogical relation between readers and texts. Books, from Freire's point of view, ought to be actively *engaged*. This means entering into a relationship of a particular kind with the text, allowing, in a sense, the text to "talk" to us while we simultaneously "talk" to it (cf. Freire, 1998a, p. 30). The creation of meaning through reading is neither entirely a product of the reader's interpretation, nor something embedded in an unambiguous way in the text. Rather, meaning emerges in the complex process of negotiation or "composition" *between* writing and reading. Reading in the manner intended by Freire is also always a process of writing, and *vice versa*. Readers ought to both apply the ideas they en-counter in books to their own struggles and material circumstances, *and* bring their personal experiences to bear in interpreting and "rewriting" texts. Reading, for Freire, entails "seizing" or "grappling" with the text, both challenging it and being prepared to *be* challenged by it (see further, Roberts, 1993, 1996c).

THE MULTIDIMENSIONAL WORD IN FREIREAN THEORY

Freire's approach to adult literacy education relied on a dynamic in-tegration of oral and literate modes of communication. Learning to *read* the word, for the adults with whom Freire was working, emerged from purposeful discussion of generative words and codifications through the medium of the spoken word. Dialogue provided the *bridge* between oral and literate forms of interpreting, understanding, and transforming the world. In fact, there was no rigid separation between "speaking" and "writing" in Freire's literacy work, at least not into clearly defined "stages" in the literacy process. Generative words were simultaneously an object for dialogue through speech and the means through which this speech was reflected on and modified in a "lettered" way (see Freire, 1976; 1996, p. 128).

The word-world relationship was dialectically redefined through this process. Freire stresses that no one comes to read the word without first having read the world (1994, pp. 78–79). Not all readings of reality, though, are especially critical. Freire argues that many participants in his literacy programs tended to view or interpret—that is, "read"—their world "magically," attributing the overtly oppressive conditions they en-dured to fate or God's will. Introducing the written word in unison with critical discussion via the spoken word allowed this reading to be *re-read*—that is to say, transformed. At the same time, the lettered world of coordinators was demystified: as participants learned to combine syl-lables from generative words to form new words, the (perceived) magical character of writing itself was deconstructed (even if only in a rudimentary way, given the time available).

Writing, Freire observes in *Teachers as Cultural Workers* (1998a, pp. 24–25), is often seen as a burden to be shunned or feared. This stems, in part, from the artificial separation of writing from reading and speaking: a process that often begins in early childhood and continues through the schooling system into adulthood. Writing, like many other human activities, needs to be carefully nurtured and practiced if it is to mature and flourish. Good writers—they may be poets, novelists, scientists, or philosophers—need to be read and studied as learners seek "beauty, simplicity and clarity" in expressing their own ideas (p. 24). In any literacy program, then, every effort should be made to encourage learners to create their own written texts at the earliest opportunity. It is not, for Freire, a case of speaking first, then developing reading skills, and then learning to write; rather, speaking, reading, and writing should be seen as intertwined elements in the quest for knowledge and social transformation.

Freire's integration of speech, reading, writing, and action is effectively captured in the notion of the multidimensional word. In a literacy program which is truly dialogical these different elements become intertwined. There is a constant interaction between the spoken word, written words, and *true* words in the process of learning to read and write. The word, for Freire, *is* a praxis: a synthesis of reflection and action, "in such radical interaction that if one is sacrificed—even in part—the other immediately suffers" (Freire, 1972a, p. 60). Word, work, and praxis are interchangeable terms for Freire: all imply conscious transformation of reality, through relationships with others. Speaking the word—which is not merely a verbal but an active process—is a *primordial* human right (p. 61). It follows for Freire that *literacy* belongs to all human beings *as* human beings. *To be human* is to be literate, if we understand literacy in Freire's special sense. Speaking the word—which includes, but is not limited to, reading and writing the printed word—is, Freire (1972b, p. 30) stresses, a basic right for *all* human beings, and should not be the privilege of an elite few.

The word-world relationship is crucial in understanding Freire's concept of literacy. Freire does not suggest that there is no difference between word and world, or text and context: He simply identifies and discusses different *kinds* of words (spoken, written, and "true") and texts (written texts and the text that is social reality itself). The world, for Freire, is more than simply a complex collection of dancing signifiers; reality has a concrete, objective, material dimension. The world in the word-world relation comprises the reflective activity of human beings, the social institutions human beings create, the relationships they forge with each other, and the material sphere of the objective world. These are the dimensions of reality to be transformed when Freire talks of "speaking a true word." Words are both a part of the world and the means through which it is shaped and transformed. Speaking a word, of any kind, always implies a process, or an act, and a *relationship* with others and with the world. Hence, it is the larger world on which the word works, and this is a necessarily social process.

Thus, words are always but one element of the larger world; that is, they are necessarily "in" the world. But the world is also always in the word. This is a difficult idea to grasp, but it is pivotal in understanding the Freirean concept of literacy. Words—whether in the form of speech, writing, or reflective action—are always spoken or written in a given context, within a particular set of material circumstances, subject to specific ideological influences, and as part of a distinct web of social relationships. But these features, which mark out the "setting" or the "context" or the "framing" for speaking or writing the word, also *live through* the word itself. For words are not lifeless formations which arise seemingly from nowhere; they are forged, created, and conditioned by the world in which they evolve.

EXTENDING LITERATE HORIZONS: CRITICAL READING AND WRITING

The overriding feature of all of Freire's literacy work is his emphasis on the importance of being *critical* in reading and writing. In both his practical work with illiterate adults and his numerous theoretical statements on literacy, Freire always upheld the worth of a critical approach toward both the word and the world. This not only applies to adults, but also to children: "No matter the level or the age of the students we teach, from preschool to graduate school, reading critically is absolutely important and fundamental" (Dillon, 1985, p. 19). Even where Freire talks about the aesthetic moment in reading, the beauty of books, or the emotions involved in literate activity, these things are defined against the dominant theme of becoming critical (see, for example, Horton and Freire, 1990, pp. 23–27, 31–32). Reading is joyous to the extent that it becomes an active, dialogical, critical process; books become beautiful when critically engaged. Unless it is critical, reading cannot become an act of *knowing* (Freire, 1983, pp. 10–11; Dillon, 1985, pp. 18–20).

In Freire's earlier work (Freire, 1972b, p. 42; 1976, p. 43), the critical aspect of literacy was defined in relation to the concept of conscientization. In the literacy programs with which Freire was involved, the aim was for illiterate adults to move from a state of either magical or naive consciousness toward (an ever-evolving) critical consciousness. More specifically, Freire's goal was "to make it possible for illiterates to learn quickly how to write and to read, and simultaneously learn also the reasons why the society works in this way or that way" (Horton and Freire, 1990, p. 84). In other theoretical discussions, Freire constantly stresses the need for a certain attitude in the literacy process. We are advised to approach texts in a searching, questioning, curious, restless manner (see, for instance, Freire, 1985, pp. 2–3). It is the *quality* of reading, not the number of books read, that matters (Freire, 1983, p. 9; Freire and Shor, 1987, pp. 83–85).

Becoming, and being, critically literate in a Freirean sense implies the development of a particular orientation toward the world. Reading *texts* critically, from a Freirean point of view, necessitates, and is only possible through, a critical reading of a given *context*. Word and world become dynamically intertwined in Freirean critical literacy. Critical reading involves a constant interplay between text and context. Contextualizing a text demands, for example, that the author's historical circumstances be taken into account in analyzing a book; on the other hand, a text can allow the reader to reinterpret aspects of his or her world. The aim, then, is to develop a more critical understanding of text *and* context through interrogating one in relation to the other (cf. Roberts, 1997c).

At a deeper level, however, the conventional distinction between text and context can be collapsed in Freirean critical literacy. Although texts can be taken as the equivalent of "books" in many of Freire's discussions of reading, there is also a much broader notion of text in his writings. Freire talks of praxis—transformative, reflective action—as a process of "speaking a true word" (1972a, p. 61). "True words," as the earlier discussion indicated, represent the dialectical synthesis of theory and practice, action and reflection, word and world. The text to be read and written or rewritten in speaking a true word is social reality itself (see further, Peters and Lankshear, 1994; Macedo, 1993). Freirean critical literacy can thus be seen as a form of, or an aspect of, transformative, reflective social action. More specifically, critical literacy implies a conscious, practical, dialogical attempt to understand, challenge, and change oppressive social structures.

Hence, a Freirean view of critical literacy is inclusive of, but also goes beyond, the notion of (merely) critically analyzing and evaluating books. Freire does not deny the value of identifying key themes and ideas, questioning and problematizing pivotal assumptions, and dissecting an author's arguments; in fact, he explicitly recommends that readers adopt such practices (see, for instance, Freire, 1985, pp. 1–4). But there is more to Freire's ideal than this. For Freire, critical literacy can be seen as a mode of discursive practice: a way of being in (and with) the world. To read and write critically is to engage in a form of dialogical praxis. It is to enter history as a critically conscious Subject, naming and transforming both the word and the world. Critical literacy, as Freire understands it, is one element in the struggle for liberation from oppression. Learning to read and write (in the conventional sense) does not in itself bring about the overthrow of oppressive attitudes, practices, and structures, but it can contribute to this process.

A Freirean notion of critical literacy is, in short, concerned with the development of a particular mode of *being* and *acting*—not simply a way of dealing with books. Reading is just one of the myriad activities to which a critical approach might be applied. This is where the real significance of Freire's construct of "reading the word and the world" lies. Critical literacy, for a Freirean educator, has to do with much *more* than reading and writing in the conventional (technical) sense. In many ways, the actual reading of texts is secondary to the emergence of a new epistemological, ontological, and ethical consciousness in a literacy program. Texts are not humanizing; people humanize themselves—in part, through engaging books and other written texts, but, more profoundly, through reading (i.e., interpreting, reflecting on, interrogating, theorizing, investigating, exploring, probing, questioning, etc.) and writing (acting on and dialogically transforming) the social world.

CONCLUDING COMMENTS

This chapter has suggested that for Freire, critical literacy education implies both the learning of letters, words, and sentences, and the development of a particular orientation toward the world. It is clear that Freire's work presents a view of literacy that differs markedly from the positions typically espoused by politicians, reading psychologists, most adult literacy program planners, and many literacy studies theorists. To become literate in the sense Freire intends requires not merely the mastery of signs and symbols, but also a willingness to participate in the process of building and rebuilding one's society. This point is elegantly conveyed by Giroux in his Introduction to Freire and Macedo's *Literacy: Reading the Word and the World*:

> Central to Freire's approach to literacy is a dialectical relationship between human beings and the world, on the one hand, and language and transformative agency, on the other. Within this perspective, literacy is not approached as merely a technical skill to be acquired, but as a necessary foundation for cultural action for freedom, a central aspect of what it means to be a self and socially constituted agent. Most importantly, literacy for Freire is inherently a political project in which men and women assert their right and responsibility not only to read, understand and transform their own experiences, but also to reconfigure their relationship with wider society. (Giroux, 1987, p. 7)

The expansiveness of Freire's view of reading and writing is reflected, and partially encapsulated, in his assessment of the Nicaraguan literacy crusade. Making the link between literacy and praxis quite explicit, Freire maintains:

> Literacy in the case of Nicaragua started to take place as soon as the people took their history into their own hands. Taking history into your own hands precedes taking up the alphabet. Anyone who takes history into his or her own hands can easily take up the alphabet. The process of literacy is much easier than the process of taking history into your own hands, since this entails the "rewriting" of your society. In Nicaragua the people rewrote their society before reading the word. (Freire and Macedo, 1987, pp. 106–107)

On other conceptions of literacy, this quotation might appear contradictory. It seems odd, on the surface, to talk of writing or rewriting society before one is "able" to read and write. But, for Freire, *all* human beings are readers and writers of the world (though some are more critical than others in this). In this respect, Freire's views are compatible with those who prefer to speak not of literacy as a single set of abilities but of *literacies* as complex social practices (see, for example, Street, 1984; Lankshear with Lawler, 1987; Roberts, 1995b). Reflecting on (reading), and transforming (writing, or rewriting), reality has been a feature—indeed, the defining characteristic—of humankind for thousands of years. In a society such as prerevolutionary Nicaragua, however, the impediments to liberating social transformation were enormous. The rewriting of Nicaraguan history, culminating in the insurrection of 1979, represented a momentous moment in the struggle to reclaim the word by changing the world. Freire would have said, perhaps, that the Nicaraguans who participated in this process spoke a "true word," through the communicative word of dialogue, thereby furnishing the conditions for learning the written word. In "taking up the alphabet," Nicaraguans acquired the means to continue "rewriting" their society in the sense of (literally) rewriting the history of Nicaragua.

In one sense, then, we can speak of reading and writing playing a *part* in the wider process of social transformation. At another level, however, literacy—as a reading and writing, which is to say a "naming," of both word and world—is the transformative process itself. This speaks directly to the link between Freire's literacy work and the narrative of hope discussed in the Introduction and chapter 2. Literacy is humanizing to the extent that it becomes critical, dialogical, and praxical. This quest involves multiple struggles, often against seemingly insurmountable odds, yet it is precisely through confronting such challenges that the spark of hope—Freire's utopian dream—remains alive.

CHAPTER 6

Critiques of Freire's Modernism

Although Freire's work has been widely admired, his pedagogy has, as has been noted in earlier chapters, also attracted strong criticism in some quarters. This chapter summarizes some of the major critiques from the last three decades, and considers possible responses to them. The most searching questions asked of Freire are those pertaining to his modernism. Freire acknowledged the importance of a number of postmodern insights, but in many respects remained a modernist thinker. In this chapter and the two that follow, I find fault with aspects of Freire's work, but also defend him against some of the charges of his harshest critics. The present chapter begins with an overview of the criticisms advanced by Bowers, Berger, and Walker who, in different ways, problematize the form of educational intervention advocated by Freire. This is followed, in the second section, by a brief account of issues raised by Ellsworth and Weiler, who argue against the "universalist" language employed by Freire and other critical pedagogues. The third section assesses some of the strengths and weaknesses of these critiques and comments on the way Freire positions himself in relation to postmodernism in his later writings. A more detailed response to Bowers, arguably the most important of Freire's critics, is provided in chapter 7. Chapter 8 highlights problems with the construal of conscientization as a stage-related process of "consciousness raising" and offers an alternative interpretation: one combining the postmodern notion of multiple subjectivities with the Freirean ideal of humanizing praxis.

PROBLEMATIZING FREIREAN INTERVENTION:
BOWERS, BERGER, AND WALKER

One of Freire's most persistent critics has been C. A. Bowers. In a series of publications dating from the early 1980s, Bowers has mounted a comprehensive attack on Freire and the assumptions allegedly underpinning his work. His essay published in *Teachers College Record* in 1983, "Linguistic Roots of Cultural Invasion in Paulo Freire's Pedagogy," is especially noteworthy and provides the main focus here. In the next chapter, I identify weaknesses in both the structure and the substantive content of Bowers's critique. I acknowledge, nevertheless, that Bowers's writings are helpful in highlighting the potential dangers educators face in involving themselves in the lives of others. Bowers was one of the first critics to put the question of Freirean intervention (i.e., whether it could be justified) squarely on the agenda, and his arguments about the dominance of one worldview over others prefigured later concerns with metanarratives and universalist philosophical principles. For these reasons, among others, Freirean scholars owe a considerable debt to Bowers, irrespective of their agreement or disagreement with his views.

Bowers argues that Freire's pedagogy imposes a Western mode of thought on traditional cultural groups. He sees Freire as a "carrier" of a Western mind-set. This is perpetuated by Freire's references to liberation, critical reflection, praxis, and social transformation. Bowers believes Freire takes for granted Western assumptions about the progressive nature of change, the importance of critical reflection, and the moral authority of individualism. He supports Freire's focus on the life world of learners in literacy programs, and sees the dialectical relating of thought to action within specific cultural settings as a major strength of Freirean pedagogy. He concedes that much of Freire's work has been in politically volatile, revolutionary situations—where indigenous cultures have already been colonized—but suggests that greater consideration needs to be given to the possibility of preserving elements of traditional belief systems (pp. 935–939).

Bowers draws a comparison between Freire and the Chipewyan of Canada in sketching two distinct worldviews. The Chipewyan, Bowers reports, tend to think more holistically than Westerners, eschewing the segmentation of knowledge and experience into component parts. Nonintervention is fostered, and freedom from dependence on other people is sought. Where Freirean literacy education encourages a form of distancing and abstraction from the gestalt of the lifeworld, the Chipewyan adopt an integrative and practical approach to knowledge. Freire advocates the continuous problematization of everyday life; the Chipewyan, on the other hand, try to avoid being in situations which are likely to lead to a questioning and renegotiation of existing beliefs (pp. 939–941).

Bowers links Freire with what Weber described as the "emissary prophecy" tradition in Western thought. Thinkers such as Freire subscribe to the view "that one possesses a truth that must be shared with, and even imposed on, others in order to save them" (p. 942). Bowers aligns Freire with Christian missionaries, marxists, and bourgeois liberals in describing examples of the emissary prophecy at work. Missionaries no longer exert the influence they once did, but have been replaced by secular authorities who also provide a moral justification for intervening in the lives of others. Thus there are marxists, who wish to eliminate the social injustices associated with capitalism and traditional (non-Western) belief structures; on the other hand, there are bourgeois liberals, who support democracy and public education on moral and social grounds. Freirean intervention has both a moral and an ontological basis, and is premised on a distinctly Western set of assumptions about the value of critical reflection, change, progress, and revolution.

Taking Freire's letters to Mario Cabral on education in Guinea-Bissau (Freire, 1978) as his reference point, Bowers also mounts an attack on modernization, secularization, and the role of the state in social organization. Bowers maintains that the connection between modernization and secularization "can be understood in terms of the increasing privatization of religious beliefs and the use of utilitarian principles and a purposive mode of rationality to justify the moral basis of social policy" (1983, p. 944). There are, Bowers suggests, four issues to be addressed by people adopting a Freirean pedagogical approach. These are the tension between Freirean individualism—based on critical reflection—and traditional religious beliefs and moral codes; the possible contribution of secularization to the rise of a new class of intellectuals and technocrats; the question of how democratic and collective decision making can be maintained when purposive rationality becomes the only acceptable basis for public discourse and value clarification; and the rise of state ideology over traditional forms of religious control (p. 946).

Bowers claims that Freire would want to privatize religious beliefs or replace them with rational thought. There is a "double-bind" in Freire's view of individualism. The first aspect of this relates to Freire's uneasy attempt to reconcile a "planned society" with the Enlightenment notion of the rational, critical, responsible individual; the second difficulty lies in the promotion of a kind of "subjectivism," where traditional forms of knowledge and morality give way to subjective feeling as the only source of authority (see pp. 947–948). In Bowers's opinion, Freire's stress on the importance of "making history" glorifies the individual's right to overturn tradition. At the same time, Bowers contends, Freire also supports state control over the population: promoting universal literacy is one means of securing this end. Freire's Western conception of the state— "with its emphasis on change, growth, and centralized planning"—does not appear to comfortably mesh with the ideal of "re-Africanizing" thought in Guinea-Bissau (p. 950). Bowers concludes that Freire's pedagogy "carries a powerful and seductive message" and "will undoubtedly have a modernizing effect" (p. 952). When applied in non-Western settings, however, Freirean ideas and practices can be seen as "a continuation of Western domination" (p. 950).

Peter Berger's main focus is Freire's concept of conscientization. Berger, like many other opponents (and supporters) of Freire, construes conscientization as a process of "consciousness raising." He suggests that programs adopting consciousness raising as a guiding principle assume that "lower-class people do not understand their own situation, that they are in need of enlightenment on the matter, and that this service can be provided by selected higher-class individuals" (Berger, 1974, p. 113). Freirean literacy programs set up a dichotomy between an intellectual vanguard and "the masses," the former taking it for granted that they possess the knowledge and the means necessary to liberate the latter. Intervention in the lives of others is seen as necessary to assist in raising their consciousnesses to a level sufficient to transform conditions of oppression. Berger accuses Freire of setting up a cognitive and ontological hierarchy, with illiterate peasants being portrayed as less fully human than those organizing literacy programs. Despite the ostensibly democratic character of Freirean methods, in Berger's view,

> it is hard to imagine a more "elitist" program (and, for that matter, a more "paternalistic" one) than one based on the assumption that a certain group of people is dehumanized to the point of animality, is unable either to perceive this condition or rescue itself from it, and requires the (presumably selfless) assistance of others for both the perception and the rescue operation. (p. 116)

For Berger, Freire's approach to adult literacy education is akin to an act of *conversion*, where one group imposes their truth on others in order to save them (p. 118). Berger concedes that one person's consciousness might be said to be "higher" or "more useful" than someone else's on specific topics or within particular settings (p. 116). He points out, however, that "the peasant knows his world far better than any outsider ever can" (p. 117). Different people make sense of the world in different ways; it is, therefore (Berger concludes), impossible to talk of raising someone's consciousness because no one can be said to be "more conscious" than anyone else (p. 118).

Further problems are identified by Walker (1980), who contends that "Freire's praxis does not have the liberating potential it aspires to." In pointing to a number of contradictions in Freire's theory, Walker argues that Freirean approaches to adult education are likely to be antidialogical. Walker sees a tension in Freire's pedagogy between two influences: existentialist Christianity on the one hand, and marxist/socialist national liberation theory on the other. Of the two, Walker claims that the former is more fundamental for Freire's practice (p. 150). This creates difficulties for Freire in dealing with the concrete realities of structured oppression and class conflict. Abandoning the notion of workers rising against the capitalist class of their own accord, Freire adopts the concept of "class suicide," whereby members of the petit bourgeoisie renounce their class origins and join with the oppressed as organizers and leaders of the resistance (p. 134). Where for Marx the struggle between dominator and dominated is to be played out dialectically (with the inevitable contradiction between the two groups eventually being negated through revolution), for Freire the answer lies in dialogue between leaders (formerly from the dominating class) and the oppressed (p. 137). Freire's faith in dialogue as a means for addressing class conflict is, in Walker's view, misplaced. Dialogue is initiated by the leaders, not the oppressed, through a process in which "the enlightened reach out to the unenlightened." Walker acknowledges the (educational and ethical) worth of dialogue, but suggests that the genuine political equality necessary for its effective functioning is absent in Freire's pedagogical theory (see p. 146).

AGAINST UNIVERSALS: ELLSWORTH AND WEILER

Bowers, Berger, and Walker all deal with problems pertaining to pedagogical intervention. Their arguments seem to suggest that Freire thinks he knows better than the oppressed the nature of their difficulties, is better placed than "the people" themselves to organize their struggles, and is, accordingly, justified in imposing his own set of cultural beliefs and practices on participants in his literacy programs. In questioning these (alleged) assumptions, Bowers, Berger, and Walker foreshadowed a not dissimilar line of critique by postmodern educational theorists. The elevation of the rational, unified Subject to a supreme position in modern thought has, in postmodern scholarship, been supplanted by a view of humans as beings constituted within multiple, sometimes contradictory, discourses of power. Postmodernists reject all claims to transcendental, universalist, or essentialist truth, distrusting "metanarratives" such as "the dialectics of Spirit, the hermeneutics of meaning, the emancipation of the rational or working subject, or the creation of wealth" (Lyotard, 1984, p. xxiii). Suspicious of any ethical theory laying claim to a unity of experience, postmodernists focus on the politics of difference, the specificities of oppression, and the importance of local and "little" narratives.

One well-known example of postmodern theorizing in the field of education is provided by Elizabeth Ellsworth (1989), who asserts that appeals to universal propositions "have been oppressive to those who are not European, White, male, middle class, Christian, able-bodied, thin, and heterosexual" (p. 304). She argues that the abstract language of critical pedagogy creates a barrier between educators and students, reducing the possibility of genuine dialogue and social transformation (of racism, sexism, classism, and other oppressive practices). Making reference to the work of Freire and Shor, Giroux, McLaren, and others, Ellsworth describes the rationalist ideals (empowerment, student voice, dialogue, etc.) espoused in the literature on critical pedagogy as "repressive myths" which serve to perpetuate rather than overturn relations of domination (p. 298).

Citing examples from her own experience as a university professor working with a diverse group of students in a course on antiracism, Ellsworth chronicles the obstacles she came up against in attempting to put "liberating" pedagogical ideas into practice. Among other things, she had to acknowledge her own position of power as a teacher, and recognize that as a White, middle-class woman she "could not unproblematically 'help' a student of color to find his/her authentic voice as a student of color" (p. 309). Her understanding of racism, she believed, would "always be constrained by . . . [her] white skin and middle-class privilege" (p. 308). Class discussion was inhibited by the dissonance participants felt in having to call up contradictory social positionings. Women, for example, "found it difficult to prioritize expressions of racial privilege and oppression when such prioritizing threatened to perpetuate their gender oppression" (p. 312). Dialogue was also stifled by fears of being misunderstood, by memories of unfortunate previous experiences of speaking out, by uncertainties about the allegiances of other class members, and by resentment of the concentration on racism at the expense of other oppressions. According to Ellsworth, "[d]ialogue in its conventional sense is impossible in the culture at large because at this historical moment, power relations between raced, classed, and gendered students and teachers are unjust" (p. 316). Other pedagogical forms, where students would be given the opportunity of speaking without interruption, were pondered. A coalition of affinity groups developed, eventually giving rise to several protest efforts in the campus library mall and administrative offices (pp. 319–320).

In his classic work, *Pedagogy of the Oppressed*, Freire (1972a) speaks of oppression, liberation, humanization, and dehumanization in universalist terms. This has drawn criticism from Weiler, who regards Freire's largely abstract treatment of these concepts as inadequate for confronting the specifics of oppression for particular groups (1991, p. 453). In positing humanization (and, concomitantly, conscientization, dialogue, and praxis) as a universal ethical ideal, Freire glosses over the layered and contradictory positions of privilege and oppression people experience (p. 450). A peasant male, for example, might be oppressed by a land-owner but simultaneously oppress his wife (p. 453). The Freirean notion of grounding adult literacy (and other) educational efforts on the experiences of learners also takes on a new face if the homogeneity of oppression cannot be taken for granted. Freire's hope that the oppressed will engage in collective, united action arising from critical reflection on their own experiences becomes problematic if such reflection throws up conflicting, divided experiences, interests, and solutions. Weiler emphasizes the importance of locating claims about oppression and liberation in particular lived social and historical contexts (p. 469). She shares the Freirean ethical imperative of educators "siding with" the oppressed, and does not want to abandon the goals of "social justice" and "empowerment." There is a need, however, for coalitions of common goals to be formed which do not deny difference and conflict. This, for Weiler, "suggests a more complex realization of the Freirean vision of the collective conscientization and struggle against oppression, one which acknowledges difference and conflict, but which, like Freire's vision, rests on a belief in the human capacity to feel, to know, and to change" (p. 470).

ADDRESSING FREIRE'S CRITICS

Chapters 7 and 8 deal with Bowers's and Berger's arguments in more detail. Here I concentrate on Walker's charge of antidialogue in Freire's pedagogy and the criticisms of universalist thought advanced by Ellsworth and Weiler. I conclude with brief comments on Freire's interpretation of postmodernism, his defense of the thesis of "unity in diversity," and his strong opposition to the politics of neoliberalism and global capitalism.

Dialogue within Limits

A dialogical approach was supposed to underpin almost every aspect of Freire's Brazilian literacy program, including the selection of generative words, the discussion of experiences and political reality, and the formulation of transformative alternatives to existing social structures. The notion of choosing the initial words for a literacy program on the basis (at least in part) of what mattered to participants was a relatively novel one in the early 1960s. Sylvia Ashton-Warner (1966) pioneered a similar approach with her organic vocabularies and key words in working with Maori children in New Zealand, and the Cuban literacy crusade of 1961 was built around themes and words tied to revolution and national reconstruction (see Kozol, 1978). But the dominant approach to literacy work, exemplified in both school classrooms and programs of adult education, was unquestionably "top-down" in emphasis: The words and themes of school journals and adult literacy primers were selected in their entirety by people other than those learning to read and write. It was the "experts"—curriculum planners, government policy makers, and occasionally academic researchers—who were considered best placed to decide the content of reading programs. Frequently the major words, story lines, and themes bore little relation to the lived reality of those learning to read. This philosophy resulted in some memorable failures in adult literacy schemes, chief among them a number of highly visible and comparatively expensive Unesco campaigns.

The Freirean approach was, without doubt, a giant step away from this tradition. Freire did, of course, have to satisfy certain linguistic criteria in his selection of generative word lists to allow the "technical" features of the program to be realized. In this sense, the selection process was a negotiation between the technical requirements and the need for words to be intimately connected to participants' lives. With this there can surely be little complaint. The success of the Freirean program depended on both of these requirements being met. Other features of the campaign, however, require stronger justification.

First, and ironically, Freire's insistence that coordinators replace the monological methods of old with a dialogical form of pedagogy was itself an exercise which had to be conducted in a rather nondialogical way. There is little evidence of *negotiation* over this issue. Although Freire cautions that the elaboration of agendas "should serve as mere aids to the coordinators, never as rigid schedules to be obeyed," the commitment to a dialogical approach was unflinching: "coordinators must be *converted* to dialogue." For this to occur, pedagogical instructions "must be followed by dialogical supervision, to avoid the temptation of antidialogue on the part of the coordinators" (Freire, 1976, p. 52). Freire says nothing about the possibility of different coordinators using alternative teaching practices with different groups of illiterate adults: dialogue, and a particular type of dialogue at that, was to be *the* method across the whole campaign.

The description of aspects of the program as "nondialogical" rather than "antidialogical" is deliberate. It is difficult to see how Freire could have avoided some nondialogical moments in his literacy work, given the educational ideal he espouses and the ethical assumptions that underpin this. In not wanting to risk dialogue being compromised, watered down, only partially instituted, or completely ignored in favor of more traditional banking methods, dialogue over the form the program would take had, to a certain extent, to be curtailed. For coordinators and participants, then, it was a case of accepting dialogue within certain predefined boundaries. There would be dialogue in discussing the codifications, generative words, and themes from Brazilian daily life, but not dialogue over the merits of (Freirean) dialogue as a pedagogical form. Thus, dialogue was fostered, but the framework for that dialogue was already presupposed. It was dialogue *within* given parameters that was promoted, rather than dialogue that might lead to a rejection of those parameters altogether. Freire could not *logically* have accepted other pedagogical styles, given his theory of education; indeed, it would not have been an "educational" program at all, from Freire's point of view, had it not been based on the principle of dialogue.

Of even greater interest than this was the next stage of the program: the introduction to the concept of culture. Ostensibly an open exploration of themes arising from the codifications (which depicted aspects of the illiterates' world), it is important to note that it was a *particular* notion of "culture" that was under investigation. Indeed, it was a specific theory of human beings and the world that illiterates were encouraged to consider. The ideas covered in discussions of the codifications, if Freire's description of these in *Education: The Practice of Freedom* (1976) is taken as representative of the program generally, were essentially the same as those found in Freire's ontology, ethic, and epistemology. The distinctions between humans and animals, the notion of transforming nature through work, the idea of human beings relating to each other are the themes at the heart of the discussions of codifications and are also central to Freire's philosophy. The second stage of the program opened up the possibility of participants discussing any themes, questions, problems, and issues associated with the pictorial representations, but a particular way of understanding the world was presupposed in their construction.

A similar point could be made, however, with regard to almost any educational program. For there to be an educational program at all, something must be put forward by someone to allow discussion and study to proceed. It is important to repeat that Freirean educational dialogue does not imply an "anything goes" discussion of whatever happens to be of interest to participants. To the contrary, as was noted in chapter 3, Freire always stressed the structured and purposeful nature of dialogue in liberating education. Freire would, I think, have been quite happy to admit that he *did* have an "agenda" (of a kind) in his work with illiterate adults. For him, literacy was potentially important (but not sufficient on its own) in creating a more humane, less oppressive Brazilian society. The locating of discussion around such themes as reflective transformation, then, was no accident. In Freire's view, it was precisely in coming to see the world this way that participants might realize their own capacity to contribute to the process of social change.

It is also important to remember that Freire's theory was informed by his practice. The correspondence between the codification themes and pivotal theoretical principles in Freire's written work is hardly surprising. Freire consistently underscored the importance of linking theory and practice (see, for example, Freire, 1985, pp. 155–157; Freire and Shor, 1987, pp. 135–137; Horton and Freire, 1990, pp. 21–22, 31–32). He likewise always insisted that the teaching-learning relationship is a reciprocal one, with teachers and coordinators not only teaching but also learning from other participants (whether they are students in a school classroom or illiterate adults) in the educative process. It is quite possible, therefore, that Freire's theoretical statements on the differences between humans and animals, the nature of culture and work, and the transformation of reality through critical reflection and action were influenced as much by his involvement in adult literacy programs as his reading of Marx, Hegel, and other theorists. Indeed, in an interview with Carlos Alberto Torres in 1989, Freire claimed: "I write about what I do. . . . my books are as if they were theoretical reports of my practice" (Torres and Freire, 1994, p. 102).

To some extent, Freire's hope that his literacy efforts would allow adults to move toward a more critical apprehension of reality embraced—through the very nature of the ideal he was espousing—the possibility of participants rejecting his view of the world if they so wished. Taking Freire's advice about the value of critical thought to heart, adults might see fit to revise or repudiate his depiction of nature, culture, work, humans and animals, and so on, and to find fault with his framing of political issues. Yet, the very act of critically analyzing the Freirean philosophy in this way represents more an endorsement than a dismissal of Freire's ideal. So long as people display the qualities outlined by Freire as characteristic of critical consciousness—even if in so doing they criticize the notion of critical, dialogical reflection and action for transformation—the Freirean ideal is being met. Rejection of Freirean assumptions through Freirean approaches does not overcome the concerns expressed by Bowers, Berger, and Walker: to the contrary, this form of disavowal would, for these critics, confirm the impositional character of Freirean literacy campaigns. I address this problem in more detail in the next chapter.

Oppression, Liberation, and Political Commitment

Ellsworth's essay has become an important reference point in debates over postmodernism and education. Her analysis is, however, not without its difficulties. It is not clear, for example, exactly what it is that makes certain groups "oppressed." Details of what "liberation" might mean for the oppressed groups she mentions are similarly sparse. Of course, one of Ellsworth's chief messages is that it is not the job of teachers or critical pedagogues to inform oppressed "Others" of the nature of their oppression. But, having taken this premise on board, Ellsworth appears to accept without question that people are oppressed either simply because they say they are, or by virtue of their gender, sexuality, body shape, and so on alone. That is, it appears to be sufficient for Ellsworth to decree that person is oppressed if that person is (for example) a woman, or gay, or overweight. This means that *all* women, *all* homosexuals, and *all* overweight people are *necessarily* oppressed in certain ways. Conversely, all males, heterosexuals, and thin people *necessarily* enjoy certain advantages. The notion that all individuals from certain groups are necessarily oppressed can be supported on a range of theoretical and empirical grounds,[1] yet, despite the fact that her entire argument turns on this issue, Ellsworth has surprisingly little to say about what those grounds might be. She is quick to point out the difficulties for individuals in reconciling their oppressed and nonoppressed spheres, noting her own affiliation to one oppressed group (women) together with her connection to several privileged classes (Whites, the able-bodied, the thin, etc.). But without an elucidation of underlying ethical and political assumptions, the result is an expansive typology of oppressor-oppressed groupings, with little idea of how the different levels or layers of oppression and privilege might interconnect or cancel each other out.

The categories of class, race, and gender have formed the backbone of much of the work in critical pedagogy and sociology of education concerned with questions of oppression and liberation. Ellsworth expands on these three, mentioning at different places in her essay: sexual-orientation, age, religion, body-shape, (dis)ability, and language of origin. Why stop there though? A case might be made for looking at the unemployed as a distinct oppressed group; or attention could be turned to the deaf, the blind, war veterans, victims of domestic violence, those subject to environmental pollution, or people forced to work under conditions of increasing insecurity with the growth of casualized labor markets. The dangers of thinking purely in terms of (an ever-increasing number of) "lines" of oppression become readily apparent here. Paradoxically, in focusing on an ever-increasing number of specific groups, the need for some sort of explanatory framework which links all of these together comes to seem all the more necessary. Ellsworth says little about whether her list of lines of oppression is meant to be exhaustive, or whether there are certain features which all groups she does identify have in common.

Somewhat ironically, having just presented an exhaustive critique of abstract universals, Ellsworth nevertheless offers what appears to be a normative principle not unlike those she finds so objectionable in the critical pedagogy literature. Seeking to locate pedagogical forms, which address "a commonality in the experience of difference without compromising its distinctive features," Ellsworth concludes:

Right now, the classroom practice that seems most capable of accomplishing this is one that facilitates a kind of communication across differences that is best represented by this statement: "If you

can talk to me in ways that show you understand that your knowledge of me, the world, and 'the Right thing to do' will always be
partial, interested, and potentially oppressive to others, and if I can
do the same, then we can work together on shaping and reshaping
alliances for constructing circumstances in which students of difference can thrive." (Ellsworth, 1989, p. 324)

This opens up two possibilities which have previously (apparently) been
closed in Ellsworth's study. First, the notion of students "thriving" is
introduced. As this arrives in the last sentence of the essay, it is impossible to ascertain what "thriving" might entail. Even so, mere mention
of the word implies a concern with some form of ethical ideal which
ought to apply to all students. Second, where up until this point dialogue
between students from different oppressed groups has been portrayed
as (at best) difficult, now the differences between students do not seem
like such an insurmountable constraint to collective action. Without these
final remarks, Ellsworth's analysis leaves educators with few avenues for
solidarity, unity, or praxis. Giroux's (1988, p. 177) assessment of Ellsworth's "separatism" as "a crippling form of political disengagement"
may be too harsh, but the danger of inadvertent passivity through fragmentation cannot be ignored.

Ellsworth claims that no teacher is free of "learned and internalized
oppressions," such as sexism, racism, classism, and ableism (pp. 307–
308). Freire, I'm sure, would have been in broad agreement with this.
His entire pedagogy was built around the assumption that we live in a
deeply oppressive world. In participating in the social institutions of
daily life, oppressive attitudes, values, beliefs, modes of consciousness,
and actions become inscribed in our very being. However, he and Ellsworth part company in their responses to the recognition of internalized
oppressions. Ellsworth accentuates the constraints "white skin and
middle-class privilege" (p. 308) place on understanding racism and other
forms of oppression, and finds the contradictions, tensions, and clashes
between different oppressive realities pedagogically debilitating. She
points out that she cannot "unproblematically 'help' " students from oppressed groups other than her own find their "voices" as members of
those groups, just as she cannot "unproblematically 'affiliate' " with
these students (p. 309). Freire would have accepted Ellsworth's view that
none of these processes are "unproblematic," but would also have
stressed the importance of taking action and getting involved in addressing oppression.

Acknowledging the different privileges enjoyed by teachers (and students) and recognizing contradictory subject positionings does not have
to lead to despair and political immobility; instead, it can provide the
basis for new forms of critical pedagogical practice. Ellsworth's analysis

furnishes helpful insights in allowing significant gaps and points of un-derdevelopment in Freire's theory of oppression, liberation, and educa-tion to be highlighted. Freire's approach to liberating education, on the other hand, provides an equally sobering antidote to Ellsworth's pessi-mism and pedagogical paralysis. If it is Ellsworth who draws our atten-tion to difficulties associated with addressing the question, "What ought I (or we) to do?" in the postmodern educational world, it is Freire who reminds us that this question can still be answered, even if only in pro-visional and contingent ways. On the Freirean view, taking a risk-laden, potentially contradictory, always constrained stand against oppression is almost invariably preferable to taking no stand at all.

In a dialogue published in McLaren and Leonard's *Paulo Freire: A Crit-ical Encounter* (1993a), Donaldo Macedo draws Freire's attention to the concerns raised by Weiler and other feminist scholars:

> [Feminists] . . . point out that your goals for liberation and social and political transformation are embedded in universals that, at some level, negate both your own position of privilege as an intel-lectual man and the specificity of experiences which characterize conflicts among oppressed groups in general. That is to say, in the-orizing about oppression as universal truth you fail to appreciate the different historical locations of oppression. (Freire and Macedo, 1993, p. 170)

Macedo advances the view that there exists "a hierarchical structure of oppression that ranges from being a white middle-class woman to an underclass black woman who may also be a peasant" (p. 173). Women are an oppressed group (given their relationship with men in a patriar-chal society), but Black women are *more* oppressed than White women because they experience racism as well. Working-class Black women bear an additional burden in a classist world. Working class Black peasant women are the most oppressed of all (using the categories supplied by Macedo), enduring sexism, racism, classism, and the hardships engen-dered by geographic and political isolation, together perhaps with ex-ploitation by ruthless landlords.

Freire claims agreement with Macedo's notion of a hierarchy of op-pression, but stresses that his major preoccupation in early work was class oppression (pp. 172–173). Earlier in the same volume, Freire main-tains that he has "always challenged the essentialism reflected in claims of a unitary experience of class and gender," and speaks of the need to acknowledge "the multiplicity of modes of oppression suffered by women and people of color" (1993b, p. x). Without denying the specific-ities of oppression, however, Freire stresses the need for solidarity in a "collective war against all oppression" (Freire and Macedo, 1993, p. 174).

From a Freirean standpoint, there are strategic as well as ethical reasons for avoiding a purely particularist approach to liberation struggles:

> If the oppressed women choose to fight exclusively against the oppressed men when they are both in the category of the oppressed, they may rupture the oppressor-oppressed relations specific to both women and men. If this is done, the struggle will only be partial and perhaps tactically incorrect. (p. 174)

Freire's position might be summarized as follows. There are certain features all oppressed groups have in common which transcend the particularities of their specific oppressive situations. By implication, there is an overriding vision of liberation beyond the particulars of local struggles. There are distinctive forms of oppression (e.g., sexism as opposed to racism), and localized liberation movements with concerns which differ from other movements. At a further level still, there are specific examples of oppression within given forms. Sexism in the workplace, for instance, might differ from sexism in the home; or, to be even more specific, sexism in *this* home might contrast in important ways with sexism in *that* home; and so on. But the local and the specific only make sense in relation to some larger conception of oppression and liberation. Where the postmodern turn of mind appears to privilege the particular over the universal, for Freire both depend on each other for their intelligibility. We cannot know that sexism and racism are both examples of oppression without some broader theory of oppression. On the other hand, a theory of oppression only gains its authenticity through reference to particular forms of oppression. That is, it would not be a theory of oppression at all unless it could apply to more than one type of oppression and myriad specific examples of oppressive situations and practices.

Peters (1999) draws attention to the Hegelian logic in Freire's work, noting in particular the driving force of the dialectic behind Freire's philosophy of history and the opposition between "the oppressor" and "the oppressed." Similarly, Giroux (1993, p. 180) argues that Freire's ideas were "sometimes constrained in totalizing narratives and binarisms that de-emphasized the mutually contradictory and multiple character of domination and struggle." McLaren and Leonard (1993b, pp. 2–3) see Freire as a utopian humanist in the Marxist tradition who shares with postmodernists and many feminists a rejection of Eurocentrism and a critique of totalitarian elements in grand theory and technocapitalism. There is a propensity among some postmodern theorists to make sweeping generalizations about modernism, allowing significant differences between ideas and theoretical perspectives to be glossed over. As Beilharz (1991, pp. 112–113) notes, many discussions of postmodernism fall back on the same dualistic thinking that allegedly underpins modernism. Hassan (1993, p. 152), for example, lays out a table of differences between modernism and postmodernism, using opposites such as purpose/play, hierarchy/anarchy, centering/dispersal, signified/signifier, and so on. Peters, Giroux, and McLaren and Leonard all avoid these pitfalls. They see Freire as a modernist thinker, yet in acknowledging the complexity of his philosophical and pedagogical position also identify significant points at which Freirean and postmodern projects meet.

Freire was not a relativist, in either an ethical or an epistemological sense. He believed some ideas and certain modes of human existence were "absolutely" better than others. A critical, dialogical, praxical approach in understanding and living in the world is clearly preferable, from a Freirean point of view, to a passive, or monological, or oppressive approach. The renunciation of "essentialist" ethical and metaphysical principles creates the impression that social theory can do without absolutes. But if there are no absolutes, then, paradoxically, there must be at least one absolute; namely, the premise that there are no absolutes. Having no absolutes means that there can be no absolute acceptance of the proposition that there are no absolutes. If one cannot be sure that this proposition (i.e., that there are no absolutes) is true, then one cannot be sure that there are no absolutes. The only alternative to having no absolutes is having (one or more) absolutes. The postmodernist who disavows absolutes must therefore concede that it is at least *possible* that there are absolutes. The postmodern era signals not the disappearance of absolutes altogether but the replacement of one set of taken-for-granted assumptions with another. All postmodernists and poststructuralists appear to agree that the unified subject is now dead; difference is inevitably celebrated; and "Reason" is invariably seen more as a "culture-specific" construct than a transcendental notion. Absolutes can *never* be avoided in theory; they simply appear in different guises under different paradigms.

Freire on Modernism and Postmodernism

Freire's stance on postmodernism is succinctly captured in the "Opening Words" to *Pedagogy of Hope*:

> *Pedagogy of Hope* . . . is written in rage and love, without which there is no hope. It is meant as a defense of tolerance—not to be confused with connivance—and radicalness. It is meant as a criticism of sectarianism. It attempts to explain and defend progressive postmodernity and it will reject conservative, neoliberal postmodernity. (1994, p. 10)

Stylistically, the most overtly postmodern of Freire's texts is his Foreword to McLaren and Leonard's (1993a) edited collection, *Paulo Freire: A Critical Encounter*. Freire's language in this piece contrasts sharply with his earlier writings. He speaks of the need to avoid "both the totalizing Eurocentric and androcentric logic with its Hegelian roots, and the pessimism that comes from a critical theory solely trapped within a philosophy of non-identity." Advocating a "postcolonial politics of ethics and compassion" as a means of contingently grounding identity in a postmodern world, Freire wants to "make presently unassailable and impenetrable cultural borders indeterminate," encourage "new forms of political redress," and create "new self-formative practices and cultures of resistance that are capable of establishing new grounds of enfranchisement for all peoples" (Freire, 1993b, p. xii). In *Pedagogy of Hope*, Freire embraces a concept of postmodernism both as an attitude and a set of structural changes and material practices. Near the beginning of the second chapter, he declares, "[L]et us be postmodern: radical and utopian" (1994, p. 51). He urges educators to become more tolerant, open and forthright, critical, curious, and humble, describing these qualities as "indisputably progressive, much more postmodern . . . than modern" (p. 80). A progressive postmodern attitude is necessary if marxists are to overcome their "smug certainty that they are *modern*" (p. 96). In substantive terms, there are at least two forms of postmodern political practice:

> Postmodernity, as I see, has a different, substantially democratic, way of dealing with conflict, working out its ideology, struggling for the ongoing and ever more decisive defeat of injustice, and arriving at a democratic socialism. There is a postmodernity of the Right; but there is a postmodernity of the Left, as well, nor does the latter—as is almost always insinuated, if not insisted—regard postmodernity as an altogether special time that has suppressed social classes, ideologies, Left and Right, dreams, and utopias. And one of the basic elements of the postmodernity of the Left is the reinvention of power—and not its mere acquisition, as with modernity. (p. 198)

It is the exaggerated certainties, the arrogance, the intolerance of some forms of modernist thought to which Freire objects. These qualities persist in neoliberal discourses, which Freire describes as "chock-full of 'modernity' " (p. 41). Freire also objects to the fatalism of neoliberal "flighty postmodern pragmatism" (1998c, p. 26), and is heavily critical of intellectuals who portray the current obstacles to liberation as inevitable and insurmountable (1997a, p. 43).

Progressive postmodernism, as Freire defines it, avoids both a naive optimism and a depressing pessimism in assessing the current moment in history. Interestingly, Freire does not see postmodern thought and dialectical thought as contradictory. In *Politics and Education* (1998b), he suggests that progressive postmodernism is dialectical in its understanding of confrontation and conflicts, and in this sense stands opposed to a domesticated conception of a new history without social classes, ideology, struggle, utopia, and dreams. Dialectical postmodernism allows us to appreciate the radical nature of being: "It is not possible to understand me only through the lens of class or race or gender; on the other hand, my position in terms of class, the color of my skin, and my gender, through which I have arrived into the world, cannot be forgotten in an analysis of what I do, what I think, and what I say" (p. 21). No *one* aspect of being human can explain who and what we are, even if some dimensions of our existence may assume greater significance than others in some contexts. Race may have been a crucial feature in dividing South Africans under apartheid, but policies of racial oppression in that country also had the effect of exacerbating class differences. Gender oppression, moreover, was practiced across class lines. From a Freirean point of view, these conflicts and contradictions make education all the more necessary. Educators have an important role to play in highlighting issues and examples of discrimination, exploitation, and oppression (Freire, 1996, p. 177). For Freire, all discrimination is immoral. Discriminatory practices, whether racist, sexist, or of any other kind, "offend the essence of human dignity and constitute a radical negation of democracy" (Freire, 1998c, p. 41). To struggle against discrimination is "a duty whatever the conditionings that have to be confronted." It is, Freire says, "in this very struggle and duty that the charm, even the beauty, of our humanity resides" (p. 60). An educational setting provides one arena within which such humanizing activity can be pursued.

In a number of his later works, Freire (1994, 1996, 1997a, 1998b) argues for a position of "unity in (or within) diversity" when addressing the politics of difference. Freire justifies this ideal on ethical, political, and educational grounds. He notes:

> Our struggle as women, men, blacks, workers, Brazilians, North Americans, French, or Bolivians, is influenced by our gender, race, class, culture, and history, conditionings that mark us. Our struggle, nevertheless, departs from these conditionings and converges in the direction of being more, in the direction of universal objectives. Or else, for me at least, the fight would make no sense. (1996, pp. 164–165)

Freire argues that without some sort of unity, the more powerful, pragmatically unified Right will prevail over all oppressed groups. In *Pedagogy of the Heart*, Freire points out that "[w]e speak of *the lefts* in the plural and *the right* in the singular." He maintains that while those on the Right are able to put their differences aside in the face of threats from political opponents, union among those on the Left is always "difficult and cumbersome." This is because the Right is only sectarian against progressive thought and practice, whereas members of the Left are sectarian among themselves (1997a, p. 76). Freire advocates dialogue among diverse groups and across differences. When groups on the Left cannot work *with* difference, but instead allow their differences to work *against* them, they can lose sight of the deeper ethical imperatives which bind all oppressive groups together.

Education should, in Freire's view, be concerned with delineating, debating, and (as far as possible) *addressing* differences—not with allowing them to prevent any productive discussion from occurring (see Escobar et al., 1994, p. 91). Provided teachers work to inculcate the progressive virtues Freire identifies as necessary for liberating education—humility, respect, openness, curiosity, commitment, rigor, a willingness to listen, and so on—tensions within and between groups can be turned to positive educational effect. Indeed, certain forms of cultural tension are, Freire (1994, p. 156) argues, essential in a democratic society. Dialogue *depends* on difference, as well as a particular kind of sameness for its very existence. It is our different experiences with, interpretations of, and social relations within the world that provide the substance for interactivity between two or more people. From a Freirean point of view, both (or all) parties in a dialogue share the same ontological vocation—and are "called" by this vocation to dialogue—and some form of common ground must be established for meaningful communication to occur. There must be a certain linguistic, communicative, and experiential compatibility between partners for dialogue to begin, but it is the differences between participants that allow a mere conversation to grow into the sort of rigorous, structured, purposeful engagement Freire sees as necessary in liberating education.

Diverse oppressed groups are united, if in no other way, by their very diversity—they share the fact that they are different from each other. It is *in* rather than *against* their differences that people pursue, through their myriad activities as creators of history and culture, their shared vocation of humanization. They become united in educational terms when they make these differences the basis for posing problems, asking difficult questions, and debating contentious issues. They become *politically* united when they act on the realization that the so-called "minorities" in most societies are, when they work together, almost always the *majority*. In refusing to work with each other, different oppressed groups allow the Right to exercise one of its principal strategic objectives: a policy of "divide and rule." As Freire sees it, "[w]hen a so-called minority refuses to join forces with another minority, it reveals a prejudiced certainty: that of the other's natural inability to be fair and decent" (1997a, p. 86). Freire confesses that he cannot understand why, in Brazil, feminist, Black, Indian, and working-class groups mount separate struggles, fighting their own battles instead of struggling against "the main enemy" (pp. 85–86).

Freire was firmly of the view that at no time in human history has the need for political unity among Left and oppressed groups been greater than it is now. In the last years of his life, he saw his nation's and the world's wealth being concentrated into the hands of fewer and fewer people, and witnessed the brutal effects of neoliberal policies on those who were already oppressed under capitalism. In a number of countries, the combination of neoliberal economic "reform" and a conservative cultural restoration had created a powerful force on the Right. At the same time, many groups on the Left had allowed their differences to become the source of division and disrespect, easing the process of forming a pragmatic political unity on the Right. In so doing, they confused "reconcilable" differences with fundamentally "antagonistic" differences (cf. p. 85). Under such circumstances, Freire saw a need for not just local liberation initiatives, but an ethically grounded and politically unsettling unity among diverse oppressed groups within regions and nations and across the globe.

Freire is adamant that neither social classes nor the ideologies of the Right and the Left have disappeared. In the early 1970s, he endured attacks from doctrinaire Marxists and Maoists for advocating dialogical principles of political organization over mechanistic models of revolutionary change. Regarded as a naïve idealist by those who believed the class struggle had its own logic independent of human interaction and intervention, Freire was always as critical of dogmatism and sectarianism on the Left as he was of entrenched conservatism, reactionary cultural politics, and dictatorial arrogance on the Right. In later works, he makes much of the suppression of dissent and diversity under neoliberalism. The same intolerance, however, continues to haunt some on the Left. Freire makes it plain that the leftist dogmatism of the past—with its "outdated language," reliance on slogans, indoctrinatory teaching procedures, and elitist leadership structures (pp. 77, 82)—will be even less effective in waging a political war against the well-organized, well-funded right-wing coalitions of our present age. Freire tries to offer *truths*, but does not claim to possess *"the* truth" (1998a, p. 47); dogmatic leftists are, by contrast, too certain of their certainties to uphold the "revolutionary virtue" of tolerance.

Postmodernity does not signal the end of history but rather the continuation of earlier themes and tasks in new forms. By way of example, Freire (1996, pp. 130–131) mentions the theme of "knowledge." He accepts that practical knowledge is important in preparing men and

women for productive activities, and acknowledges the growing importance of technical and scientific knowledge. Under neoliberalism, however, the development of technoscientific knowledge is typically reduced
to a narrow exercise in training, and students are discouraged from
learning anything other than techniques. In making this a generative
theme for educative discussion and debate, it becomes possible to put
alternative conceptions of knowledge in postmodernity forward for consideration. Freire's "progressive" answer is to refuse to separate "technical ability from philosophical reason, manual skill from mental
exercise, practice from theory, economic production from political production" (p. 131).

Freire sees capitalism as "intrinsically evil" (1998c, p. 114). He never
relinquished the belief that the capitalist mode of production poses deep
structural impediments to humanization: Capitalism is by its very nature
exploitative and oppressive. In *Letters to Cristina*, he asserts: "To make
capitalism more human is an impossible dream to which angelic spirits
or incorrigible deceivers are devoted" (1996, p. 188). He continued to call
himself a socialist in the 1990s, despite the claim by some that such an
"outdated" and "unfashionable" ideal is no longer relevant after the
thawing of the Cold War (cf. p. 114). He saw the struggle for socialism
as an urgent requirement for oppressed groups in Brazil and other countries. He believed, however, that if this struggle was to be liberating, the
Left would have to shed its authoritarian elements, recognize differences,
and work toward constructing less bureaucratic and more democratic
social forms (p. 165).

FINAL REMARKS

Although Freire accepted a number of insights from progressive and
radical postmodernists, the modernist roots of his ontology, epistemology, and ethic could still be detected in his last works. In his later
publications, he eschewed, as he always had, the relativism of those who
say there are no legitimate grounds for preferring (justifying) one way
of understanding and being in the world over another. He favored a
stance of respectful tolerance in the expression of political difference, but
this did not make him a supporter of "anything goes" pluralism. He
defended the democratic principle of allowing all political voices to be
heard but insisted on his right to make judgments about the worth and
accuracy of different contributions. He problematized the romantic conception of education as a social equalizer and smooth path to enlightenment, yet also saw progressive teaching and learning as a potentially
important dimension of the wider process of social change. He continued, on occasion, to speak of "*the* dominant ideology" and "*the* dominant
class" (Freire, 1998a, p. 6) despite postmodern discomforts with such lan-

guage, seeing good reasons for doing so in an era when societies were increasingly being defined by the dictates of one (ever-smaller) class of corporate elites. He retained a utopianism that, for all its radical features, still owed something to a humanist tradition scorned by many postmodernists. He spoke of multiple perspectives on, and readings of, the word and the world, yet also urged scholars to seek out a text's "deeper significance." For Freire, there *was* more to life than the play of dancing signifiers: surface appearances, in his view, could be—and needed to be—distinguished from deeper realities. Freire believed his respect for cultural differences should not prevent him, as an educator, from intervening in some situations of oppression, and he never tired of reasserting the primacy of critical reflection, dialogue, and transformative action to human existence.

That Freire remained essentially a modernist is perhaps most vividly highlighted in *Pedagogy of Freedom*, where he argues for a "universal human ethic" (1998c, p. 23). This is, in essence, a reinterpretation of the notion of humanization in response to both new forms of global capitalism and the increasing fragmentation of oppositional movements. Freire insists that we should not be afraid to condemn the policies and practices of neoliberalism, nor to speak of the illusions, lies, and ideological manipulation necessary to maintain gross inequalities under globalization. Neoliberalism represents a *perversion* of the quest to become more fully human. Freire speaks of every country on the planet becoming "suffocated" by the ethics of the market (pp. 24–25). He reiterates fundamental ethical principles from his earlier writings, emphasizing the human capacity to "take stock of, compare, evaluate, give value to, decide, break with, and dream" (p. 26) as the basis for resisting the marketization of everyday life.

Neoliberals are dominant among the fatalistic voices of our age, leading many to believe that imbalances in the comparative wealth of nations, along with mass unemployment, widespread hunger, exploitation, discrimination, poverty, and misery are acceptable and inevitable: a necessary price to pay for the "freedoms" afforded by the market. Freire leaves little doubt about his ethical priorities: "The freedom of commerce," he says, "cannot be ethically higher than the freedom to be human" (p. 116). If the latter is to be upheld over the former, legislative changes and a transformation in the social relations of production within and between nations must be instituted. From Freire's point of view, the prime beneficiaries of "liberalized" trade are multinational capitalists. When factories close because they cannot compete with cheaper goods produced in other countries, numerous people suffer. It is not just the factory owners, but the workers, their families, and the overseas employees (who receive the lower wages necessary to make the goods competitive) who lose. The dominance of the market as the model for all economic and social activity constitutes a dictatorship, driven by the relentless drive for greater profits—the "unfettered greed of the power minority who control the world today" (pp. 115–116). For Freire, the workings of the market have no regard for the "ethical code that is common to us all" (p. 116). Unity and solidarity will, in his view, be essential if this distortion of our ontological vocation is to be effectively analyzed, resisted, and overturned.

NOTE

1. On Marx's view of class, for example, *all* workers under the capitalist mode of production are oppressed given the part they play in the production process. Workers do not own the means of production and are forced to sell their labor power to capitalists in exchange for a wage. Irrespective of the particulars of given industrial situations, the wage paid to workers is never sufficient to enable them to break out of this oppressive cycle. Rather, it is always just enough to enable them to nourish and sustain themselves to continue laboring (that is, to continue creating surplus value) for capitalists. See Marx (1976).

CHAPTER 7

Defending Freirean Intervention

The work of C. A. Bowers poses a formidable challenge for Freirean scholars and practitioners. If Bowers's views are accepted, doubt is cast not only on Freirean pedagogical principles, but on the very assumptions underpinning many programs of education in the Western and non-Western world. Freire never provided a detailed response to Bowers, though he does mention him briefly in places. In *Pedagogy of Hope*, for example, he notes that he and Bowers met for a debate at the University of Oregon in July 1987, and although they disagreed "almost across the board," they were able to do so "without having to offend or abuse each other." "We simply argued for our respective, mutually contradictory positions," Freire says, and "did not have to distort anything in each other's thinking" (1994, pp. 182–183). The arguments advanced in this chapter are offered in the same spirit of debate.

Perhaps the greatest strength of Bowers's analysis lies in the significance of the questions he raises. For Bowers calls into question precisely those characteristics often most valued in Freirean education: critical reflection, the questioning of established beliefs and authority structures, the dialogical problematization of everyday life, and the commitment to social transformation. Bowers draws attention to one of the deepest concerns facing teachers, namely, the question of how their actions as educators might impact on the lives of their students. His work serves as a reminder that there is always a fine line between affirming and denying the experiences of others. In according the problem of intervention a central place in his investigation, Bowers anticipates later work by postmodern theorists on the dangers of attempting to speak for, or even with, others. Bowers thus addresses issues of fundamental importance not only for Freireans, but all educationists, and, in this respect, his discussion is stimulating and helpful.

Nevertheless, I hope to show that Bowers's critique is flawed, both in its structure and arguments. The chapter falls into five related parts. In the first section, I examine some of the difficulties associated with the binary division between 'Western' and "non-Western" cultures in Bowers's analysis. I concentrate on Bowers's homogenizing of diverse Western ideas and practices, and draw attention to the danger of romanticizing non-Western and traditional cultures. This is followed, in the second section, by a discussion of the comparison between Freire and the Chipewyan, which I see as highly problematic. The third and fourth parts of the chapter address the relationship between education, intervention, and change. I stress the importance of change as a fundamental educational aim, highlight potential tensions and contradictions in a non-interventionist system of education, and defend the particular *form* of change initiated by Freirean pedagogical intervention in situations of oppression. Finally, I point to some of the dangers, as I see them, in Bowers's cultural conservatism.

WESTERN AND NON-WESTERN CULTURES

Bowers employs the general category "Western" in buttressing many of his claims about the nature of Freirean pedagogy. He talks, for example, of "Western culture," "[the] Westernizing mode of consciousness," "the Western episteme," "Western assumptions about progressive change," "the dominant pattern of Western thinking," "the traditional Western pattern of thinking," "the Western mind set," "this Western view of literacy," and "Western ideology" (1983, pp. 935, 937, 938, 939, 940, 947, 949, 951). This is problematic. In speaking of *the* Western mode of consciousness, episteme, pattern of thinking, mind-set, and so on, Bowers glosses—to the point of grossly reifying the term "Western"—the complexities, contradictions and deep divisions between different theoretical perspectives in Western thought. There *is* no uniform Western mind set, no single "dominant pattern of Western thinking," no view of literacy that is typically Western.

In assuming such homogeneity in Western ways of thinking and acting, some of Bowers's examples border on the absurd. He draws a contrast, for instance, between Chipewyan and Western approaches to learning how to drive a road grader. Bowers claims that "the Western approach . . . would involve reading operating manuals and listening to someone else explain the steps of the operation" (p. 940). The Chipewyan, on the other hand, used a quite different strategy:

[They] sat on the side of the road watching the operation of the road grader. After watching for several days, the man operated the grader with skill and ease. In interviewing the man [it was found that] . . . he could not explain how he operated the machine. The integrative way of thinking enabled him to learn from direct experience, and to be able to explain the operation in abstract, to have knowledge in our sense, was useless—particularly in terms of other Chipewyans who would trust only what they learned from their own experience. (p. 940)

The way this example is constructed, it is as if no Westerners ever learn via direct experience, or through practical example, or informal apprenticeship. All or most Westerners, Bowers would have us believe, use abstract, print-based, linear, or lock-step approaches to learning, even where the task is an obviously practical one such as driving a grader. In using references to "the" Western way of doing things as a bludgeon in criticizing Freire, this example is highly ironic. For Freire was one of the best-known advocates of learning through experience. Freire's approach to adult literacy education was built around words, themes, and codifications which derived directly from, or related to, the existential reality of participants (see Freire, 1976, pp. 41–84; 1972a, pp. 81–95; 1972b, pp. 29–47). As I argued in chapter 2, Freire advances a profoundly *anti*abstract theory of knowledge. Knowledge, from a Freirean point of view, can only be acquired, or, more correctly, authentically *constructed*, through practical experience; that is, through one's interaction with others and with the objective world (cf. Freire, 1976, p. 99). Westerners make sense of the world in an enormous variety of different ways, as do those in traditional and non-Western societies. As Freire recognized, there is no one way of learning, understanding, or educating in the West. Some approaches to learning had Freire's support (those which were critical, dialogical, praxical, problem-posing, etc.); others, also prevalent in the West, were the object of Freire's critique. Freire was highly critical, for example, of antidialogical and authoritarian systems of learning, and often noted with regret the frequent separation of theory from practice in schools and other institutions.

Bowers's very act of positioning himself against (supposedly) Western assumptions contradicts his own thesis on the Western mind-set, for although he admits that he too "cannot escape entirely" (Bowers, 1983, p. 944) Western categories of thought, his analysis attempts to do precisely this, from a Western setting, in a Western publication, for predominantly Western readers. Lest Bowers claim that he is a lone battler against the tide, his citation of the work of several other accomplished scholars in this piece and other articles provides further evidence that within "the" Western tradition, there are many thinkers who advance views which radically oppose the individualism, liberal rationalism, and marxist view of history he finds so objectionable. In addition to Bowers himself and the writers he refers to, of course, there are literally thousands of others who have undertaken detailed critiques of, and in many cases advanced alternatives to, the elements within Western scholarship with which Bowers deals.

Bowers says very little about the way ideological and material forces impact on cultural practices, attitudes, and patterns of thought. He does speak in places (e.g., p. 935) about the "hegemonic" influence of Western culture. Although he does not elaborate on what the notion of "hegemony" means in his account (e.g., whether it closely approximates the classic Gramscian rendition, or derives from some other source), the implication is that representatives of "Western Culture" have often colonized the consciousnesses of those in non-Western cultures, wittingly or unwittingly imposing a Western way of thinking in place of traditional belief structures: this is a form of cultural domination. On ideology, Bowers is even less forthcoming. He admits at one point, however, that he has been conditioned by humanist ideology (p. 949), and he clearly wants to say that Freire has likewise been shaped in his thinking by liberal, existentialist, marxist, and humanist strands in the Western mind-set. Indeed, according to Bowers, Freire is so immersed in these Western traditions, he cannot detect their (pervasive) influence on his pedagogical thinking.

Bowers says virtually nothing, however, about the ways in which ideological processes operate in traditional or non-Western societies to shape attitudes, practices, and ideas. In commenting on traditional societies, Bowers adopts a peculiarly decontextualized, depoliticized, and ahistorical view of social practice and the formation of consciousness. Ideology, hegemony, and domination all seem to be features of Western societies and the Western mind-set. In non-Western and traditional societies, they appear curiously absent (in Bowers's account). Although Bowers does not claim that everything about Western culture is undesirable, he certainly finds a great deal that is problematic in the Western mind-set. Non-Western cultures, by contrast, appear remarkably free of faults—to the point, in fact, of being almost "pure" by comparison with their opposite in Bowers's binary. Bowers anticipates this criticism (p. 943), but does not *address* it, leaving himself open to the charge of romanticizing traditional cultures and of positing an idealized notion of community.

FREIRE AND THE CHIPEWYAN

Bowers attributes to Freire a number of ideas which neither Freire's written works nor his practice bear out. In part, this is a result of the rhetorical device of collapsing diverse intellectual traditions, practices and ways of life into two clearly opposing groups: Western and non-Western. Bowers's argument depends on Freire being placed squarely with the former—at least as far as the pivotal assumptions in Freire's philosophy and educational practice are concerned. The Chipewyan are juxtaposed against Freire as a logical "Other" in undermining ostensibly "Western" patterns of thought. Freire gains a form of "guilt by association," where both aspects of the association and the portrayal of that with which he is allegedly associated are questionable. At the most fundamental level, the very nature of the comparison between Freire's approach and Chipewyan belief structures is problematic.

Bowers aligns Freire with certain strands of Western thought, alludes to some of the problems in these views, and then asks, in effect, "*What if* Freire's form of pedagogy were to be applied to the Chipewyan context?" Bowers then proceeds to show how Freirean theory and Chipewyan conceptions of reality do not comfortably mesh, and concludes that it would be problematic to "use" Freire's pedagogy "in an Islamic culture or one [such as the Chipewyan's] not already partially assimilated to the Western mind set" (p. 943). At best, then, Bowers's critique allows us to draw a lesson about where a Freirean educational program might not work. In making this point, however, Bowers fails to heed Freire's warnings about the dangers of decontextualization.

Freire never (to the best of my knowledge) provided any detailed comment on the Chipewyan context, and certainly never "used" his pedagogy in working with Chipewyan people. Leaving aside problems pertaining to the term "use" here, it is imperative to recognize Freire's insistence on dealing with each setting for a major educational initiative in its proper historical, social, and cultural context. Some of the beliefs Bowers outlines as integral to the Chipewyan worldview are certainly at odds with elements of Freire's ethical ideal, but before Freire could comment on how he might interpret or respond to these beliefs he would have insisted—if his approach to adult literacy education is taken as evidence—that he first be given the opportunity to learn something of the people with whom he might potentially be working. On the "nonquestioning" and "noninterventionist" qualities of Chipewyan thought, for example, Freire might have said that one would have to examine the *way* in which these attributes had developed before any decision could be made as to whether and how they ought to be challenged. This would involve considering these patterns of thought in relation to the wider cultural and social mores, structures, practices, and relations which characterize Chipewyan society.

Despite Freire's repeated warnings that his pedagogical ideas should never simply be transported or transposed from one context to another, and notwithstanding the fact that Freire has never discussed the complexities of Chipewyan culture, Bowers states unequivocally:

> If a revolutionary socialist government were to come to power in Canada and invite Freire to use his adult literacy program with the Chipewyan, he would undoubtedly welcome the opportunity to emancipate another group from the oppression of their own history. Even if it were possible to establish dialogue, the pedagogy would involve the most fundamental forms of cultural intervention. (p. 942)

This is pure speculation, however, for neither Bowers nor Freire have established whether and in what ways the Chipewyan *are* (or have been) oppressed. The extent to which dialogue might be possible, and the precise form that dialogue might take, could only be gauged on assessment of the concrete realities of Chipewyan life, with due regard being given to the nature of any proposed educational program.

Bowers's differentiation between the Chipewyan's "integrative form of knowing" and Freire's emphasis on the importance of gaining rational distance from the everyday tide of experience is also problematic. Bowers notes with regard to Freire's view, "[t]he same pattern of thought, when carried to an extreme, is expressed in the activities of technocrats who have reified the power of abstract-theoretical thought" (p. 941). Bowers concedes that Freire is "highly critical" of the nondialectical and authoritarian nature of abstract theory, but asserts nonetheless that "the cultural episteme underlying his pedagogy is based on the same epistemological assumption that can easily lead to the extreme forms of technological culture that he criticizes" (p. 941). The point is, though, that Freire did *not* extend his ideas on rational/critical thought processes—and in particular those pertaining to the notion of human beings gaining "distance" from their social surroundings—to a technocratic form of rationality. Freire would have argued that human beings can never completely separate themselves from what Bowers (p. 941) calls "the ongoing flow of experience" (McLaren and da Silva, 1993). Even if it were true that Freire and technocrats begin from similar premises about rational distance, there would still be no logical reason to draw the connections Bowers does, for many of the *other* theoretical assumptions (about dialogue, the nature of knowledge, dialectical thinking, etc.) which give Freire's views on rationality their sense contrast markedly with, and in some cases diametrically oppose, technocratic views. (See chapters 2 and 8 of this volume.) Fundamental premises on rational distance *may or may not* lead to "extreme forms of technological culture," and with respect to Freire, they demonstrably do not.

EDUCATION, OPPRESSION, AND INTERVENTION

I turn now to those aspects of Bowers's analysis which bear directly on Freirean pedagogical intervention. Bowers argues that Freire's approach to pedagogy has a "bias" toward change (Bowers, 1983, p. 942). Yet, the same could be said of any educational program, and indeed of any educational process. Education, on a variety of liberal and radical positions, and on some conservative accounts as well, is necessarily concerned with changing those being educated. Indeed, change is one of the few themes that binds otherwise disparate groups commenting on education together. Although there are deep disagreements over the nature and direction of that change, and over questions as to whether it is personal or social or structural in character, most commentators on pedagogical matters argue that some sort of transformation ought to occur through education. Hence, if the term "program" is taken to mean any structured, organized form of pedagogy or system of education, then change is always a fundamental objective and intervention a logical necessity. Whether examining an educational program in schools, in prisons, for the elderly, or with adults learning to read and write, it would not be a program at all unless it was assumed that people would change in some way as a result of their participation or involvement.

Bowers is particularly critical of Freire's stress on the importance of change through critical reflection, questioning, and problematization. If a principle of nonquestioning is endorsed, it is instructive to contemplate what might properly count as "the process of education" when the principle is coupled with a policy of nonintervention. One possibility is that educational processes become those in which existing forms of knowledge are transmitted. But the notion of transmission is problematic here, because this implies a transmitter and someone to whom ideas are transmitted: such a relationship is ruled out by the nonintervention requirement. Even the broader notion of "passing on" existing knowledge must be rejected, because this still implies someone doing the passing and someone receiving. It might be more accurate, therefore, to talk of educational processes as those activities through which the accepted beliefs, values, practices, and so on are acquired or *learned*, by experience. If a policy of nonintervention is strictly applied, this must be a wholly spontaneous process. Even if there might be occasions in which adults might override this policy in, for example, protecting a child from physical harm, the general attitude would be one, as in the Chipewyan's case, of "*rarely* exercising control" over children's activities (Bowers, 1983, p. 940). Individuals would be largely, and *on principle*, free to learn whatever they wished, when they wished, as they pleased.

But what if, in encouraging children to "learn by their own experience"

(p. 940), a child, on the basis of this experience, questioned or challenged some aspect of the existing belief system? This would pose a dilemma, for if the imperative of nonintervention is to be met, no one ought to step in to prohibit such questioning, or even to dissuade it. Bowers points out that the Chipewyan try to avoid being in situations that lead to the questioning and renegotiation of beliefs (p. 941). It seems highly unlikely, though, that such instances could be entirely eluded. Indeed, given the curiosity children often display in spontaneously investigating the wonders of everyday life, it seems probable that questioning of established beliefs, ideas, practices, and forms of authority—even if in a relatively unsophisticated way—might occur quite regularly. In the case of adults, if, despite the discouragement of problematization, one or two people *did* question accepted views or existing modes of practice, what steps would be taken to censure this questioning? The moment at which *any* move is made to stem the problematization or renegotiation of beliefs, the principle of nonintervention is subverted. A similar difficulty might arise in a situation where one member of the group *did* intervene in the activities of others (e.g., in helping a child). If other members of the group intervene to prevent this intervention, the principle of nonintervention is violated. On the other hand, if they do not intervene, this allows the original intervention to continue. In his analysis of Chipewyan society, Bowers says nothing about how such contradictions might be resolved, or when they might be justified, or which principles override others under given circumstances.

Some answers to these questions can be found in Scollon and Scollon's *Linguistic Convergence* (1979), the book to which Bowers refers in discussing Chipewyan culture. Scollon and Scollon note that Chipewyan children are given the opportunity to observe a wide range of adult activities, and are restrained only when there is a risk of serious injury. Children are expected to emulate the model of noninterference exemplified by adults, and "any intervention by adults is taken as a very serious matter." Learning is noninterventionist in two senses:

> As educator, the teacher does not directly intervene in the activities of the student. The child . . . is expected to watch and learn without active intervention on the part of the teacher. On the other hand, the learner is expected to learn how to do things without immediately intervening in their operation. That is, learning is holistic and not incremental. (p. 202)

An apparent contrast with the Freirean concept of education is evident here. Freire (1998c, p. 99) sees education as "that specifically human act of intervening in the world." The term intervention, as used in this context, is not restricted to the actions of one particular political group, or one form of education. Both leftist radicals and right-wing reactionaries become interventionists when they educate. Educational intervention may take the form of revolutionary societal change, but it may also be exemplified in subtle changes in human relations, ways of thinking, or modes of acting among small groups of people. On the Freirean view, a teacher or educator (Freire uses these terms interchangeably) not only has a right but a *responsibility* to become involved in the lives of others. All forms of teaching, whether via direct instruction in a formal class-room or by example in informal settings, are interventionist. Kevin Harris adopts a similar stance:

> The simple reality is that one cannot be a teacher and neutrally lay out options or for ever hold one's peace. To teach, which can in-clude academics stating their cases in highly privileged legitimated contexts like journals and books ... is to be interventionary: it is to state one's views, or at the weakest to place one's ideas "on the agenda," and to do so from a position of privilege from which power and ascribed status cannot be removed. (1990, pp. 180–181)

If an "educator" is a person who intends or hopes that others will learn from him or her, or gain in some way from participating in an educative relationship, then such people cannot exist in a strictly non-interventionist system. Even the notion of being a "facilitator" must be ruled out, for there is still an element of intervention present in attempt-ing to set up the conditions for others to learn. In fact, there can be no hint of deliberate guidance of any kind, for *intentional* assistance in the learning process necessitates intervention in the lives of others. From a Freirean point of view, the entire process of education must be aban-doned under such conditions. Freire argues that "[i]f we have nothing to put forward, or if we simply refuse to do it, we really have nothing to do with the practice of education" (Freire and Faundez, 1989, p. 34). The question for Freire is not "How can one, as an educator, avoid in-tervening in the lives of others?," but "What *form* will this intervention take?"

In addressing the relationship between education and nonintervention in Chipewyan society, much hinges on how the terms "teacher" and "educator" are understood. For Freire and Harris, teaching is a neces-sarily interventionist process. If their view of teaching is accepted, either Scollon and Scollon must be seen as mistaken in designating the adults from whom Chipewyan children learn "teachers," or an element of in-tervention is still present despite the claim that learning in Chipewyan society is noninterventionist. The latter possibility seems to provide a sounder basis for rendering Bowers's and the Scollons' account of Chip-ewyan attitudes and practices problematic. In contemplating this line of argument, an incident recounted by Scollon and Scollon (but not Bowers) is revealing. Noting that it is wrong, in Chipewyan culture, to "take any distance from oneself," Scollon and Scollon recall the case of "a mother who taped over a mirror on a baby's toy because the baby was looking at herself in it" (1979, p. 188). This suggests that intervention is practiced, and seen as justifiable, in situations where a key feature of what Scollon and Scollon call the Chipewyan's "bush consciousness" is threatened. In this example, intervention was seen as necessary to discourage a form of reflexiveness which contravened the integrative dimension of the Chipewyan's worldview. In setting up conditions for children to learn about the entropic, integrative, individualistic, and nonintervening aspects of Chipewyan thought, Chipewyan adults practice a form of pedagogical intervention.[1] Thus, intervention of a certain kind, at particular times, becomes necessary in encouraging children to become minimally interventionist—in some respects—as adults. Hence, rather than claiming that the Chipewyan are noninterventionist, it might be more accurate to say that the *kind* of intervention they exercise is of a different order to that practiced by Freire (and others). I turn now to the question of whether the particular form of intervention initiated by Freire in Brazil in the late 1950s and early 1960s was justified.

PEDAGOGICAL INTERVENTION IN SITUATIONS OF OPPRESSION

Bowers, in building a case for nonintervention, effectively avoids some of the most difficult practical and ethical questions facing Freire (and other educators). What would he do if he were in Freire's position? In the literacy program for which he gained international recognition, Freire was not dealing with the Chipewyan—the group upon which so much of Bowers's analysis depends—but with illiterate adults in Brazil in the early 1960s, the majority of whom were severely impoverished. Even a fleeting glimpse at Brazil's history provides sobering reading. Despite rapid industrial expansion in Brazil between 1956 and 1961, much of the wealth remained concentrated in the hands of relatively few people. In 1960, the share of the total national income of the lower 50 percent of the population was only 14.5 percent; the lowest 10 percent of income earners enjoyed only 1.9 percent of the country's wealth. By 1970, these figures had decreased even further to 13.9 percent and 1.2 percent for the lower 50 percent and lowest 10 percent, respectively.[2] The poor, in both urban and rural areas, endured horrific hardships. The northeast of Brazil, especially, was marked in the early 1960s by "truly appalling social conditions—60,000 square miles of suffering."[3] In sections of the northeast in the years immediately prior to Freire's appointment as director of the national literacy program average caloric intakes were at levels barely high enough to sustain life; the life expectancy was twenty-eight years for men and thirty-two for women, and infants frequently died before reaching their first year.[4] Freire speaks of malnutrition so severe that permanent damage to mental faculties resulted (1972b, p. 62). With high rates of disease, substandard housing, and minimal facilities for basic hygiene practices, living conditions for the poor in Brazil were virtually intolerable.

Freire's claim that those subject to such appalling conditions tended to see the world in "magical" terms needs to be considered against the background of Brazil's history. (The next chapter provides a detailed discussion of the different levels of consciousness identified by Freire.) Semi-intransitive consciousness was, in Freire's words, "a consciousness historically conditioned by the social structures"; it was a *dominated* consciousness (p. 62). None of the features of magical or semi-intransitive thought—passivity, fatalism, the attributing of problems to higher powers, and so on—existed in an ahistorical void. Rather, all emerged within relations in which power was structured unequally. Dominant groups—and here reference can be made to landowners, the conservative wing of the church, and the emerging class of corporate elites—exerted enormous influence over the lives of others, restricting the parameters within which illiterate adults (among other groups) could act and think. Freire argues that the dominant classes develop an insensitivity to the misery of their fellow human beings, refusing to face up to the hunger and poverty experienced by others (1996, p. 112; 1997a, p. 65). Encouraged by others to think in magical terms, peasants not only "explained" but *reinforced* their own material domination, and thus played a part—*though not an intentional one*—in perpetuating the very system that oppressed them.

It is important, of course, not to ignore or underestimate the extent of peasant resistance to oppressive structures and practices. In *Politics and Education*, Freire refers to these as the "subterfuge" of the oppressed. Educators have an important role to play in comprehending and working with different forms of popular resistance, including "parties, dances, jokes, legends, devotions, fears, semantics, syntax, [and] religiosity" (1998b, p. 47). Collectively, these activities constitute a latent, often hidden form of class struggle.[5] Yet although such modes of resistance must not be neglected—and indeed may be potentially vital in building a new, more democratic social system—they have their limits. "Merely rebellious attitudes or actions are insufficient," Freire says, "though they are an indispensable response to legitimate anger" (1998c, p. 74). Rebellious consciousness is not yet *revolutionary* consciousness (Freire, 1996, p. 118). Walls of fear can be created when dominated groups find expressions of resistance are met with brutal retaliation and the unfolding of an even more oppressive reality. Educators can, if they are not careful, reinforce these walls instead of breaking them down. In some situations,

> the violence of the oppressors and their domination is so profound that it generates a type of *existential weariness* in the popular classes which, in turn, is associated with . . . *historical amnesia,* in which one loses the idea of tomorrow as a possible project. Tomorrow becomes a repetition of today, a today that is as violent and perverse as always. (Freire, 1998c, p. 48)

This is precisely what Freire encountered in parts of Brazil during the 1950s and 1960s: large groups of people so beaten down by the violence of an unequal society that the notion of a "future" seemed inconceivable. This situation, one in which "[t]he oppressed grandchild repeats the suffering of their grandparent," with history being reduced to "an everlasting present of hopelessness and resignation," persists today in the northeast of Brazil (Freire, 1997a, p. 45).

What, then, was Freire to do, given these circumstances? With no intervention of any kind, the situation was unlikely to change; indeed, there was some evidence to suggest conditions might continue to deteriorate.[6] Should Freire wash his hands of the situation, ignore it, and not intervene at all? Or was some kind of intervention—in *this* situation—justified? If so, what direction should this take? Bowers has virtually nothing to say on these questions, yet they are surely vital from an ethical—and an educational—standpoint. As Bowers points out, if Freire was convinced that large numbers of illiterate adults were oppressed, intervention directed at transforming this oppressive situation would—given Freire's philosophical, ethical, and educational position—seem imperative (cf. Freire, 1998c, pp. 72–73). As Freire puts it, "I cannot be indifferent to the pain of those who go hungry, [and] I cannot suggest to them . . . that their situation is the result of God's will. That is a lie" (1997a, p. 45). Freire tries to clarify his position thus:

> Obviously, it is not a question of inciting the exploited poor to rebellion, to mobilization, to organization, to shaking up the world. In truth, it's a question of working in some given area, be it literacy, health or evangelization, and doing so as to awake the conscience of each group, in a constructive, critical manner, about the violence and extreme injustice of this concrete situation. (1998c, p. 75)

Bowers seems to largely sidestep the question of oppression: for him, the paramount concern is to respect the culture of certain groups. For Freire, however, inaction on the grounds of "respect for the culture" would, in the case with which he was dealing (but not every case), have amounted to *de facto* support for the status quo—and hence for the continuation of an oppressive situation. Bowers argues that Freirean adult literacy programs perpetuate Western domination, but Freire could have turned the tables on this point. He might have said that Bowers, were he to do nothing in the same circumstances, could be accused of reinforcing domination himself. Of course, Bowers might not object to intervention under such conditions. He might simply articulate cautions about the nature, and potential consequences, of educational involvement. It is difficult to know exactly what Bowers would do, however, because he never adequately addresses the relationship between oppression, education, and intervention in Brazil, Chile, and the other countries in which Freire worked.[7]

BEYOND CULTURAL CONSERVATISM

Freirean pedagogy is not without its difficulties. Of particular significance for present purposes, in promoting the ideal of critical consciousness, there is at least one dilemma from which Freire cannot easily escape. Freire argues that all ideas should be open to question. A logical corollary of this is that there are no ideas which *cannot* be questioned. All ideas, for Freire, are thus potentially subject to change. We should never, as Freire puts it, be too certain of our certainties. We should always be open to the possibility that some ideas might be rejected on the basis of critical reflection. Yet this must also include the idea that there are no ideas that cannot be questioned. But to question this idea is simultaneously to uphold this idea. In effect, then, there *is* one idea that cannot be questioned, namely, the idea that there are no ideas that cannot be questioned.[8]

Notice, however, that in saying that there are no ideas that cannot be questioned, it does not necessarily follow that all ideas should be questioned all of the time. Freire grants what might be termed "provisional" acceptance to certain ideas to allow theoretical and practical work to proceed. He recognizes that it would be quite impossible to engage in any kind of consciously directed action, or to develop a philosophy, or to advance an ethical position, without taking some ideas for granted— for the time being (see, for example, Freire and Shor, 1987, pp. 101–102). This is true whatever political stance one adopts, and applies as much to Bowers as it does to Freire. Bowers takes for granted the divisibility of cultures into Western and non-Western categories, the value of tradition, the importance of community, and so on, just as Freire assumes that reality is dialectical, that education should be dialogical, that liberation from oppression is desirable, and so on.

Nevertheless, questioning is a vital element of the Freirean ethical ideal. Freire argues for a restless, searching, investigative, *critical* orientation toward the world. Education, for Freire, should foster this critical attitude. To participate in a Freirean program of adult literacy education, then, is to be inducted into a particular way of thinking and acting. As Bowers's analysis shows, this critical orientation is likely to be different from the approach many people in "traditional" cultures adopt in understanding reality. Bowers is, I believe, theoretically astray in arguing that Freire's pedagogy reflects, reinforces, and reproduces "the Western mind set," but it is undeniable that Freirean adult literacy programs privilege (and foster) a critical mode of consciousness over what Freire regarded as passive and naïve forms of thought.

This "bias" toward critical thought can, however, be strongly defended if a moment's consideration is given to alternative positions. Bowers does not make his ethical position clear in his 1983 article, but elsewhere, in a critique of Giroux and McLaren,[9] he maintains:

> [T]here are certain beliefs, values, and practices that should not be politicized. For example, if we could arrive at a new cultural consensus on viewing our relationships with the rest of the biotic community as part of our sense of the moral order I would not recommend that teachers politicize it by encouraging each generation of students to make up their own "individualistic mind" about it. Should students be encouraged to demythologize the Constitution and Bill of Rights? Should the relativizing power of *pedagogical negativism* be directed at the emerging sense of taken for grantedness relating to the immorality of gender and racial discrimination? (Bowers, 1991a, p. 483)

This comment suggests that there are certain matters that are beyond interrogation, or that ought not to be subjected to critical reflection, or that we ought to strive to achieve a binding consensus on. Some ideas, in Bowers's view, should not be questioned, nor, it seems, even be *open* for questioning and critical debate (or "politicizing" as Bowers puts it). It is important to point out that this position is *not* explicitly conveyed in Bowers's earlier (1983) critique of Freire. Bowers's discussion of the Chipewyan *does*, however, question the value of promoting critical reflection among the young. Bowers's later call for cultural consensus on some issues does not *necessarily* follow from his earlier critique of Freirean pedagogical intervention, but it is consistent with it.

Freire would not have accepted the view that some ideas, laws, or agreements are beyond questioning or politicization. But leaving all ideas open to problematization does not mean that every view must be immediately superseded by a superior position. It is precisely through allowing ideas to be considered and compared, analyzed and evaluated, that they can be held with greater conviction. Bowers laments the lack of agreement on such issues as abortion and education in Western societies, as if these matters could somehow be definitively resolved and closed to further questioning. Freire's ethic does not preclude the possibility of a consensus on such complex problems being reached; a Freirean position simply demands that such agreement not be regarded as fixed, absolute, and binding for all groups, in every cultural or social context, for all time.

Bowers's critique is helpful in highlighting the sensitivities educationists must display in involving themselves in the lives of others. Teachers, discussion facilitators, adult literacy coordinators, and others invested with educational responsibilities are people whose actions as educators always have *consequences* (see Freire, 1998c, p. 97), some of which might be construed as "invasive" or "dominating" or "oppressive." Freire was acutely aware of this, and was very deliberate in the approach he adopted in his adult literacy work. He knew that if his program worked as he hoped it would, participants would never be the same again. The worth of a critical orientation toward the world, therefore, had to be such that it would—as far as any educator could reasonably foresee—substantially improve the lives of those among whom it was being fostered. Although participants in a Freirean adult literacy program might never be able to go back (entirely) to their former ways of thinking, in advocating an ideal of critical reflection Freire promoted the means through which people might *revisit* and *reinterpret* their old patterns of thought and behavior. Of course, as I have argued in the Introduction and earlier chapters, in reinterpreting ideas we can distort them: the frequent misrepresentation of Freirean principles is a case in point. Equally, however, some forms of reinterpretation may result in a significantly enhanced appreciation of the object of study. The development of a critical consciousness does not imply the necessary abandonment of traditional practices, rituals, customs, and forms of authority: it simply demands that these elements of the life world of any group not be above questioning.

Bowers identifies some of the most positive features of traditional worldviews, drawing attention in particular to the importance of a holistic perspective on the relationship between human beings and their wider environment. The elevation of human activity over all other forms of ecological life by some Westerners is arguably highly problematic. There is, as many Western thinkers (Bowers included) have recognized, much that might be learned from cultural groups other than our own. Yet, Bowers seems to forget that a willingness to seriously investigate alternative ways of viewing the world is one of the defining features of critical consciousness. To affirm that Freire draws on a number of Western intellectual traditions, and adopts and endorses principles favored by many other Western scholars, is not to say (as Bowers seems to suggest) that Freire is an unreflexive, "blinded," carrier of *all* Western views, or of some reified, homogenous, generalized Western mind-set. The Freirean notion of critical consciousness embraces possibilities for appreciating, understanding, and sanctioning a variety of Western and non-Western ideas.

In aligning Freire with the Western side of the Western/non-Western binary, Bowers not only is compelled to see Freire as an opponent of traditional cultures but of "tradition" itself.[10] Yet, Freire notes that among other distinguishing features, critical consciousness is defined by "receptivity to the new for reasons beyond mere novelty and by the good sense not reject the old just because it is old—*by accepting what is valid in both old and new*" (Freire, 1976, p. 18, emphasis added). This statement is absent from Bowers's account of the Freirean critical ideal. Bowers is certainly correct in arguing that Freire hoped participants in his Brazilian literacy program would develop a critical consciousness, but he fails to provide a rounded picture of what the Freirean view of critical consciousness entails. This failing needs to be seen as one aspect of a broader problem in Bowers's critique. In portraying Freire as a de facto supporter of generalized Western views on critical agency, individual freedom, rational autonomy, and so on, Bowers ignores or downplays many of the subtleties of Freire's analysis—those features which give his work its distinctiveness, and which demarcate his interpretation of such concepts as praxis, dialogue, critical reflection, knowing, and from other accounts.

Bowers wants to uphold traditional beliefs and practices because they provide a form of authority which promotes community cohesion. He claims that members of traditional cultural groups tend to adopt a more "integrated" approach to life, and to exist more harmoniously with their biotic environment, than their Western counterparts. Freire not only would have criticized Bowers's proclivity to romanticizing traditional cultures, but also questioned his uncritical valuing of group cohesion. Apparent agreements often mask subtle or deep-seated differences: consensus and harmony are often illusory. Moreover, a high degree of social cohesion can exist among groups whose actions are regarded by many as profoundly oppressive (e.g., the Ku Klux Klan, Hitler Youth, etc.). Given the existence of such groups, Freire would not have supported a position of upholding established social practices, beliefs, and forms of cultural expression at all costs; indeed, he would, I think, have been in favor of *disrupting* traditional patterns of life if these were demonstrably oppressive.

It could be argued against Freire that those who come to view their situation critically might remain as powerless as ever to effect change, given the overwhelming dominance of certain groups, but be more frustrated, more unhappy, more resentful, and more bitter than ever before.

For where in the past a magical or naive mode of consciousness might have acted as a kind of "insulating" device, allowing adults to "explain" or "rationalize" or "make sense of" their circumstances in such a way that they, in a certain sense, *accepted* them, with the development of a more critical orientation toward the social world, suddenly nothing seems so simple any more. The world is, following the emergence of a critical mode of being, rendered at once more complex and more unbearable than ever before. What, however, is the alternative to this? Freire would certainly not have defended an "ignorance is bliss" view of the world. Maintaining people in a state of ignorance about the deeper reasons behind their suffering is, from Freire's point of view, never justified. Certainly it does not provide a sufficient reason for not allowing people to see the world in a different way. In Freire's ethic, liberation cannot be equated with "happiness." Liberation involves *struggle*, sacrifice, and a profound respect for one's fellow human beings. Fighting for a better world, Freire would often say, is always filled with risks and uncertainties. If becoming more critically conscious leads to unhappiness or frustration, this is no reason to abandon the goal of critical consciousness as an ideal; rather, it is an affirmation of the need to change the structures and relations which form the object of critical reflection.

FINAL WORDS

From a Freirean point of view, education can never be neutral. Freire did not "force" participants in his literacy programs to abandon their existing customs, values, beliefs, and practices; he merely encouraged people to *consider* others ways of thinking about social reality. This chapter has highlighted the importance of addressing the question, "*Given* the situation with which Freire was dealing, to what extent was the promotion of a critically conscious mode of being justified?" Freire would have had little to gain by asking what might be done in an ideal, "pure" community, for, in his view, such communities do not, and could not, exist. Although the preceding analysis suggests that Bowers reifies, exaggerates, and distorts elements of the Freirean ideal, it is clear that Freire's orientation to the social world contrasts in important ways with that adopted by the Chipewyan and many other groups in traditional societies. In encouraging a critical approach to reading the word and the world through his adult literacy work, Freire challenged prevailing modes of thought among Brazilian peasants and the urban poor (and other groups in other programs). Freire was quite explicit in his wish to promote this change; he saw it as an authentic part of the wider struggle for liberation from conditions of oppression. From Bowers's point of view, this intervention is unacceptable, or at least (very) problematic. I have attempted to demonstrate that Bowers's critique rests on flawed foundations, and have argued that Freire's pedagogical approach was justified under the circumstances.

NOTES

1. See Scollon and Scollon (1979, pp. 178–192) for a summary of these four dimensions of the Chipewyan worldview.

2. From the 1970 Brazilian census, cited in Taylor (1993, p. 18).

3. Comments from Josue de Castro, cited in Taylor (1993, p. 16).

4. From Tad Szulc, cited in Taylor (1993, p. 17).

5. For another insightful discussion of the subtle and hidden forms of resistance in peasant societies, see Scott (1990).

6. Compare, Taylor (1993) on the changes between 1960 and 1970.

7. It is possible that different types of education may accomplish different kinds of liberation. This proposition might provide a useful starting point for further critical work on Bowers and Freire.

8. An alternative line of argument is possible here. A person might often question the idea that no ideas cannot be questioned, entertaining the possibility that there may well be some absolutes, but acknowledging that he or she hasn't found them yet. If such absolutes *are* (subsequently) discovered, that person may then change his or her view that no ideas cannot be questioned.

9. See Bowers (1991a). This article was followed by a response from Peter McLaren (1991) and a rejoinder by Bowers (1991b).

10. Bowers makes this explicit in a review of Freire's *The Politics of Education* (1985) in 1986, where he maintains: "Freire's theory, by presenting us with an oversimplified view of tradition—one he inherited from the Enlightenment, leads to an intellectual stance that would reject as reactionary any consideration of the possibility that traditions can be sources of individual meaning, empowerment, and bonding to the shared life of the community" (p. 150).

CHAPTER 8

Rethinking Conscientization

When Freire's work first began to attract international attention in the early 1970s, a new term—conscientization—found its way into educational discourse. Almost immediately, this concept was embraced by many as a miraculous solution to problems of oppression and exploitation. Freire's success with adult literacy initiatives in Brazil and Chile was taken as evidence by those who became "converted" to Freirean principles that conscientization could rapidly and dramatically change people's lives. From the beginning, however, Freire emphasized the importance of understanding conscientization in the light of his wider philosophy and in relation to the context within which the term was applied. Conscientization quickly became the object of much confusion as well as fascination.

Over the past two decades, numerous scholars have commented on the notion of conscientization, and many attempts have been made to apply the concept in First World educational settings.[1] On one view, conscientization is seen as the developmental movement of individuals through a succession of distinct stages, with each stage being defined by certain attitudes and behaviors. This chapter suggests that the "stages" model is inherently flawed, and offers an alternative position—one that draws a direct link between conscientization and praxis. The interface between Freire's modernism and the postmodernist critique of subject-centered reason is briefly examined. An individualist interpretation of critical consciousness is rejected, and the postmodernist notion of multiple subjectivities is brought to bear on a reworked concept of conscientization.

FREIRE AND THE STAGES MODEL
OF CONSCIENTIZATION

Although his name has become synonymous with the concept, Freire was not the first person to speak of conscientization. The original Portuguese term, *conscientizacao*, came into being during a series of meetings between professors at the Brazilian Institute of Higher Studies (ISEB). Although the concept had immediate appeal to Freire, and obvious relevance for his emerging pedagogical theory, it was Helder Camara who first popularized the term *conscientizacao* and gave it currency in English (Freire, 1974b, p. 575).

In his early writings on the subject, Freire relates conscientization to sociohistorical conditions in Brazil (see Freire, 1972b, pp. 57–71; 1976, pp. 17–20). Essentially, conscientization represents the movement toward "critical" consciousness from a state of either "magical" consciousness or "naïve" consciousness. Magical (semi-intransitive) consciousness predominated in rural areas. "Introverted" peasant communities, isolated from political and industrial changes taking place elsewhere in Brazil, suffered exploitative working conditions, poor nutrition, alarming levels of infant mortality and disease, and low life expectancy. Illiteracy was widespread. Freire (1976) describes the worldview typical of individuals in these communities thus:

> Their interests center almost totally around survival, and they lack a sense of life on a more historic plane . . . semi-intransitivity represents a near disengagement between men and their existence. In this state, discernment is difficult. Men confuse their perceptions of the objects and challenges of the environment, and fall prey to magical explanations because they cannot apprehend true causality. (p. 17)

The transition to "naïve" consciousness corresponded with infrastructural changes in Brazil which began after the abolition of slavery at the end of the nineteenth century. Change accelerated during the First World War and further intensified after the Second World War, with increasing development of urban areas, and with the emergence of a populist (rather than land-owner) leadership (Freire, 1972b, pp. 63–68). Freire (1976) notes:

> Naïve transitivity, the state of consciousness which predominated in Brazilian urban centers during the transitional period, is char-

acterized by an over-simplification of problems; by a nostalgia for the past; by underestimation of the common man; by a strong tendency to gregariousness; by a lack of interest in investigation, accompanied by an accentuated taste for fanciful explanations; by fragility of argument; by a strongly emotional style; by the practice of polemics rather than dialogue; by magical explanations. (p. 18)

Magical and naïve states of consciousness are contrasted with critical consciousness. Critical consciousness, characteristic of "authentically democratic regimes" (p. 18), is characterized by:

depth in the interpretation of problems; by the substitution of causal principles for magical explanations; by the testing of one's "findings" and by openness to revision; by the attempt to avoid distortion when perceiving problems and to avoid preconceived notions when analyzing them; by refusing to transfer responsibility; by rejecting passive positions; by soundness of argumentation; by the practice of dialogue rather than polemics; by receptivity to the new for reasons beyond mere novelty and by the good sense not to reject the old just because it is old—by accepting what is valid in both old and new. (p. 18)

The focus on three levels of consciousness has been taken by many as evidence that Freire intended the notion of conscientization to be conceived in terms of a "raising" of consciousness through clear, definitive stages. A detailed example of this "stages" model of conscientization is provided by William Smith (1976). According to Smith, conscientization is "a developmental process which can be divided into three distinct stages: magical, naïve, and critical consciousness" (pp. 41–42). At each stage, people interpret and act on the world in different ways. Smith categorizes characteristic responses of magical, naïve, and critical individuals to three key questions: "[W]hat are the most dehumanizing problems in your life? (NAMING); what are the causes and consequences of those problems? (REFLECTING); and, what can be done to solve those problems? (ACTING)" (p. 42). In naming their world, magically conscious individuals tend to either deny that they have problems or avoid them by situating them in the past or elsewhere (p. 46). In reflecting on their circumstances, such individuals typically explain the conditions they endure through reference to "God's will," fate, or bad luck (p. 48). Using examples from his experience with Ecuadorian farmers, Smith notes that people at this level of consciousness often either sympathize with their oppressors, or live in fear of them (p. 49). Causal explanations of difficulties are frequently simplistic. For example, peasants might say: "We can't study because we don't have any money," but not go on to inquire as to *why* they are impoverished (p. 50). Passive acceptance of harsh social conditions, rather than critical analysis and transformation, is the order of the day for those at this stage of consciousness.

People at the naïve level see reform within an existing social system as a major task. Where problems are identified, individuals (rather than social structures or systems) are often blamed (p. 52). Naïve individuals sometimes attempt to model their oppressors' behavior and distance themselves from their oppressed peers. Violence within families and among groups of people at this stage of consciousness is not uncommon (p. 58). Overcoming difficulties becomes a matter of using the system rather than changing it.

Critical consciousness is characterized by an attempt to transform oppressive social structures (p. 60). Self-esteem increases, and an understanding of and sympathy for one's peers ensues (pp. 61, 63). Connections between different oppressive structures are identified (p. 64). Self-actualization becomes possible, and cooperative dialogical relationships are sought (pp. 65–67). The critically conscious individual is willing to take risks in resisting oppression (p. 66).

For Smith, the process of conscientization is strictly sequential: "One does not begin as critical and become magical, nor move from magical to critical, nor move freely between the three stages. Development is a progression from magical to naïve to critical" (p. 79). This idea owes much to the work of Kohlberg and Mayer, who talk of development through "invariant ordered sequential stages," where all individuals are assumed to follow the same developmental path (p. 78). Environmental and personal factors influence the extent to which individuals progress through the stages of development, but the stages remain the same in all cases (p. 78). On Smith's model of conscientization, not all people will necessarily reach the stage of critical consciousness, but those who do must move through the stages in order. For example, an Ecuadorian peasant who exhibits the qualities of magical consciousness cannot "skip a stage" and move directly to critical consciousness. Magical consciousness is considered the least desirable (lowest) level and critical consciousness the most desirable (highest) stage, with naïve consciousness in the middle. Hence, under this framework conscientization can legitimately be seen as a process through which one's consciousness is *raised* from one level to the next.

The notion of "consciousness raising" has attracted some vigorous attacks over the years. As chapter 6 suggested, few have been more forthright in their denouncement of this idea than Peter Berger (1974). Kevin Harris (1979) has mounted a strong defense of Freire against Berger's criticisms. Basing his analysis of education on a rereading of Marx, Harris argues that consciousness raising is desirable in situations where it can be shown that people do not (critically) understand the situation in which they live or grasp what is in their best interests (p. 171). According to Harris, the essential idea behind consciousness raising is that

> some people's consciousness has been arrested and fixed at some point, and that others, with raised consciousness of a situation, can step in and help the former to understand the situation properly. Or, to put this just a little differently in the Marxian terms we employed earlier, some people have false consciousness, which can possibly be put right by those whose consciousness is not false. (p. 171)

For Harris, some ideas provide a better reading of reality than others. Given that the dominant ideology in capitalist societies serves to distort reality, those with higher consciousnesses are justified in attempting to provide the conditions for enlightening others with a less critical understanding of the world. Contrary to Berger's assertions, however, there is no reason why critically conscious individuals need come from the "higher" or "educated" classes. Quite the opposite, Harris claims such individuals are more likely to emerge from the "exploited and deceived" classes (p. 171). Berger forgets that consciousnesses are formed within relations of domination where certain interests are privileged over others; indeed, "[p]art of the disguise and mystification lies . . . in the implanting of the consciousness that one actually does, freely and actively, define one's own situation, and that one is perfectly well aware of what the realities of the situation are" (p. 172). Consciousness raising does not imply the imposition of one's views on others; rather, the aim is to encourage people to examine their world in a different way (p. 174). Provided dialogue is employed in place of monologue, and insofar as the starting point for any program is the lived reality of learners,

> consciousness raising can . . . be seen . . . as a viable alternative to education, allowing as it does for people to gain undistorted knowledge by interacting with the world in terms of their *own* interests. . . . The distortions normally brought about by the social dimension of knowledge production should be eliminated, such that people can come to perceive their world as it really is. (p. 176)

AN ALTERNATIVE INTERPRETATION: CONSCIENTIZATION AND PRAXIS

The stages model of conscientization, particularly as exemplified in the work of Smith, is methodical, systematic, and convenient. It allows us to categorize people according to their level of consciousness, and to explain their attitudes and behaviors in terms of preidentified characteristics. Educators appear to have an important role to play in seeking ways of assisting people from one stage to the next. Once a person has reached critical consciousness, he or she has "made it" for life. It might be expected that those who reach this stage of consciousness will continuously display the most desirable qualities of conscious development and cannot regress to earlier stages.

This portrait may exaggerate some features of the stages model, but I believe it indicates the logical direction of such an approach to conscientization. In this section, I suggest that it is the very systematization of the stages theory which gives rise to difficulties: a mechanical theory of consciousness emerges, which goes against the grain of Freire's dialectical perspective on reality. I argue that making a direct link with the notion of praxis takes us closer to Freire's intentions in using the concept of conscientization.

Under the stages model, there is a categorization of individual characteristics at each stage. For magically conscious individuals in Smith's scheme, denial of problems, passive acceptance of one's circumstances, and simplistic causal explanations are common characteristics. Critically conscious individuals, by contrast, possess high self-esteem, take risks, empathize with peers, and work dialogically with others. For each stage of consciousness, then, there are certain personal qualities—particular attitudes and modes of thinking, acting, and behaving—which are distinct from the characteristics typical of other stages. These characteristics separate the stages from one another. In Smith's theory, there is no overlap between magical, naïve, and critical consciousness. In depicting conscientization as a process of consciousness raising, the stages model is also hierarchical: naïve consciousness is a higher stage than magical consciousness, and critical consciousness is higher than naïve consciousness. Critical consciousness represents the most (ethically) desirable mode of being, and magical consciousness the least desirable.

Freire clearly intended critical consciousness to be quite separate from other levels of consciousness. He does allow, however, for a degree of overlap between magical consciousness and naïve consciousness. In *Cultural Action for Freedom*, for instance, he cautions:

> Although the qualitative difference between the semi-intransitive consciousness and the naïve transitive consciousness can be explained by the phenomenon of emergence due to structural transformations in society, there are no rigidly defined frontiers between the historical moments which produce qualitative changes in men's awareness. In many respects, the semi-intransitive consciousness remains present in the naïve transitive consciousness. (1972b, p. 65)

And in *Education: The Practice of Freedom*, Freire notes with respect to naïve consciousness: "The magical aspect typical of intransitivity is partially present here also. Although men's horizons have expanded and they respond more openly to stimuli, these responses still have a magical quality" (1976, p. 18). Naïvely conscious groups remain as dominated as those at the magical level of consciousness, with the myths perpetuated by oppressors continuing to exert a powerful influence over their lives (Freire, 1972b, p. 65). It is only when the potential for resistance to oppression among naïvely conscious groups is realized and the full flowering of critical consciousness emerges that the shackles of these myths are removed.

In Smith's analysis, the blurring of boundaries between levels disappears. The divisions between magical, naïve, and critical individuals become tidy and clear-cut. There is little attention paid to the transition from one stage to another. Where Freire finds in naïve consciousness both aspects of the former magical stage and the seeds of potential resistance to oppression, in Smith's study the two stages are presented as discrete categories with distinctive defining characteristics. For Freire, the categories of magical consciousness and naïve consciousness represent an attempt to capture the essence of general patterns of thought among contemporary and past social groups. In Smith's study, the focus is on individuals and the extent to which their attitudes and behaviors conform to predetermined characteristics for given stages. Smith begins with the characteristics identified by Freire, making slight modifications in an effort to develop a systematic code for "measuring" conscientization. Alschuler summarizes this approach in his Foreword to Smith's study:

> We needed to define *conscientizacao* . . . more concretely than Freire's abstruse philosophizing. We reasoned that if we could create an operational definition of *conscientizacao*, in other words, a way of measuring it, we would have reached a clear understanding of the term. And, we would have a method of accurately gauging the level of consciousness in situations before and after efforts to raise consciousness. (1976, pp. vi–vii)

This systematization is fraught with problems. As I argued in the Introduction and chapter 3, the danger of domesticating Freire's work is ever-present in attempts to convert his pedagogy into a method or set of methods. Freire offers a distinctive approach to education—one informed by a particular understanding of human beings, knowledge, and the nature of reality—but he refuses to systematize his pedagogical ideas into clear-cut rules, steps, or methods for effective teaching, learning, and development. The goal of accurately measuring levels of consciousness betrays a behaviorist view of human consciousness and activity, and a technocratic conception of education. The professed hope that an "operational" definition would provide a "clear" understanding of conscientization is, I believe, ill-founded. This interpretation of conscientization

certainly simplifies the notion (by ridding it of its contextual and theoretical "baggage"), and perhaps furnishes a certain clarity in that respect.
But, given Freire's explicit rejection of behaviorism and technocratic reductionism (see chapters 2 and 7), this is obviously not a form of lucidity
he would support: in systematizing conscientization in this manner, the
concept is arguably stripped of the very features that give it its educational significance. What, then, can be offered as an alternative interpretation?

Freire's discussion of magical consciousness and naïve consciousness
is largely confined to two early works, *Education: The Practice of Freedom*
(1976) and *Cultural Action for Freedom* (1972b). In his classic text, *Pedagogy
of the Oppressed*, new terms such as "critical thinking," "real consciousness," and "potential consciousness" emerge, but there is little overt talk
of magical and naïve stages of consciousness (see Freire, 1972a, pp. 65,
85). The need for a critical approach in understanding reality remained
a key theme in Freire's work throughout his publishing career, and in
some of his later works (1994, 1996, 1998c), he started commenting in a
little more detail on conscientization again. Freire refers to the continuing
propensity among some illiterate communities to view their social circumstances in fatalistic terms, and speaks of the ongoing need for conscientization in addressing problems such as hunger (1996, pp. 182–183).
Although references to naïve thinking can be found in many of Freire's
books, the concept of naïveté appears broader in later statements than
the initial formulation in *Education: The Practice of Freedom* and *Cultural
Action for Freedom*. Freire's construction of descriptive statements for
three contrasting levels of consciousness in these early texts is not duplicated in his later works. The important point, for present purposes, is
that the categories of magical consciousness and naïve consciousness
were originally developed by Freire to explain *specific* situations (namely,
the conditions that prevailed in urban and rural areas in Brazil during
and before the early 1960s). Some of the features of these modes of consciousness persist in places today, but Freire never intended the categories to be taken as descriptors of ahistorical, universal stages for all
individuals in every society to pass through.

It is also instructive to note that Freire has usually avoided using the
term "consciousness raising" in his books, articles, and interviews. Given
the relatively small number of exceptions to this, it is possible that where
the term has emerged under Freire's name (e.g., Freire, 1975; 1994, p. 104)
it has been as a result of the translation from Portuguese to English. It
is undeniable that Freire regarded critical consciousness as an ethically
preferable mode of being for Brazilian adults when compared with magical and naïve modes of consciousness. In this sense, it could be said that
he hoped illiterates would "raise" their consciousnesses to a "higher"
level. But Freire avoids talk of the logical corollary to this, namely, the

notion that some people are at a "lower" level of consciousness than others. It would be more accurate, I believe (despite Berger's criticisms), to say that Freire simply identified different ways of making sense of the world, some of which were less likely than others to disrupt the status quo. He is careful (again, contra Berger and Bowers) not to denigrate the people with whom he was working by declaring them lower beings. His point in identifying magical and naïve modes of consciousness is that these forms of thought are shaped by, and serve the interests of, oppressor classes. If there is any group at risk of being "denigrated" by Freire, it is those who deliberately promote a view of the world that reproduces an oppressive social order.

Although Freire's initial use of the concept of conscientization in *Education: The Practice of Freedom* and *Cultural Action for Freedom* exhibited some features of what I have called "the stages model," subsequent (and other) work lends support to an alternative interpretation of conscientization. In his essay, "The Process of Political Literacy," for example, Freire suggests that conscientization involves "a constant clarification of what remains hidden within us while we move about the world." Conscientization "cannot ignore the transforming action that produces this unveiling," and "occurs as a process at any given moment" (in Freire, 1985, p. 107). This suggests that Freire intended conscientization to be seen not as a progression through a finite series of steps with a fixed set of attitudes and behaviors to be achieved, but rather as an ever-evolving process. This construct of conscientization stands in marked contrast to a theory based on distinct stages of consciousness. The stages model depends for its very intelligibility on the idea of sets of characteristics which endure for some period of time: There is no consideration of the possibility that people shift, from moment to moment, from one level to another. The process of moving from one stage to the next is gradual, difficult, and (for Smith) irreversible. On the alternative interpretation to be considered here, conscientization occurs incessantly, with no firm, fixed demarcations between levels or stages, and no end to the process.

I wish to extend this line of argument and draw a more overt connection between conscientization and praxis. I argued in chapter 2 that praxis is the pivotal concept in Freire's ethical ideal. We humanize ourselves, Freire argues, to the extent that we engage in praxis. The pursuit of one's humanization through praxis is, on the Freirean view, an inevitably incomplete process: the transformed reality which results from reflective action always presents a fresh set of (material or social) conditions, requiring further reflection. Freire, it will be recalled, stresses the fluid nature of both the material world and subjective reality. Not only are all aspects of the material world in motion; so too are consciousnesses always changing. Rejecting both mechanical objectivism and solipsistic idealism, Freire emphasizes the interaction between inner and outer dimensions of reality. We change the objective world through consciously directed activity, but our ideas are also shaped by material phenomena, processes, and activities. Aware of the need to avoid both activism and verbalism, Freire saw praxis as the *synthesis* of reflection and action.

Freire speaks of conscientization as "the process by which human beings participate critically in a transforming act" (p. 106), and stresses "there is no conscientization outside of praxis, outside the theory-practice, reflection-action unity" (p. 160). Conscientization, Freire notes elsewhere, "can only be manifested in the concrete praxis (which can never be limited to the mere activity of the consciousness)" (1976, p. 147). I propose, therefore, that rather than separating the two concepts out, as many people attempting to apply Freirean ideas do, conscientization and praxis ought to be seen as *necessarily* intertwined. Conscientization, I submit, is the reflective dimension of praxis. Hence, when one engages in praxis, one is of necessity being conscientized. Conscientization occurs in the transforming moment where critical reflection is synthesized with action.

Constant change in the world around us demands a continuous effort to reinterpret reality. As we have seen in previous chapters, Freire urges learners to take a restless, curious, searching, questioning stance in reading, writing, and thinking. He maintains that to the extent that reality is always changing, one can never know the object of one's study absolutely: one's knowledge of the world is necessarily incomplete. It is possible, however, to strive for an ever-deeper understanding of the essence or reason behind the object of study. These basic epistemological and educational ideas inform Freire's concept of conscientization. Conscientization demands a constant effort to probe beneath surface appearances. It is as if Freire wants us to peel back layer after layer of reality, searching all the time for a better understanding of the world. For Freire, knowledge is, in one sense, always *provisional*; it is that which we understand of reality as it exists at any given moment. The process of *searching* for knowledge, though, is continuous—a part of our ontological vocation as incomplete, inquiring beings. It is necessary, on the Freirean view, to see the posing and addressing problems, the asking of questions, the practice of dialogue, and the transformation of social reality as fundamental defining features of human existence. Conscientization can be seen as the educative process through which these related forms of human activity are brought together.

Freire's use of the concept of conscientization must be understood in relation to the original context within which it was applied. In promoting an alternative to the stages model, it is important to stress the *political* nature of conscientization in Freire's early work. The goal was critical reflection upon, and active transformation of, oppressive social structures and practices within Brazilian (and, later, Chilean) society. Conscientization, then, was tied directly to an explicit political agenda where it was assumed that certain groups were oppressed and that certain forms of praxis were necessary to address this oppression. The praxis championed by Freire was not simply reflective action designed to change *any* aspect of the world; rather, the aim was to foster critical teaching, learning, and dialogue relevant to the specific concerns of peasant communities and the urban poor in northeast Brazil. Freire was quite open about the political intentions of his literacy work, observing that all education serves certain interests, and he paid a heavy price—enforced exile—for this.

POSTMODERNISM, INDIVIDUALISM, AND CONSCIENTIZATION

I have identified two constructs of conscientization in Freire's work: a particular version of the stages model tied to an explicit political project, and a dialectical representation of conscientization as a continuous reflective process. Whereas the former conception is underwritten by behaviorist assumptions, the latter opens up the possibility of a reformulated notion of conscientization—one that is linked to the ideal of praxis but sensitive to criticisms of universalist thought and subject-centered reason. In this section, I argue against an individualist interpretation of critical consciousness, and reinterpret conscientization in the light of the postmodernist notion of multiple subjectivities.

Where modern thought has placed the unified, autonomous subject at its center, postmodern social philosophy decenters the subject and rejects the ideal of a self-directing, self-knowing, individual agent. Postmodernists underscore the multiplicity of (sometimes contradictory) subject positions assumed by human beings (Weiler, 1991). We become, as it were, an amalgam of many different "selves." There is no "essential" or "unencumbered" self. All individuals are constituted within discourses or sign systems (Gee, 1993). In the face of these challenges to fundamental modernist principles, Smith's categorization of individuals into neatly defined, closed "boxes" (as magical, naïve, or critical) seems quaint and artificial. From a postmodernist perspective, it becomes impossible to conceive of a quintessentially magical (or naïve, or critical) individual. Smith's portrayal of conscientization as a *linear* progression through successive, irreversible stages is equally worrying given the postmodernist view of history as discontinuous, disorderly, and nonsequential (cf. Benhabib, 1991).

These concerns also apply, to a certain extent, to Freire's early writings on conscientization. Elements of Freire's work resonate with some ideas on texts and contexts advanced by postmodernists in such fields as literary criticism and cultural studies (Peters, 1999). However, as I argued in chapter 6, the ontological, epistemological, and ethical principles which underpin Freire's pedagogy work are essentially modernist. The demise of subject-centered reason (Peters and Marshall, 1993) poses particular difficulties for Freirean theory. Freire explicitly situates the knowing, praxical, dialogical human Subject (the capitalization is Freire's) at the center of his ethic, and in the notion of conscientization, we find the educational manifestation par excellence of this ideal. Education on the Freirean view should (among other things) enable people to more deeply perceive the contradictions of social life, probing beneath the superficiality of surface appearances, while simultaneously entering the historical process as a critically conscious Subjects. Becoming critically conscious affirms humans as beings who create history and culture. The critically conscious person thus appears, at first glance, to be the very embodiment of the self-knowing, self-directing, self-contained subject so central to the Enlightenment project. Critical consciousness not only implies an ability to transform the world, but a *self-conscious, reflective, rational* process of change.

Bowers (1983, p. 943) maintains that Freirean adult literacy programs are built on an existentialist-humanist view of individualism, from which Freire derives the notion that "rational thought should govern individual choice." Freire begins with the liberal Enlightenment construct of the individual as a "self-forming and directing being" (Bowers, 1986, p. 151). Building on the shift from a medieval to a modern Western consciousness, which carried with it an attack on received traditions of authority (Bowers, 1983, p. 945), Freire's pedagogy privileges personal and social change over tradition and continuity. The constant problematization of daily life implied by Freire's ethic, and by critical consciousness in particular, is, in Bowers's view, characteristically Western and unavoidably individualist. Freire moderates his ideal of critical reflection by "saying that learning to think must lead to democratic and mutually responsible forms of community" (p. 937), but he does not resolve the tension between the authority of individual judgment and "the forms of authority that give community a sense of coherent identity and purpose" (Bowers, 1986, p. 150).

Bowers's claim that "consciousness raising" (to use the term he generally employs) is an individualist ideal is reinforced by the stages interpretation of conscientization represented in the work of such people as Smith and Alschuler. For Smith, conscientization is conceived as a process of individual development. Further support for an individualist account of conscientization is furnished by the wide variety of "empowering" pedagogies which purport to be Freirean in orientation. Many of these concentrate on *self*-empowerment and draw tacitly if not directly on the same assumptions which underpin Smith's understanding of conscientization. At stake is the ideal of an individual human being gaining greater control over his or her life through the acquisition or adoption of certain attitudes, modes of thought, and forms of behavior.

The characterization of conscientization in individualist terms does not square with Freire's stress on the collective, dialogical nature of liberating reflection and action for transformation. From his earliest writings, Freire emphasized the *social* character of conscientization: "It is sufficient to know that conscientization does not take place in abstract beings in the air but in real men and women and in social structures, to understand that it cannot remain on the level of the individual" (Freire, 1976, pp. 146–147). This point finds further support in one of Freire's last works, *Pedagogy of Freedom*, where he maintains that although the initial stimulus for a new perception of social reality may come from an individual, the experience that makes a breakthrough in awareness possible is *collective* (1998c, p. 77). The notion of dialogue is central to conscientization, as Freire conceives it, and must be understood in contextual, political terms. Dialogue, when viewed specifically as an aspect of the process of conscientization in Freirean adult literacy education, is not merely idle conversation, nor even simply an educative conversation in the general sense (i.e., a conversation through which learning takes place). Rather, it is, in part, explicitly directed toward identifying, analyzing, criticizing, and transforming conditions of oppression. The importance of collectivity for Freire cannot be overemphasized. Without it, he warns, those who wield the greatest power have a lever for fragmenting (and thus reducing the effectiveness of) struggles against dominant ideas and practices. Dialogue for conscientization implies a certain unity of purpose, originating in (what Freire sees as) the very nature of human *being* itself: the ontological vocation of humanization.

An individualist account of conscientization is (or ought to be) ontologically untenable given what it means to "truly" *be* for Freire. For being critical, dialogical, and praxical—that is to say, being a Subject in the Freirean sense—is in large part what being human entails. An individualist reading of conscientization (and Freirean theory more broadly) is also at odds with the Freirean concept of "knowing," suggesting an epistemological tension as well. As was noted in chapter 2, Freire argues that no one can "know" alone. Knowing requires the presence (though this does not have to be an immediate physical presence) of an "other" to gain its authenticity. Conscientization, apart from anything else, represents the process of coming to "know" the world in a different way. One dimension of this process is acquiring a sense of oneself as a being among others—that is, as a member of a class, or at least a group—such that personal difficulties come to be seen in their wider social context. This is a process of linking "biography" with "structure" (Mills, 1970), which is profoundly anti-individualist and which can only proceed authentically *through* a more collective (dialogical) approach toward education and the activities of daily life.

Smith and Alschuler might protest here that nothing in their analysis diminishes the importance of dialogue in Freire's ideal. One of the distinguishing features of critically conscious individuals is that they are dialogical. Naïvely conscious individuals analyze and confront the world in reformist terms, often shunning relationships with their peers and disavowing their class origins (see Smith, 1976, pp. 52, 58). Magically conscious individuals have no sense of themselves as beings *with* as well as *in* the world, and no conception of life on a more historic and social plane. Their existence is defined by the struggle to survive rather than the need to flourish (compare, Freire, 1976, p. 17). Yet, in locating the process of conscientization within the discourse of individualism—and more specifically (in Smith's case) within the Kohlbergian approach to developmental psychology—a significant break from Freire's overall intentions in employing the term conscientization has already been made. Freire does not deny that individuals will (or ought) to change through the conscientization process, but this must be seen alongside the wider phenomenon of *social* transformation. The "I think" is only possible (Freire believes) through a corresponding "we think." Thus, to speak of conscientization as a movement in patterns of thought or behavior among individuals without tying this to a broader shift in collective consciousness is nonsensical from the Freirean point of view.

Bowers, however, would argue that the ethical assumptions underpinning concepts such as "dialogue" in Freire's philosophy are Western to the core and thus *necessarily* individualist. This idea, as I argued in the previous chapter, turns on a particular construction of "the" Western tradition and Freire's relationship to this (and place in it). Bowers assumes that underlying or "driving" all of Freire's theorizing is a specific way of looking at the world: a mode of consciousness which can be described as the Western mind-set. At the heart of this mind-set are certain presuppositions about (the value of) rationality, control, agency, and change. Dialogue may involve discussion between two or more people—and Freire may talk of the importance of fostering collective relationships, an awareness of class, and a sense of community—but Bowers might say that the modes of human thought and action which occur within dialogical and communal settings are still centered on the individual.

Although the characteristics of critical consciousness outlined in *Education: The Practice of Freedom* bear some resemblance to ideals often associated with liberal individualism, Freire's statements must be read in conjunction with other sections in this text, studied alongside other writings, and examined in light of Freire's *practice* of conscientization in his adult literacy work. Freire's ethic is not built on the idea of unified individuals making "free," autonomous choices in a contextless vacuum. The notion of conscientization, in fact, rests in large measure on assumptions which directly oppose this view. As human beings, Freire argues, we are always socially, culturally, and politically "situated." Human consciousnesses are constituted within ideological frameworks (some identifiable, others sometimes unnoticed given our immersion within them), through relationships with others and with an ever-changing world. The very justification for conscientization depends on an acknowledgment that consciousnesses are never "pure," but always shaped or conditioned. Freire speaks—in *Education: The Practice of Freedom*, as well as in later books, of thinking, acting, and knowing as *social* events (see, for example, pp. 134–135). He is adamant that we cannot think, speak, read, write, learn, or *be* alone. *To be human* is to be a social being. Humans are beings of relationships: beings whose very existence cannot be comprehended without reference to others.

Freire explicitly rejects the Cartesian notion of self-identical, self-knowing "I" and replaces it with the dialogical, socially constituted "we." Clearly, then, he does not embrace a pure, "atomistic" notion of individual rational autonomy. Bowers would concede this, but argue that in placing the reflective Subject at the center of his ethic, Freire cannot avoid fostering a certain form of individualism. The critical reflection in Freirean dialogue, Bowers would argue, presupposes an "individual-like intentionality" (Bowers, 1986, p. 150). This, I believe, is a distortion of the Freirean ideal. It is true that Freire conceives of consciousness—and, by implication, reflection—as "intentionality toward the world," but this is not an "individual-like" intentionality. When we turn to world to examine it, or attempt to step back from our immediate surroundings to more clearly perceive the nature of our problems, we do so with a reflective intentionality that is already, and necessarily, socially formed. Consciousnesses are created in a social world, through interaction with that world. We can strive to know or understand ourselves in relation to the world, but we cannot autonomously constitute ourselves as knowers. As McLaren and Hammer (1989) argue, and this is consistent with Freire's position, human beings are *self-conscious* rather than *self-constituting*. Although we do not individuate our own consciousnesses, we can nevertheless become *sufficiently* self-conscious to "recognize our own constitution outside of the exigencies of our own volition." Crucially, it is our self-consciousness of the constitution of selves which *makes liberation possible* (p. 49).

An important element of conscientization is precisely this: the development of a deeper (self-conscious) understanding of the ways in which we are *not* merely isolated, self-constituting individuals. Dialogue, the means through which this growing realization emerges, can never be simply a collection of individual consciousnesses. Consciousnesses are

socially constituted before dialogue even begins, and they are reconstituted through purposeful communication with others. The ideas generated
through dialogue are more than the sum of individual contributions:
they are the *synthesis* of a dialogical relation, mediated by an object of
study, between two or more partially self-conscious Subjects seeking to
know and to transform the world.

Freire does not use the language of discourse analysis, but his theory
of conscientization—when viewed in relation to his philosophy as a
whole, and considered in the light of his later writings—is compatible
in many respects with insights from work in this area. All of us, Freire
wants to say, operate within and through multiple discourses. (The term
"discourse" here is used in the broadest sense to mean "a way of being
in the world.") Conscientization is, to some extent, concerned with ex-
panding the range of discourses within which people might actively and
reflectively participate. This is not merely a shift in "sign systems," but
a change in the concrete practices of everyday life. There is thus a material as well as an "intellectual" basis to conscientization. Being critically
conscious implies a continuous process of transformation. People who
undergo conscientization are constantly being reconstituted, as they critically reflect on reality, act, change both themselves and the world
around them, reflect again on the new reality which results from transformation, carry out further actions as necessary, and so on.

The conscientized Freirean Subject is therefore a subject "on the
move," a being who both shapes reality and is shaped by it. The subject
remains the "home of consciousness" (Oliver, 1991, p. 178) in Freirean
theory, but the consciousness which "resides" in a given subject is never
stable. The subject for Freire is neither completely self-constituting and
self-directing nor a totally decentered network of crisscrossing desires
(cf. Eagleton, 1985, pp. 71–72). Freire retains the view that people can
resist oppressive structures, ideas, and practices—consciously, reflectively, and deliberately. Such resistance, though, which is at the heart of
conscientization, always takes place within ideological and political limits, must be forged dialogically with others, and is necessarily incomplete. The Freirean conception of agency, especially as represented in the
notion of conscientization, thus falls between the liberal individualist
view and a fully developed postmodern position.

The postmodernist notion of multiple subjectivities suggests a reorien-
tation in thinking about conscientization. Individuals can certainly no
longer be neatly categorized into "personality types," nor adequately
described as being at a (single) particular level of consciousness. For, on
the postmodernist view of subjectivity, we live in and through a plethora
of different discourses. In his later years, Freire acknowledged that these
discourses are frequently contradictory. If the original construct of conscientization as a process of moving from a state of either magical or

naïve consciousness toward "critical" consciousness is reconsidered, a postmodernist perspective implies constant movement between the three levels. The assumption that one cannot display characteristics of more than one stage of consciousness in any given period becomes highly questionable.

Taking Freire's initial list of characteristics at each stage as a starting point, imagine the case of a Brazilian peasant supposedly at a magical level of consciousness. Under a strict stages model, such an individual would not be expected to display any of the characteristics typical of critical consciousness. "Depth in the interpretation of problems," "the testing of one's 'findings,' " "openness to revision," and the avoidance of distortion in the perception of problems are all features of critical consciousness (see Freire, 1976, p. 18). Peasants might not display these characteristics with respect to their understanding and evaluation of political problems, but it is surely possible that such qualities would be in evidence in their management of land and crops. Making the most of the land involves balancing a complex range of factors pertaining to soil, plants, the weather, irrigation, crop rotation, and so on. The depth in interpretation of the various elements necessary for effective crop production is likely to have been considerable; many peasants would have "tested" their "findings" in employing different methods of using the soil from year to year; and revision of planting or harvesting procedures in the light of experience would have been almost essential.

The notion of occupying multiple stage positions by displaying characteristics from several levels not only seems possible but probable, given a moment's reflection on everyday experiences. Conceivably, a person might be classed as magical, naïve, *and* critical, depending on the sphere of that person's life under examination. People might display the qualities associated with critical consciousness within one discursive setting, while acting in typically magical or naïve ways in other situations. I may develop a sophisticated, critical understanding of party politics, yet at the same time explain events in my family life in terms of fate or the workings of some higher power. Or, I may exhibit all the qualities of critical consciousness in my professional life (e.g., as a teacher), yet display a naïve understanding of environmental issues. At any given moment, a person thinks, feels, and acts in a particular way, within a discursive framework which constructs limits and possibilities for being and doing. Almost simultaneously, however, a specific orientation toward the world can be transformed as people shift from one discourse to another, or move between different "moments" within a single discursive setting.

There are thus no fixed stages of consciousness with clear-cut distinguishing characteristics at each level. People experience, engage, and construct social reality in different ways within different discourses, ma-

terial circumstances, and historical moments. We do not remain perma-
nently conscientized, or "locked in" to a particular way of thinking;
conscientization takes place as a momentary process. The focus is no
longer on a single, "self-contained," self-knowing human subject directing his or her life in an increasingly critical fashion. If there is no essential
self, then we can only talk of a person as he or she "is" at any given
moment engaging in reflective action. Through conscientization, a person
shifts his or her "position" in the world, though not in the ordered,
sequential, behaviorist fashion implied by the stages model.

CONCLUDING COMMENTS

If the original impetus for, and purpose of, conscientization is to be
retained, particular emphasis must be placed on enhancing possibilities
for moments of dialogical, critical reflection on conditions of oppression.
To denude conscientization of its political character and liberatory intent
is to destroy the very purpose for which the term was initially employed.
In *Letters to Cristina*, Freire claims that the ideal of a revolutionary critical
consciousness, although more difficult to uphold, "continues to be essential and possible" (1996, p. 119). He points to significant gains during
the "lost" decades of the 1980s and 1990s, such as land rights for the
landless and new community schools for those previously denied the
opportunity of a formal education, while also highlighting the enormous
impediments to further change (political corruption, drug dealing, corporate greed, continuing poverty, etc.). As time has passed, responses to
conscientization have shifted. "Yesterday," Freire observes, "conscientization was seen as a devilish instrument, and I was seen as the devil
himself, threatening the suffering souls of so many innocents with destruction." Now "immobilists" cast conscientization, dreams, and utopias
aside in favor of scientific and technical efficiency (p. 136). Fatalistic neoliberal discourses, along with new forms of capitalist hegemony under
globalization and the saturation of everyday life by carefully constructed
media images, give the project of conscientization renewed significance
(cf. Freire, 1998c, pp. 55, 114, 124; Mayo, 1996). Conscientization remains,
in Freire's words, "a requirement of our human condition" (Freire, 1998c,
p. 55).

The postmodern turn in social theory does not, to my way of thinking,
rule out the possibility of *attempting* to understand—and act within and
upon—the world in ever more critical ways. From a postmodernist point
of view, however, any effort to act or think in a particular manner must
be recognized as partial, incomplete, and possibly contradictory. Indeed,
an important dimension of critically conscious activity is the process of
reflecting on the embeddedness of one's own views within multiple discourses. This demands an exhaustive attempt to examine processes of

discursive construction and the historical formation of subjectivities—especially those associated with modes of oppression and liberation. Critical theoretical analysis, political commitment, and social action may all be inevitably provisional in postmodern times, but this does not make them any less necessary. Three decades have passed since Freire published his first thoughts on conscientization, and many new challenges to humanization now exist. As we confront these challenges, and those of the future, there is potentially much that might be gained in rethinking the concept of conscientization as an educational ideal and in applying it as a powerful force for social change.

NOTE

1. See, for example, Lloyd (1972); Sanders (1972); Gleeson (1974); Elias (1974); Plunkett (1978); Bock (1980); Shor (1980); Kilian (1988); O'Hara (1989); and Burstow (1989).

Bibliography

Alschuler, A. (1976) Foreword, in W. Smith, *The Meaning of Conscienti-zacao: The Goal of Paulo Freire's Pedagogy*, pp. v–viii. Amherst, MA: Center for International Education.

Aristotle (1976) *Ethics* (The Nicomachean Ethics), revised ed., trans. J. A. K. Thomson. Harmondsworth: Penguin.

Aronowitz, S. (1993) Paulo Freire's radical democratic humanism. In P. McLaren & P. Leonard (eds.), *Paulo Freire: A Critical Encounter*, pp. 8–24. London: Routledge.

Ashton-Warner, S. (1966) *Teacher*. Harmondsworth: Penguin.

Bartolome, L. I. (1994) Beyond the methods fetish: towards a humanizing pedagogy. *Harvard Educational Review*, 64 (2), pp. 173–194.

Bee, B. (1980) The politics of literacy. In R. Mackie (ed.) *Literacy and Revolution: The Pedagogy of Paulo Freire*, pp. 39–56. London: Pluto Press.

Beilharz, P. (1991) Back to postmodernity. *Thesis Eleven*, 29, pp. 111–118.

Benhabib, S. (1991) Feminism and postmodernism: An uneasy alliance. *Praxis International*, 11 (2), pp. 137–149.

Berger, P. (1974) "Consciousness raising" and the vicissitudes of policy. In *Pyramids of Sacrifice: Political Ethics and Social Change*, pp. 111–132. New York: Basic Books.

Bloom, A. (1988) *The Closing of the American Mind*. New York: Simon and Schuster.

Bock, S. (1980) Conscientization: Paulo Freire and class-based practice. *Catalyst*, 6, pp. 5–24.

Boler, M. (1999) Posing some feminist queries to Freire. In P. Roberts (ed.), *Paulo Freire, Politics and Pedagogy: Reflections from Aotearoa-New Zealand*, pp. 61–69. Palmerston North: Dunmore Press.

Bowers, C. A. (1983) Linguistic roots of cultural invasion in Paulo Freire's pedagogy. *Teachers College Record*, 84 (4), pp. 935–953.

——. (1984) The problem of individualism and community in neo-Marxist educational thought. *Teachers College Record*, 85 (3), pp. 365–390.

——. (1986) Review of Freire, P., *The Politics of Education: Culture, Power, and Liberation*. (Mass.: Bergin and Garvey, 1985). *Educational Studies*, 17 (1), pp. 147–154.

——. (1991a) Some questions about the anachronistic elements in the Giroux-McLaren theory of critical pedagogy. *Curriculum Inquiry*, 21 (1), pp. 239–252.

——. (1991b) Critical pedagogy and the "arch of social dreaming": A response to the criticisms of Peter McLaren. *Curriculum Inquiry*, 21 (4), pp. 479–487.

Brady, J. (1994) Critical literacy, feminism and a politics of representation. In P. McLaren and C. Lankshear (eds.) *Politics of Liberation: Paths from Freire*, pp. 142–153. London: Routledge.

Brandes, D. (1971) Education for liberation: An interview with Paulo Freire. Transcript of an interview conducted for the Canadian Broadcasting Corporation television programme "Something Else," June 18.

Brown, C. (1974) Literacy in 30 hours: Paulo Freire's process in northeast Brazil. *Social Policy*, 5 (2), pp. 25–32.

Bruss, N., and Macedo, D. (1985) Toward a pedagogy of the question: Conversations with Paulo Freire. *Journal of Education*, 167 (2), pp. 7–21.

Buber, M. (1958) *I and Thou*, trans. R. G. Smith. Edinburgh: T. and T. Clark.

——. (1961) *Between Man and Man*, trans. R. G. Smith. London: Fontana.

Burstow, B. (1989) Conscientization: A new direction for ex-inmate education. *International Journal of Lifelong Education*, 8 (1), pp. 25–45.

Cabral, A. (1980) *Unity and Struggle*. London: Heinemann.

Castells, M., Flecha, R., Freire, P., Giroux, H. A., Macedo, D., and Willis, P. (1999) *Critical Education in the New Information Age*. Lanham, Md.: Rowman and Littlefield.

Chesterfield, R., and Schutz, P. (1978) Nonformal continuing education in rural Brazil. *Lifelong Learning: The Adult Years*, 2 (2), pp. 12–16.

Coben, D. (1998) *Radical Heroes: Gramsci, Freire and the Politics of Adult Education*. New York: Garland.

Connolly, R. (1980) Freire, praxis and education. In R. Mackie (ed.), *Literacy and Revolution: The Pedagogy of Paulo Freire*, pp. 70–81. London: Pluto Press.

Darling, J. (1994) *Child-Centred Education and Its Critics*. London: Paul Chapman.

Davis, R. (1980) Education for awareness: a talk with Paulo Freire. In R. Mackie (ed.), *Literacy and Revolution: The Pedagogy of Paulo Freire*, pp. 57–69. London: Pluto Press.

Declaration of Persepolis (1976). In L .B. Bataille (ed.), *A Turning Point for Literacy*, pp. 273–276. Oxford: Pergamon Press.

Descartes, R. (1931) *The Philosophical Works of Descartes*, Vol.1, trans. E. S. Haldane and G. R. T. Ross. London: Cambridge University Press.

Dillon, D. (1985) Reading the world and reading the word: An interview with Paulo Freire. *Language Arts*, 62 (1), pp. 15–21.

Eagleton, T. (1985) Capitalism, modernism and postmodernism. *New Left Review*, 152, pp. 60–73.

Elias, J. L. (1974) Social learning and Paulo Freire. *Journal of Educational Thought*, 8 (1), pp. 5–14.

———. (1994) *Paulo Freire: Pedagogue of Liberation*. Malabar, Fla.: Krieger.

Ellsworth, E. (1989) Why doesn't this feel empowering? Working through the repressive myths of critical pedagogy. *Harvard Educational Review*, 59 (3), pp. 297–324.

Escobar, M., Fernandez, A. L., Guevara-Niebla, G., and Freire, P. (1994) *Paulo Freire on Higher Education: A Dialogue at the National University of Mexico*. Albany: State University of New York Press.

Fanon, F. (1967) *The Wretched of the Earth*, trans. C. Farrington. Harmondsworth: Penguin.

Findsen, B. (1999) Freire and adult education: Principles and practice. In P. Roberts (ed.), *Paulo Freire, Politics and Pedagogy: Reflections from Aotearoa-New Zealand*, pp. 71–82. Palmerston North: Dunmore Press.

Fonseca, C. (1973) Paulo Freire in Bombay. *New Frontiers in Education*, 3 (2), pp. 92–98.

Freire, A. M. A., and Macedo, D. (1998) Introduction. In Freire, A. M. A. and Macedo, D. (eds.) (1998a), *The Paulo Freire Reader*, pp. 1–44. New York: Continuum.

Freire, P. (1969) Cultural liberty in Latin America. *International Catholic Auxiliaries News*, 7 (1), pp. 2–6.

———. (1970a) Cultural action. Lecture delivered at CIDOC, Cuernavaca, January.

———. (1970b) Showing a man how to name the world. *New World Outlook*, August, pp. 16–17.

———. (1970c) Development and educational demands. *World Christian Education*, 25 (3), pp. 125–126.

———. (1971a) By learning they can teach. *Studies in Adult Education*, 2, pp. 1–9.

———. (1971b) Education as cultural action: an introduction, in L. M. Colonnese (ed.), *Conscientization for Liberation*, pp. 109–122. Washington, D.C., Division for Latin America.

————. (1972a) *Pedagogy of the Oppressed*. Harmondsworth: Penguin.

————. (1972b) *Cultural Action for Freedom*. Harmondsworth: Penguin.

————. (1972c) The third world and theology. *LADOC*, March, pp. 1–3.

————. (1974a) Research methods. *Literacy Discussion*, Spring, pp. 133–142.

————. (1974b) Conscientisation. *Month*, May, pp. 575–578.

————. (1975) Oppression. *LADOC*, September-October, pp. 16–19.

————. (1976) *Education: The Practice of Freedom*. London: Writers and Readers.

————. (1978) *Pedagogy in Process: The Letters to Guinea-Bissau*. London: Writers and Readers.

————. (1979) Letter to adult education workers. In *Learning by Living and Doing*, pp. 27–32. Geneva: IDAC.

————. (1981) The people speak their word: Learning to read and write in Sao Tome and Principe. *Harvard Educational Review*, 51 (1), pp. 27–30.

————. (1983) The importance of the act of reading. *Journal of Education*, 165 (1), pp. 5–11.

————. (1985) *The Politics of Education*. London: Macmillan.

————. (1987) Letter to North-American teachers. In I. Shor (ed.), *Freire for the Classroom*, pp. 211–214. Portsmouth, NH: Boynton/Cook.

————. (1993a) *Pedagogy of the City*. New York: Continuum.

————. (1993b) Foreword. In P. McLaren and P. Leonard (eds.), *Paulo Freire: A Critical Encounter*, pp. ix–xii. London: Routledge.

————. (1994) *Pedagogy of Hope: Reliving Pedagogy of the Oppressed* New York: Continuum.

————. (1996) *Letters to Cristina: Reflections on My Life and Work*. London: Routledge.

————. (1997a) *Pedagogy of the Heart*. New York: Continuum.

————. (1997b) A response. In P. Freire, J. W. Fraser, D. Macedo, T. McKinnon, and W. T. Stokes (eds.), *Mentoring the Mentor: A Critical Dialogue with Paulo Freire*, pp. 303–329. New York: Peter Lang.

————. (1998a) *Teachers as Cultural Workers: Letters to Those Who Dare Teach*. Boulder, Colo.: Westview Press.

————. (1998b) *Politics and Education*. Los Angeles: UCLA Latin American Center Publications.

————. (1998c) *Pedagogy of Freedom: Ethics, Democracy, and Civic Courage*. Lanham, Md.: Rowman and Littlefield.

————, and Faundez, A. (1989) *Learning to Question: A Pedagogy of Liberation*. Geneva: World Council of Churches.

Freire, P., and Fraser, J. W., Macedo, D., McKinnon, T. and Stokes, W. T. (eds.), (1997) *Mentoring the Mentor: A Critical Dialogue with Paulo Freire*. New York: Peter Lang.

Freire, P., and Macedo, D. (1987) *Literacy: Reading the Word and the World*. London: Routledge and Kegan Paul.

———. (1993) A dialogue with Paulo Freire. In P. McLaren and P. Leonard (eds.), *Paulo Freire: A Critical Encounter*, pp. 169–176. London, Routledge.

———. (1995) A dialogue: Culture, language, and race. *Harvard Educational Review*, 65 (3), pp. 377–402.

———. (1999) *Ideology Matters*. Lanham, Md.: Rowman Littlefield.

Freire, P. and Shor, I. (1987) *A Pedagogy for Liberation*. London: Macmillan.

Fromm, E. (1984) *The Fear of Freedom*. London: Ark.

Gee, J. P. (1988) The legacies of literacy: from Plato to Freire through Harvey Graff. *Harvard Educational Review*, 58 (2), pp. 195–212.

———. (1993) Postmodernism and literacies. In P. McLaren and P. Leonard (eds.), *Critical Literacy: Politics, Praxis, and the Postmodern*, pp. 271–296. Albany: State University of New York Press.

Gerhardt, H-P. (1993) Paulo Freire. *Prospects*, 23 (3/4), pp. 439–458.

Giroux, H. A. (1981) *Ideology, Culture, and the Process of Schooling*. London: Falmer.

———. (1985) Introduction. In P. Freire, *The Politics of Education*, pp. xi–xxv. London: Macmillan.

———. (1987) Introduction. In P. Freire and D. Macedo, *Literacy: Reading the Word and the World*, pp. 1–27. London: Routledge.

———. (1988) Border pedagogy in the age of postmodernism. *Journal of Education*, 170 (3), pp. 162–181.

———. (1993) Paulo Freire and the politics of postcolonialism. In P. McLaren and P. Leonard (eds.), *Paulo Freire: A Critical Encounter*, pp. 177–188. London: Routledge.

Gleeson, D. (1974) "Theory and practice" in the sociology of Paulo Freire. *Universities Quarterly*, 28 (3), pp. 362–371.

Goodman, P. (1971) *Compulsory Miseducation*. Harmondsworth: Penguin.

Graff, H. J. (1987) *The Labyrinths of Literacy*. London: Falmer.

Gramsci, A. (1971) *Selections from the Prison Notebooks*, Eds. Q. Hoare and G. Nowell Smith. London: Lawrence and Wishart.

Harris, K. (1979) *Education and Knowledge*. London: Routledge and Kegan Paul.

———. (1990) Empowering teachers: Towards a justification for intervention. *Journal of Philosophy of Education*, 24 (2), pp. 171–183.

Hassan, I. (1993) Toward a concept of postmodernism. In T. Docherty (ed.), *Postmodernism: A Reader*, pp. 146–156. London: Harvester Wheatsheaf.

Hill, B. (1974) When I met Marx, I continued to meet Christ on the corners of the street. *Age*, 19 April.

Holt, J. (1969) *How Children Fail*. Harmondsworth: Penguin.

———. (1970) *How Children Learn*. Harmondsworth: Penguin.

———. (1971) *The Underachieving School*. Harmondsworth: Penguin.

Horton, M. and Freire, P. (1990) *We Make the Road by Walking: Conver-*

sations on Education and Social Change, Eds. B. Bell, J. Gaventa, and J. Peters. Philadelphia: Temple University Press.

Illich, I. (1971) *Deschooling Society.* Harmondsworth: Penguin.

Janmohamed, A. R. (1994) Some implications of Paulo Freire's border pedagogy. In H. A. *Giroux* and P. McLaren (eds.), *Between Borders: Pedagogy and the Politics of Cultural Studies,* pp. 242–252. London: Routledge.

Jay, G. and Graff, G. (1995) A critique of critical pedagogy. In M. Berube and C. Nelson (eds.), *Higher Education under Fire: Politics, Economics, and the Crisis of the Humanities,* pp. 201–213. New York: Routledge.

Kilian, A. (1988) Conscientisation: An empowering, nonformal education approach for community health workers. *Community Development Journal,* 23 (2), pp. 17–123.

Kozol, J. (1978) A new look at the literacy campaign in Cuba. *Harvard Educational Review,* 48, pp. 341–377.

Lankshear, C. (1982) *Freedom and Education.* Auckland: Milton Brookes.

———. (1988) In whose interests? The role of intellectuals in New Zealand society. *Sites,* 17, pp. 3–21.

———. (1993) Functional literacy from a Freirean point of view. In P. McLaren and P. Leonard (eds.), *Paulo Freire: A Critical Encounter,* pp. 90–118. London: Routledge.

———. (1994a) Literacy and empowerment: discourse, power, critique. *New Zealand Journal of Educational Studies,* 29 (1), pp. 59–72.

———. (1994b) Afterword: Reclaiming empowerment and rethinking the past. In Escobar, M., Fernandez, A. L., Guevara-Niebla, G., with Freire, P., *Paulo Freire on Higher Education: A Dialogue at the National University of Mexico,* pp. 161–187. Albany: State University of New York Press.

———, with Lawler, M. (1987) *Literacy, Schooling and Revolution.* London: Falmer.

———, and McLaren, P. (1993) Preface. In C. Lankshear and P. McLaren (eds.), *Critical Literacy: Politics, Praxis, and the Postmodern,* pp. xii–xx. Albany: State University of New York Press.

Lister, I. (1973) Towards a pedagogy of the oppressed. *Times Higher Education Supplement,* September 13, pp. 13–14.

Lloyd, A. S. (1972) Freire, conscientization, and adult education. *Adult Education,* 23 (1), pp. 3–20.

Lopes-Correa, A. (1976) MOBRAL: Participation-reading in Brazil. *Journal of Reading,* 19 (7), pp. 534–539.

LP News Service (Lima, Peru) (1971) Conscientization, not magic, warns Paulo Freire. August 6.

Lyotard, J-F. (1984) *The Postmodern Condition: A Report on Knowledge,* trans. G. Bennington and B. Massumi. Minneapolis: University of Minnesota Press.

Macedo, D. (1993) Literacy for stupidification: the pedagogy of big lies. *Harvard Educational Review*, 63 (2), pp. 196–197.

———. (1994) Preface. In P. McLaren and C. Lankshear (eds.), *Politics of Liberation: Paths from Freire*, pp. xiii–xviii. London: Routledge.

Mackie, R. (1980a) Introduction. In R. Mackie (ed.), *Literacy and Revolution: The Pedagogy of Paulo Freire*, pp. 1–11. London: Pluto Press.

———. (1980b) Contributions to the thought of Paulo Freire. In R. Mackie (ed.), *Literacy and Revolution: The Pedagogy of Paulo Freire*, pp. 93–119. London: Pluto Press.

Makins, V. (1972) Interview with Paulo Freire. *The Times Educational Supplement*, October 20, p. 80.

Mao Tse-tung (1968) *Four Essays on Philosophy*. Peking: Foreign Languages Press.

Marx, K. (1970) *A Contribution to the Critique of Political Economy*. Moscow: Progress Publishers.

———. (1976) *Capital*, vol.1, trans. B. Fowkes. Harmondsworth: Penguin.

———, & Engels, F. (1967) *The Communist Manifesto*. Harmondsworth: Penguin.

———, & Engels, F. (1976) *The German Ideology*. Moscow: Progress Publishers.

Mayo, P. (1993) When does it work? Freire's pedagogy in context. *Studies in the Education of Adults*, 25 (1), pp. 11–30.

———. (1994) Gramsci, Freire and radical adult education: A few "blind spots." *Humanity and Society*, 18 (3), pp. 82–98.

———. (1995) Critical literacy and emancipatory politics: The work of Paulo Freire. *International Journal of Educational Development*, 15 (4), pp. 363–379.

———. (1996) Transformative adult education in an age of globalization: A Gramscian-Freirean synthesis and beyond. *Alberta Journal of Educational Research*, June, pp. 148–160.

———. (1997) Tribute to Paulo Freire (1921–1997). *International Journal of Lifelong Education*, 16 (5), pp. 365–370.

McLaren, P. (1991) The emptiness of nothingness: Criticism as imperial anti-politics. *Curriculum Inquiry*, 21 (4), pp. 459–477.

———, and Hammer, R. (1989) Critical pedagogy and the postmodern challenge: Toward a critical postmodernist pedagogy of liberation. *Educational Foundations*, 3 (3), pp. 29–62.

McLaren, P., and Lankshear, C. (eds.), (1994) *Politics of Liberation: Paths from Freire*. London: Routledge.

McLaren, P., and Leonard, P. (eds.), (1993a) *Paulo Freire: A Critical Encounter*. London: Routledge.

———. (1993b) Absent discourses: Paulo Freire and the dangerous memories of liberation. In P. McLaren and P. Leonard (eds.), *Paulo Freire: A Critical Encounter*, pp. 1–7. London: Routledge.

McLaren, P., and Silva, T. T. da (1991) Language, experience and pedagogy: A tribute to Paulo Freire. *Access*, 10 (1), pp. 38–48.

———. (1993) Decentering pedagogy: Critical Literacy, resistance and the politics of memory. In P. McLaren and P. Leonard (eds.), *Paulo Freire: A Critical Encounter*, pp. 47–89. London: Routledge.

Mills, C. W. (1970) *The Sociological Imagination*. Harmondsworth: Penguin.

Moreira, C. (1985) Planning literacy and post-literacy programmes for the implementation of basic education: The case of Brazil. In G. Carron and A. Bordia (eds.), *Issues in Planning and Implementing National Literacy Campaigns*, pp. 338–357. Paris: Unesco.

New Citizen (1974) Freire on free space. May 30.

O'Cadiz, M. del P., Wong, P. L., and Torres, C. A. (1998) *Education and Democracy: Paulo Freire, Social Movements, and Educational Reform in Sao Paulo*. Boulder, Colo.: Westview Press.

O'Hara, M. (1989) Person-centered approach as conscientizacao: The works of Carl Rogers and Paulo Freire. *Journal of Humanistic Psychology*, 29 (1), pp. 11–36.

Oliver, K. (1991) Fractal politics: How to use "the subject." *Praxis International*, 11 (2), pp. 178–194.

Peters, M. (1999) Freire and postmodernism. In P. Roberts (ed.), *Paulo Freire, Politics and Pedagogy: Reflections from Aotearoa-New Zealand*, pp. 113–122. Palmerston North: Dunmore Press.

———, and Lankshear, C. (1994) Education and hermeneutics: A Freirean interpretation. In P. McLaren and C. Lankshear (eds.), *Politics of Liberation: Paths from Freire*, pp. 173–192. London: Routledge.

Peters, M., and Marshall, J. (1993) Beyond the philosophy of the subject: Liberalism, education and the critique of individualism. *Educational Philosophy and Theory*, 25 (1), pp. 19–39.

Plato (1974) *The Republic*, 2d ed., trans. H. D. P. Lee. Harmondsworth: Penguin.

Plunkett, H. D. (1978) Modernization reappraised: The Kentucky mountains revisited and confrontational politics reassessed. *Comparative Education Review*, 22 (1), pp. 134–142.

Postman, N., and Weingartner, D. (1971) *Teaching as a Subversive Activity*. Harmondsworth: Penguin.

Reimer, E. (1971) *School Is Dead*. Harmondsworth: Penguin.

Roberts, P. (1993) Philosophy, education and knowledge: some comments on Bloom. *New Zealand Journal of Educational Studies*, 28 (2), pp. 165–180.

———. (1994) Education, dialogue and intervention: Revisiting the Freirean project. *Educational Studies*, 20 (3), pp. 307–327.

———. (1995a) Education, literacy and political commitment in post-modern times. *The Review of Education/Pedagogy/Cultural Studies*, 17 (1), pp. 55–73.

———. (1995b) Defining literacy: Paradise, nightmare or red herring? *British Journal of Educational Studies*, 43 (4), pp. 412–432.

———. (1996a) The danger of domestication: A case study. *International Journal of Lifelong Education*, 15 (2), pp. 94–106.

———. (1996b) Structure, direction and rigour in liberating education. *Oxford Review of Education*, 22 (3), pp. 295–316.

———. (1996c) Critical literacy, breadth of perspective, and universities: Applying insights from Freire. *Studies in Higher Education*, 21 (2), pp. 149–163.

———. (1996d) Defending Freirean intervention. *Educational Theory*, 46 (3), pp. 335–352.

———. (1996e) Rethinking conscientisation. *Journal of Philosophy of Education*, 30 (2), pp. 179–196.

———. (1997a) Paulo Freire and political correctness. *Educational Philosophy and Theory*, 29 (2), pp. 83–101.

———. (1997b) The consequences and value of literacy: A critical reappraisal. *Journal of Educational Thought*, 31 (1), pp. 45–67.

———. (1997c) Political correctness, great books and the university curriculum. In M. Peters (ed.), *Cultural Politics and the University*, pp. 103–134. Palmerston North: Dunmore Press.

———. (1998a) Beyond *Pedagogy of the Oppressed*: Reading Freire holistically. *New Zealand Journal of Adult Learning*, 26 (1), pp. 32–47.

———. (1998b) Knowledge, dialogue and humanization: The moral philosophy of Paulo Freire. *Journal of Educational Thought*, 32 (2), pp. 95–117.

———. (1998c) Extending literate horizons: Paulo Freire and the multidimensional word. *Educational Review*, 50 (2), pp. 105–114.

———. (1998d) Bloom on books, reading and the determination of greatness: A critique and an alternative. *Interchange: A Quarterly Review of Education*, 29 (3), pp. 245–260.

———. (1999a) A dilemma for critical educators? *Journal of Moral Education*, 28 (1), pp. 19–30.

———. (ed.) (1999b) *Paulo Freire, Politics and Pedagogy: Reflections from Aotearoa-New Zealand*. Palmerston North: Dunmore Press.

———. (1999c) Freire, neoliberalism and the university. In P. Roberts (ed.), *Paulo Freire, Politics and Pedagogy: Reflections from Aotearoa-New Zealand*, pp. 97–111. Palmerston North: Dunmore Press.

Rowe, K. (1974) Freire speaks on Freire. *Church and Community*, 13 (4), pp. 4–7.

Sanders, T. G. (1972) The Paulo Freire method: Literacy training and conscientization. In T. J. La Belle (ed.), *Education and Development: Latin America and the Caribbean*, pp. 587–599. Los Angeles: Latin American Center.

Sartre, J-P. (1969) *Being and Nothingness*, trans. Hazel E. Barnes. London: Methuen.

Scollon, R., and Scollon, S. B. K. (1979) *Linguistic Convergence: An Ethnography of Speaking at Fort Chipewyan*. New York: Academic Press.

Scott, J. C. (1990) *Domination and the Arts of Resistance: Hidden Transcripts*. New Haven: Yale University Press.

Shallcrass, J. (1974) The politics of education. *New Zealand Listener*, April 13, p. 24.

Shor, I. (1980) *Critical Teaching and Everyday Life*. Boston: South End Press.

———. (Ed.) (1987) *Freire for the Classroom*. Portsmouth, NH: Boynton/ Cook.

———. (1992) *Empowering Education: Critical Teaching and Social Change*. Chicago: Chicago University Press.

———. (1993) Education is politics. In P. McLaren and P. Leonard (eds.), *Paulo Freire: A Critical Encounter*, pp. 25–35. London: Routledge.

———. (1996) *When Students Have Power: Negotiating Authority in a Critical Pedagogy*. Chicago: Chicago University Press.

Smith, G. (1999) Paulo Freire: Lessons in transformative praxis. In P. Roberts (ed.), *Paulo Freire, Politics and Pedagogy: Reflections from Aotearoa-New Zealand*, pp. 35–41. Palmerston North: Dunmore Press.

Smith, W. (1976) *The Meaning of Conscientizacao: The Goal of Paulo Freire's Pedagogy*. Amherst, MA: Center for International Education.

Street, B. (1984) *Literacy in Theory and Practice*. Cambridge: Cambridge University Press.

Taboo: The Journal of Culture and Education (1997) Special issue on Paulo Freire, 2 (Fall), pp. 1–188.

Taylor, P. V. (1993) *The Texts of Paulo Freire*. Buckingham: Open University Press.

Teilhard de Chardin, P. (1959) *The Phenomenon of Man*. London: Collins.

Torres, C. A. (1994a) Paulo Freire as Secretary of Education in the municipality of Sao Paulo. *Comparative Education Review*, 38 (2), pp. 181–214.

———. (1994b) Education and the archeology of consciousness: Freire and Hegel. *Educational Theory*, 44 (4), pp. 429–445.

———, and Freire, P. (1994) Twenty years after *Pedagogy of the Oppressed*: Paulo Freire in conversation with Carlos Alberto Torres. In P. McLaren and C. Lankshear (eds.), *Politics of Liberation: Paths from Freire*, pp. 100–107. London: Routledge.

UNESCO Courier (1990) Reading the world (interview with Brazilian educator Paulo Freire), December, pp. 4–10.

Walker, J. (1980) The end of dialogue: Paulo Freire on politics and education. In R. Mackie (ed.), *Literacy and Revolution: The Pedagogy of Paulo Freire*, pp. 120–150. London: Pluto Press.

Weiler, K. (1991) Paulo Freire and a feminist pedagogy of difference. *Harvard Educational Review*, 61 (4), pp. 449–474.

———. (1996) Myths of Paulo Freire. *Educational Theory*, 46 (3), pp. 353–371.

West, C. (1993) Preface. In P. McLaren and P. Leonard (eds.), *Paulo Freire: A Critical Encounter*, pp. xiii–xiv. London: Routledge.

Index

Abreu, Vincente de, 85 n.3
Absolutes, 111
Action, 42–43
Activism, 43
Alschuler, Alfred, 143, 148, 150
Aristotle, 41–42
Aronowitz, Stanley, 15, 30
Arraes, Miguel, 75
Ashton-Warner, Sylvia, 103

Basic Church Communities, 4
Behaviorism, 36, 143
Beilharz, Peter, 110–11
Bell, Brenda, 26
Berger, Peter, 19, 97, 100, 140–41, 145
Binary oppositions, 72–73
Bowers, C. A., 19–20, 97–100, 119–36, 145, 148, 150
Brazil: Brazilian Institute of Higher Studies (ISEB), 138; Brazilian Literacy Movement, 82; Brazilian Workers' Party, 60; Freire's literacy work in, 75–83, 103–6; history of, 48, 128–29, 138–39; inequalities in, 8, 128; literacy and illiteracy in, 8–9. *See also* Freire, Paulo; Illiteracy; Literacy
Brenand, Francisco, 78
Brown, Cynthia, 85 n.3

Cabral, Amilcar, 58
Cabral, Mario, 99
Camara, Helder, 138
Capitalism, 47, 116
Catholic Action Movement, 4
Chardin, Teilhard de, concept of homonization, 40
Child-centered education, 55, 70–72
Chile: Chilean Agrarian Reform Corporation, 5, 83; Freire's work in, 83–84
Chipewyan, of Canada, 98–99, 120–28, 132, 135
Class: class consciousness, 47; class suicide, 58–59, 73 n.2; class

oppression, 109; class struggle, 129

Codifications, 77

Collectivity, 149. *See also* Liberation; Solidarity; Unity

Communication: intercommunication, 90; oral and literate modes, 91–93. *See also* Dialogue

Conscientization, 16, 19, 93–94, 137–55; and praxis, 141–47; stages model, 138–4. *See also* Consciousness; Consciousness raising; Praxis

Consciousness, 36, 151; critical consciousness, 106, 131, 133–34, 139–40, 142, 153; levels of consciousness, 129, 142–45; magical consciousness, 135, 138–39, 144, 150, 153; naïve consciousness, 135, 138–40, 144, 150, 153; revolutionary consciousness, 129–30. *See also* Class; Dialectic; Epistemology; Knowledge and knowing

Consciousness raising, 9, 19, 139–141, 144–45, 148. *See also* Conscientization; Consciousness

Critical Consciousness. *See* Consciousness

Cuban literacy crusade, 103

Culture: concept of, 77–80, 105–6; culture circles, 75–76, 82; Western and non-Western cultures, 120–22, 133–34, 150. *See also* Experience; Knowledge; "Western mind-set"

"Declaration of Persepolis," 83

Dehumanization, 44–45. *See also* Humanization; Liberation; Oppression

Descartes, René, 43

Deschooling, 10

Dialectic, 35–37, 110

Dialogue, 15, 43–44, 56, 149; between readers and texts, 91; and differences, 114–15; in Freirean literacy programs, 90–91; and individualism, 150–52; on Left and Right, 114; limits of, 103–6; silence in dialogical communication, 63; as structured and purposeful, 62–64. *See also* Communication

Discourse analysis, 152

Dogmatism, 115

Education: and academic rigor, 64–65; authoritarian and laissez-faire approaches, 59–61; banking education and problem-posing education, 1–2, 11–12, 13–14, 53–55, 66, 72–73; educational programs, 125; educators and teachers, 73 n.1; Freire's concept of, 126–27; and humor, 65–66; liberating education, 55–67; as manipulation, 61; as non-neutral, political process, 57–58, 135; problem-solving education, 55–56. *See also* Learning and teaching; Methods; Pedagogy; Questioning; Teaching

Ellsworth, Elizabeth, 19, 97, 101–2, 106–9

Empowerment, 15, 148–49

Engels, Friedrich, 45, 47

Epistemology, 37–40

Epoch, epochal themes and tasks, 48

Experience, 89–90; role in Western and non-Western cultures, 120–21, 125–26. *See also* Knowledge and knowing

Facilitators: compared with educators, 127; compared with teachers, 59–60. *See also* Education; Teaching

Fanon, Frantz, 28

Faundez, Antonio, 25–26

First World and Third World, 6–8, 17–18, 26, 48

Freedom, 46; and license, 61

Freire, Ana Maria Araujo, 6

Freire, Elza, 4, 85

Freire, Paulo: biography, 3–6; contextualizing his work, 8–10; critical reading of, 16–17; criticisms of his work, 2, 9–10, 19–20, 97–103; danger of domesticating his work, 6–17, 143, 146–47; holistic reading of, 10–13, 23–33; periods in writing career, 23–30; reductionism in applying Freirean ideas, 13–16; as Secretary of Education in São Paulo, 6, 8, 27. Works: *Cultural Action for Freedom*, 5, 19, 24, 87, 142, 144–45; *Cultural Education in the New Information Age*, 33 n.3; *Education: The Practice of Freedom*, 5, 19, 24, 30, 75, 142–43, 144–45, 150–51; *Ideology Matters*, 34 n.3; *Learning to Question*, 26, 32; *Letters to Cristina*, 28–29, 61, 116, 154; *Literacy: Reading the Word and the World*, 26, 95; *Paulo Freire on Higher Education: A Dialogue at the National University of Mexico*, 27; *A Pedagogy for Liberation*, 18, 25–26, 31–33, 65; *Pedagogy in Process: The Letters to Guinea-Bissau*, 5, 18, 24; *Pedagogy of Freedom*, 29–31, 43, 117; *Pedagogy of Hope*, 2, 27–28, 30, 59, 111–12, 119; *Pedagogy of the City*, 27; *Pedagogy of the Heart*, 28–29, 113–14; *Pedagogy of the Oppressed*, 1, 5, 9–10, 18, 23–24, 28, 30–33, 102; *Politics and Educa-*

tion, 29, 113, 129; *The Politics of Education*, 17, 24; *Teachers as Cultural Workers*; 31, 92; *We Make the Road by Walking: Conversations on Education and Social Change*, 26–27, 31–33. *See also* Brazil; Education; Epistemology; Knowledge and knowing; Literacy; Pedagogy

Gaventa, John, 26

Gee, James Paul, 85

Generative themes, 82

Generative words, 76–77, 80–82, 89, 91, 104

Giroux, Henry, 37, 38, 95, 102, 108, 110–11, 132

Goulart, Joao, 76

Graff, Gerald, 31–32

Guinea-Bissau, 25–26

Harris, Kevin, 127, 140–41

Hassan, Ihab, 111

Hegel, G.W.F., 35, 106

Historical vocation, 41

Horton, Myles, 26, 59

Humans and animals, 42

Humanization, 1, 41–43, 45, 117, 145, 149

Illich, Ivan, 10, 30

Illiteracy: disadvantages of, 87–88; illiteracy and structural injustices, 8, 88; in United States, 26. *See also* Brazil; Literacy; National Literacy Program; Nicaraguan Literacy Crusade; Reading "word" and "world"

Individualism, 99–100, 148–152

Inductive moments, 62

Intervention. *See* Pedagogy

Intolerance, 115

Jay, Stephen, 31–32

Knowledge and knowing: and conscientization, 146, 149; and experience, 121; Freire's theory of, 37–40; Plato's theory of, 38–40; and postmodernity, 115–16; and technocratic thought, 124. *See also* Culture; Epistemology; Experience; "Western mind-set"

Kohlberg, Lawrence, 140

Lankshear, Colin, 15, 21 n.9, 27

Learning, and teaching, 57, 73. *See also* Education; Methods; Pedagogy; Teaching

Leonard, Peter, 110–11, 112

Liberation, 45–48, 58, 106, 135. *See also* Dehumanization; Humanization; Oppression

Limit acts, 48

Limit situations, 48

Literacy: benefits of, 87–88; in Brazil, 8–9, 88; critical literacy, 19, 93–95; Freirean adult literacy education, 75–86, 89, 133; Freirean concept of, 85, 95–96; multidimensional word, 19, 91–93; National Literacy Program in Brazil, 76; as a political phenomenon, 88–89; postliteracy, 82; in United States, 26

Lopes-Correa, Arlindo, 82

Macedo, Donaldo, 25, 30, 59–60, 67–68, 109

McLaren, Peter, 40, 102, 110–11, 112, 132

Magical consciousness. *See* Consciousness

Mao, Tse-tung, 36; Maoists, 115

Maori, people of Aotearoa-New Zealand, 28, 103

Market, 117–18

Marx, Karl, 13, 35–37, 42, 45, 47, 106; Marxists, 115; Marx's view of class, 118

Mayer, R., 140

Mechanistic objectivism, 36

Melo, Collor de, 6

Methods, 13, 67–70. *See also* Education; Pedagogy

Modernism, Freire's, 97, 116–18

Moral principles, in Freire's work, 49–51

Municipal Bureau of Education (Brazil), 6

Naïve consciousness. *See* Consciousness

Naming the world, 44

National Literacy Program (Brazil), 5

Neoliberalism, 115–18

Nicaraguan literacy crusade, 5, 95–96

North and South. *See* First World and Third World

Ontological vocation, 41–42

Oppression: C. A. Bowers and question of oppression, 130–31; and conscientization, 154–55; Ellsworth's view, 106–9; Freire's view, 44–48, 109–110, 114–15; hierarchy of, 109; resistance against, 129–30. *See also* Class; Dehumanization; Humanization; Liberation

Pedagogy, 13, 16; in different contexts, 123–24; non-neutrality of pedagogical activity, 57; pedagogical intervention, 98–101, 125–131; pedagogical principles, 70. *See also* Education; Learning; Methods; Teaching

Peters, John, 26

Peters, Michael, 110–11

Plato, 38–40, 41
Politics: and/of education, 30, 57–
    59; on Left and Right, 114–15;
    of liberation, 44–48; of literacy,
    87–89; political unity, 115. *See*
    also Brazil; Education; Illiteracy;
    Literacy
"Popular Culture Notebooks," 84
Portuguese language, 25, 84, 144
Postmodernism, 101–3; and con-
    scientization, 147–55; dialectical
    postmodernism, 113; and dualis-
    tic thinking, 110–11; Freire's
    stance on, 111–16; progressive
    postmodernism, 112–13
Praxis, 38, 42, 49–51; and con-
    scientization, 145–47. *See also*
    Conscientization; Dialectic;
    Humanization; Humans and
    Animals; Knowledge and
    knowing
Problematization, 125
Problem-posing education. *See*
    Education

Questioning: in liberating educa-
    tion, 64, 125; as part of Freire's
    ethical ideal, 131–33, 136 n.8.
    See also Education

Reading "word" and "world," 1,
    91–95. *See also* Illiteracy; Liter-
    acy
Reflection, 42–43
Reimer, Everett, 10
Relativism: epistemological, 40,
    111; ethical, 111

São Tomé and Príncipe, 84–85
Science education, interactive
    methods in, 55
Scollon, Ron, 126–28
Scollon, Suzanne B. K., 126–28

Shor, Ira, 25–26, 58, 66, 102
Silva, Luis Inacio Lula da, 6
Silva, Tomaz Tadeu da, 40
Smith, William, 139–40, 148, 150
Social Service of Industry (SESI),
    4
Solidarity, 47, 118
Solipsistic idealism, 36
Subject, Freire's concept of, 149,
    151–52

Teaching: attributes of progressive
    teachers, 66–67; in Chipewyan
    society, 127–28; taking a side in
    teaching, 58–59. *See also* Educa-
    tion; Learning; Pedagogy
Technocratic thought, 13, 124, 143.
Text and context. *See* Reading
Theory and practice, 105–6
Third World. *See* First World and
    Third World
Torres, Carlos Alberto, 37, 106
Tradition, 134, 136 n.10
True words, 44, 94

Unity, 47, 118
Unity in diversity, 113–15
Universals, 74 n.3, 98, 101–2, 107–
    8; and particulars, 110; univer-
    sal human ethic, 117
University of Recife, 4: Cultural
    Extension Service, 5

Verbalism, 43
Violence, 46–47, 130

Walker, James, 19, 97, 100–101
Weber, Max, 99
Weiler, Kathleen, 19, 32–33, 97,
    102–3, 109
"Western mind-set," 98–100, 120–
    22. *See also* Culture; Experience;
    Knowledge
World Council of Churches, 5

About the Author

PETER ROBERTS is Senior Lecturer in the School of Education, University of Auckland, New Zealand.

ISBN 0-89789-571-1

90000>

EAN

9 780897 895712

HARDCOVER BAR CODE